EARTH BEFORE US

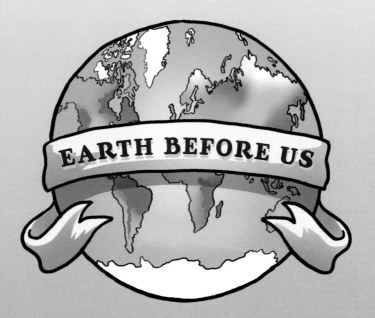

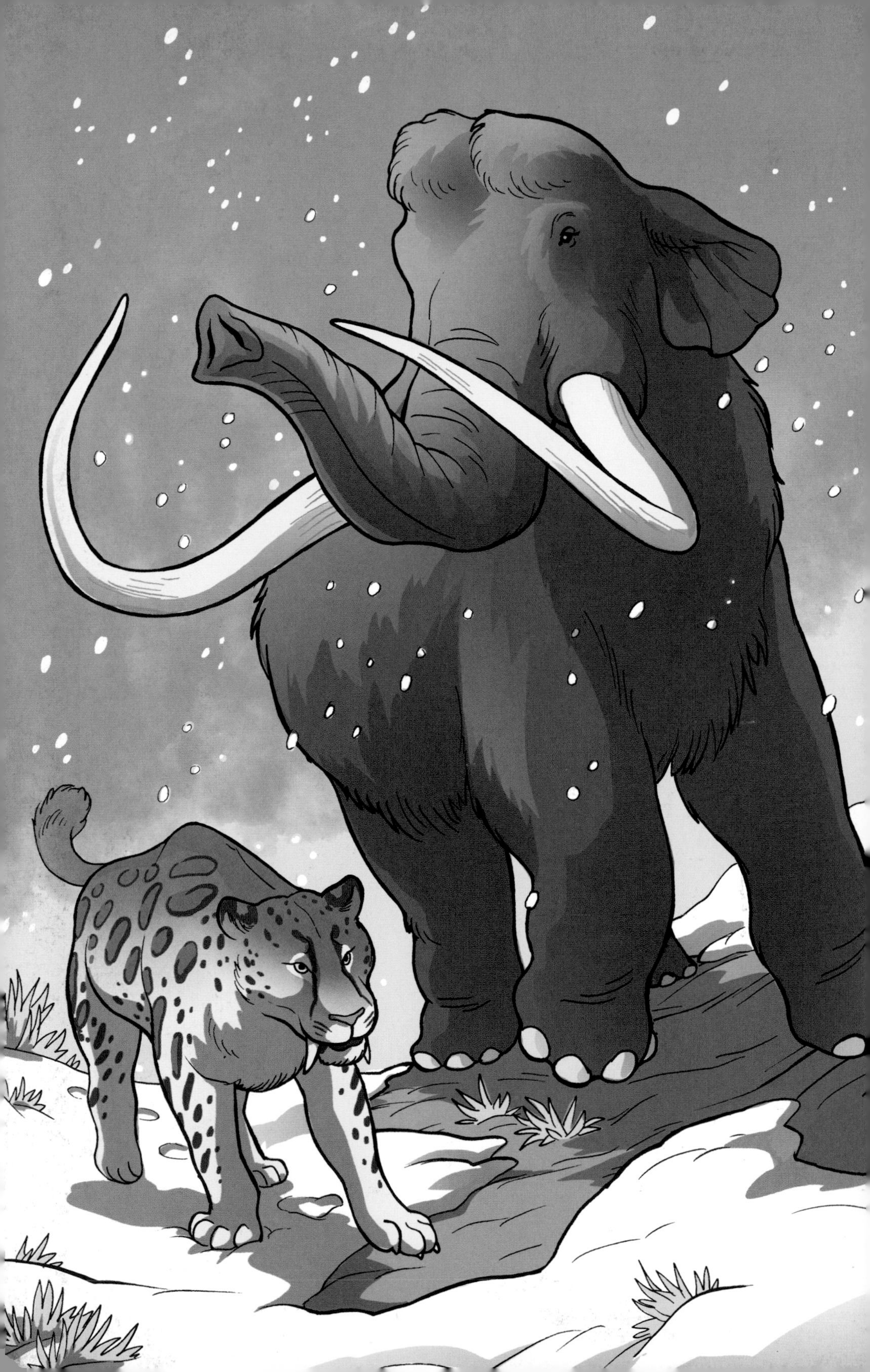

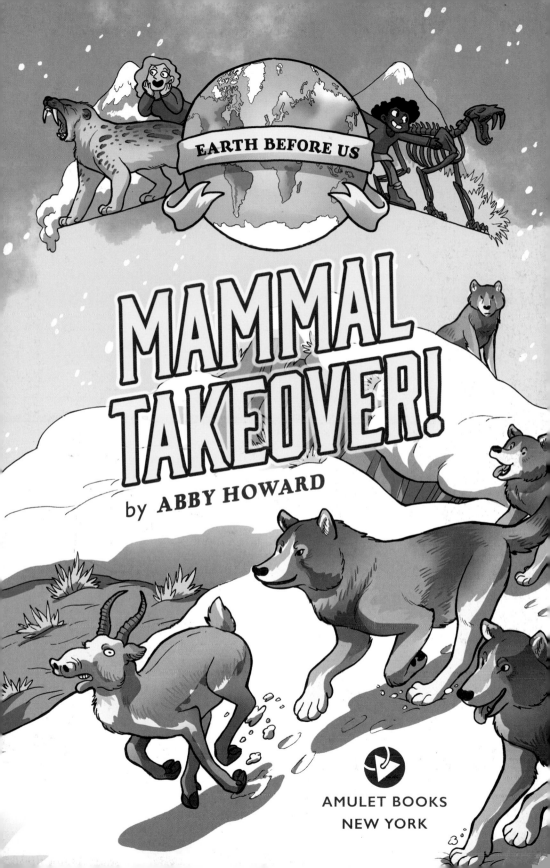

EARTH BEFORE US

MAMMAL TAKEOVER!

by ABBY HOWARD

AMULET BOOKS
NEW YORK

Special thanks to Sam Easy and Rosemary Mosco for their assistance and specialist knowledge.

Cataloging-in-Publication Data has been applied for and may be obtained from the Library of Congress.

ISBN 978-1-4197-3624-7
Library of Congress Control Number 2018047577

Printed and bound in China
10 9 8 7 6 5 4 3 2 1

Amulet Books are available at special discounts when purchased in quantity for premiums and promotions as well as fundraising or educational use. Special editions can also be created to specification. For details, contact specialsales@abramsbooks.com or the address below.

Amulet Books® is a registered trademark of Harry N. Abrams, Inc.

ABRAMS The Art of Books
195 Broadway, New York, NY 10007
abramsbooks.com

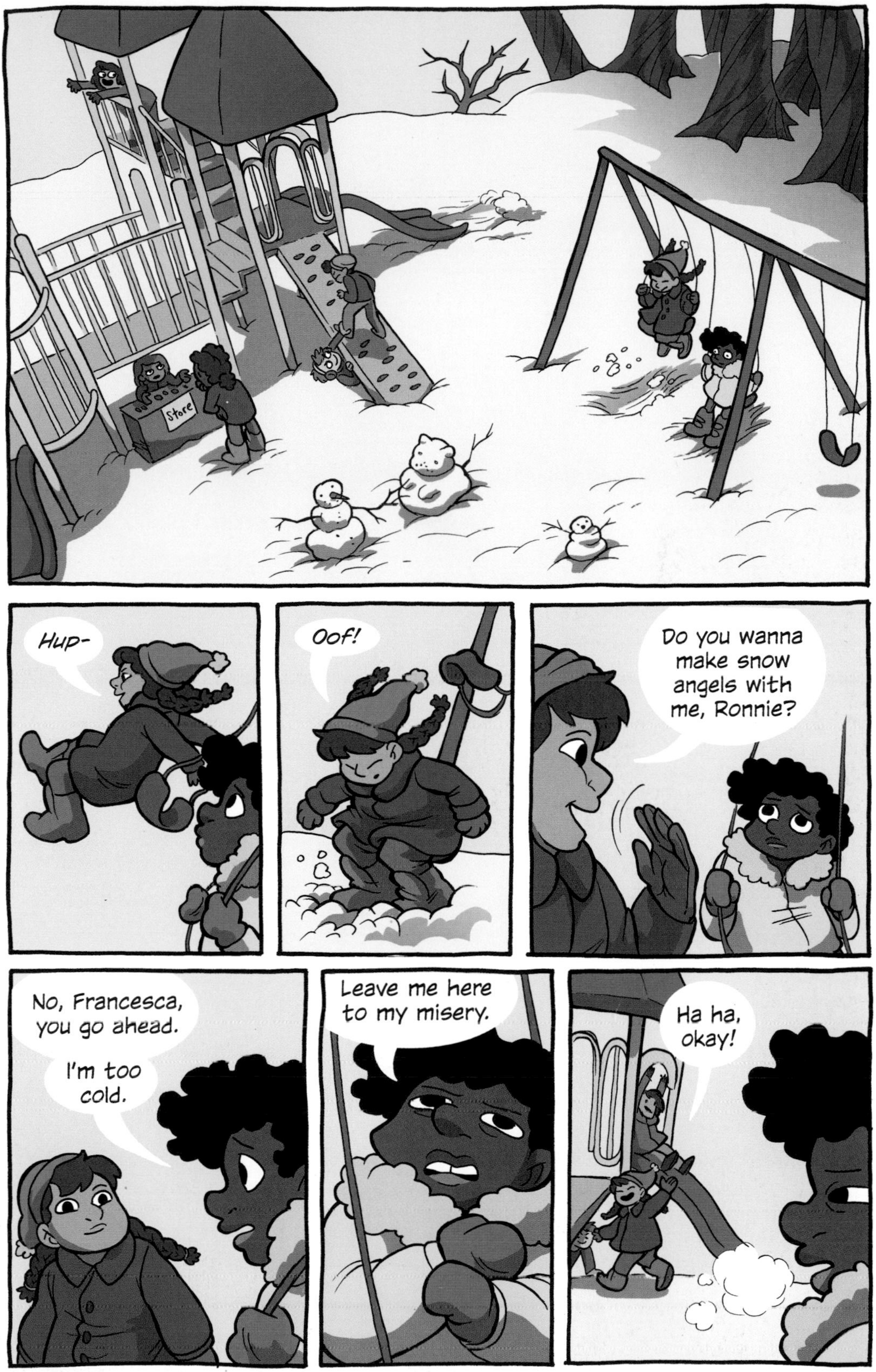
Store
Hup-
Oof!
Do you wanna make snow angels with me, Ronnie?
No, Francesca, you go ahead.
I'm too cold.
Leave me here to my misery.
Ha ha, okay!

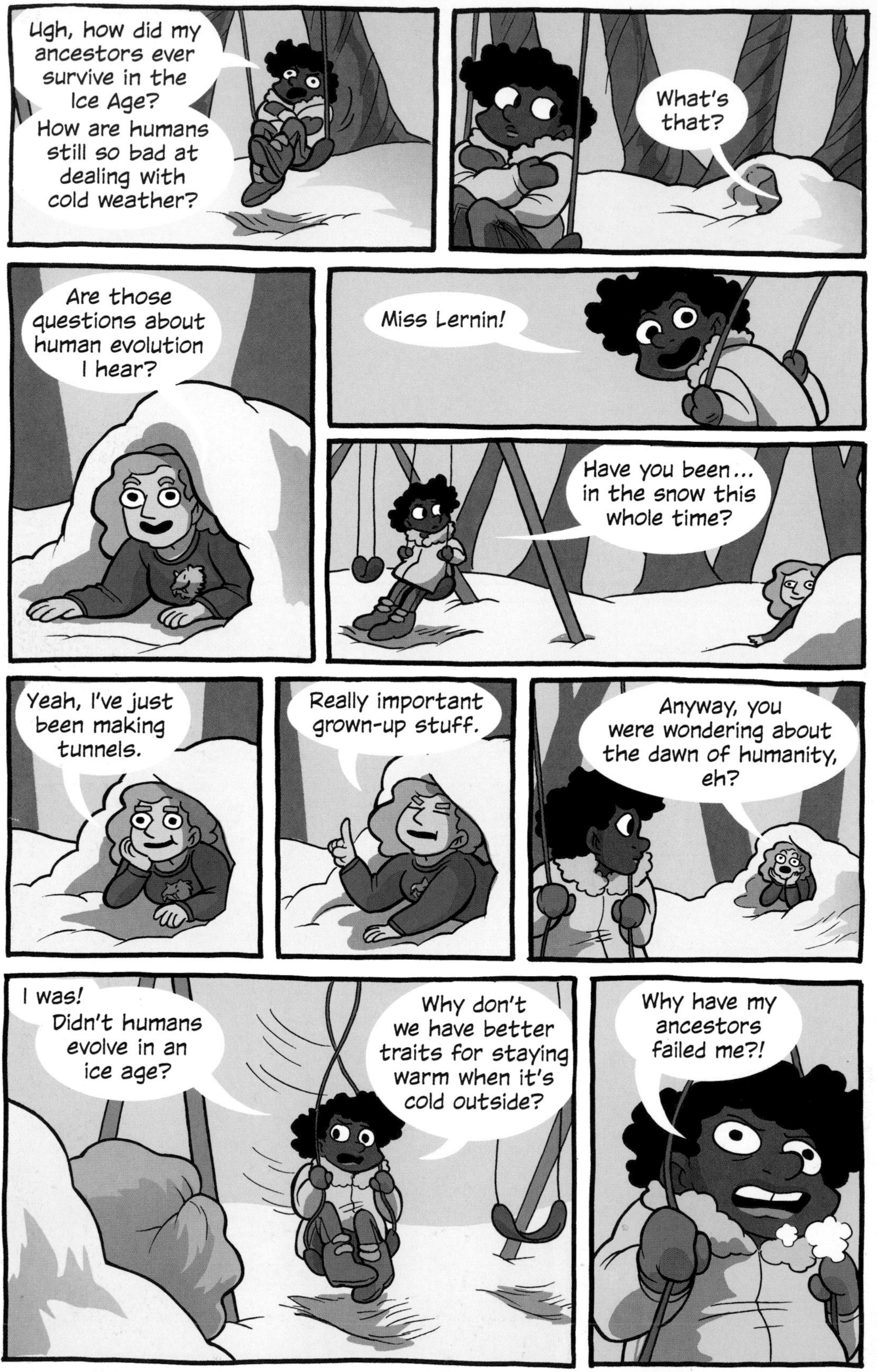
Ugh, how did my ancestors ever survive in the Ice Age?
How are humans still so bad at dealing with cold weather?
What's that?
Are those questions about human evolution I hear?
Miss Lernin!
Have you been... in the snow this whole time?
Yeah, I've just been making tunnels.
Really important grown-up stuff.
Anyway, you were wondering about the dawn of humanity, eh?
I was!
Didn't humans evolve in an ice age?
Why don't we have better traits for staying warm when it's cold outside?
Why have my ancestors failed me?!

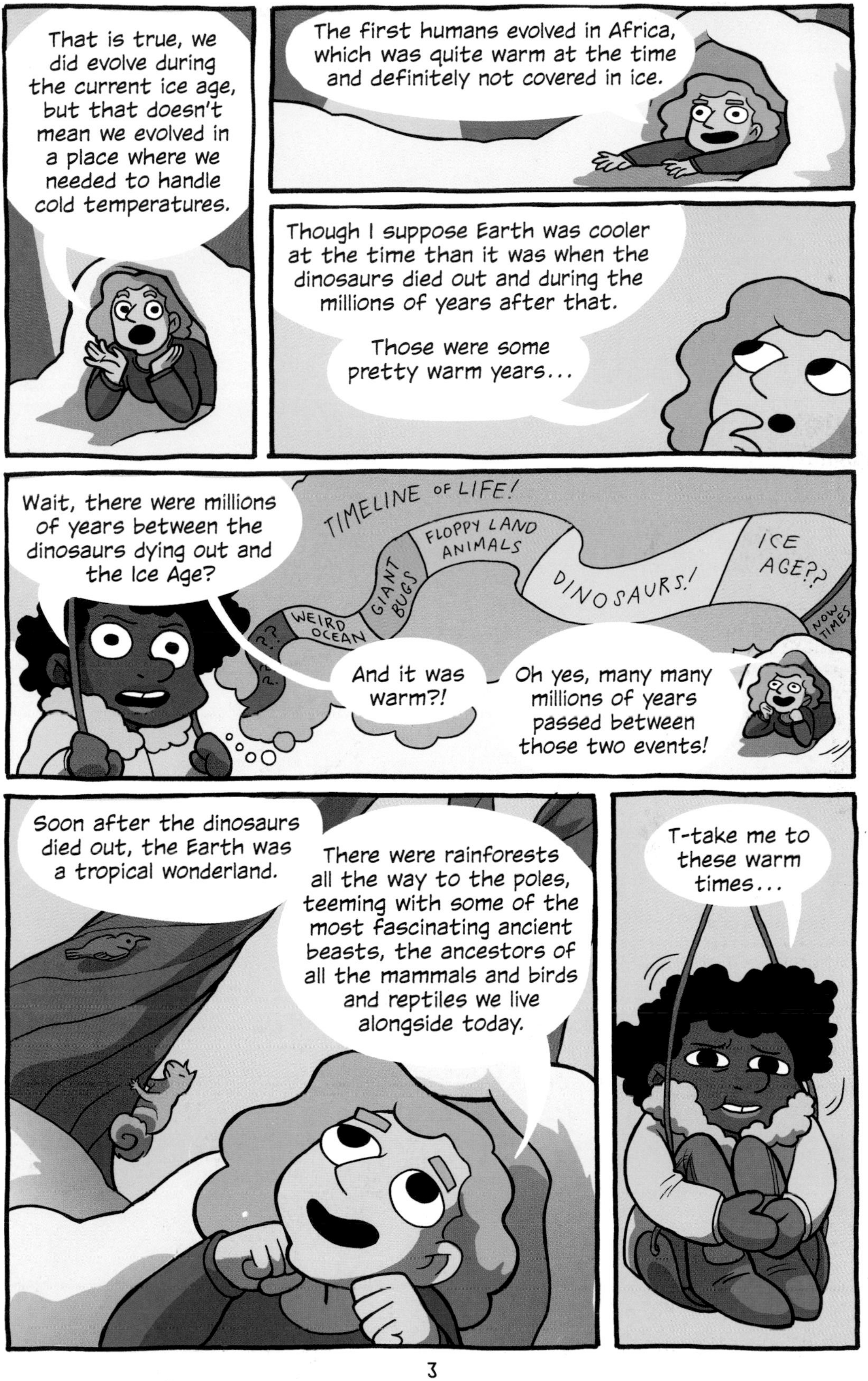
That is true, we did evolve during the current ice age, but that doesn't mean we evolved in a place where we needed to handle cold temperatures.
The first humans evolved in Africa, which was quite warm at the time and definitely not covered in ice.
Though I suppose Earth was cooler at the time than it was when the dinosaurs died out and during the millions of years after that.
Those were some pretty warm years...
Wait, there were millions of years between the dinosaurs dying out and the Ice Age?
TIMELINE OF LIFE!
WEIRD OCEAN
GIANT BUGS
FLOPPY LAND ANIMALS
DINOSAURS!
ICE AGE??
NOW TIMES
And it was warm?!
Oh yes, many many millions of years passed between those two events!
Soon after the dinosaurs died out, the Earth was a tropical wonderland.
There were rainforests all the way to the poles, teeming with some of the most fascinating ancient beasts, the ancestors of all the mammals and birds and reptiles we live alongside today.
T-take me to these warm times...

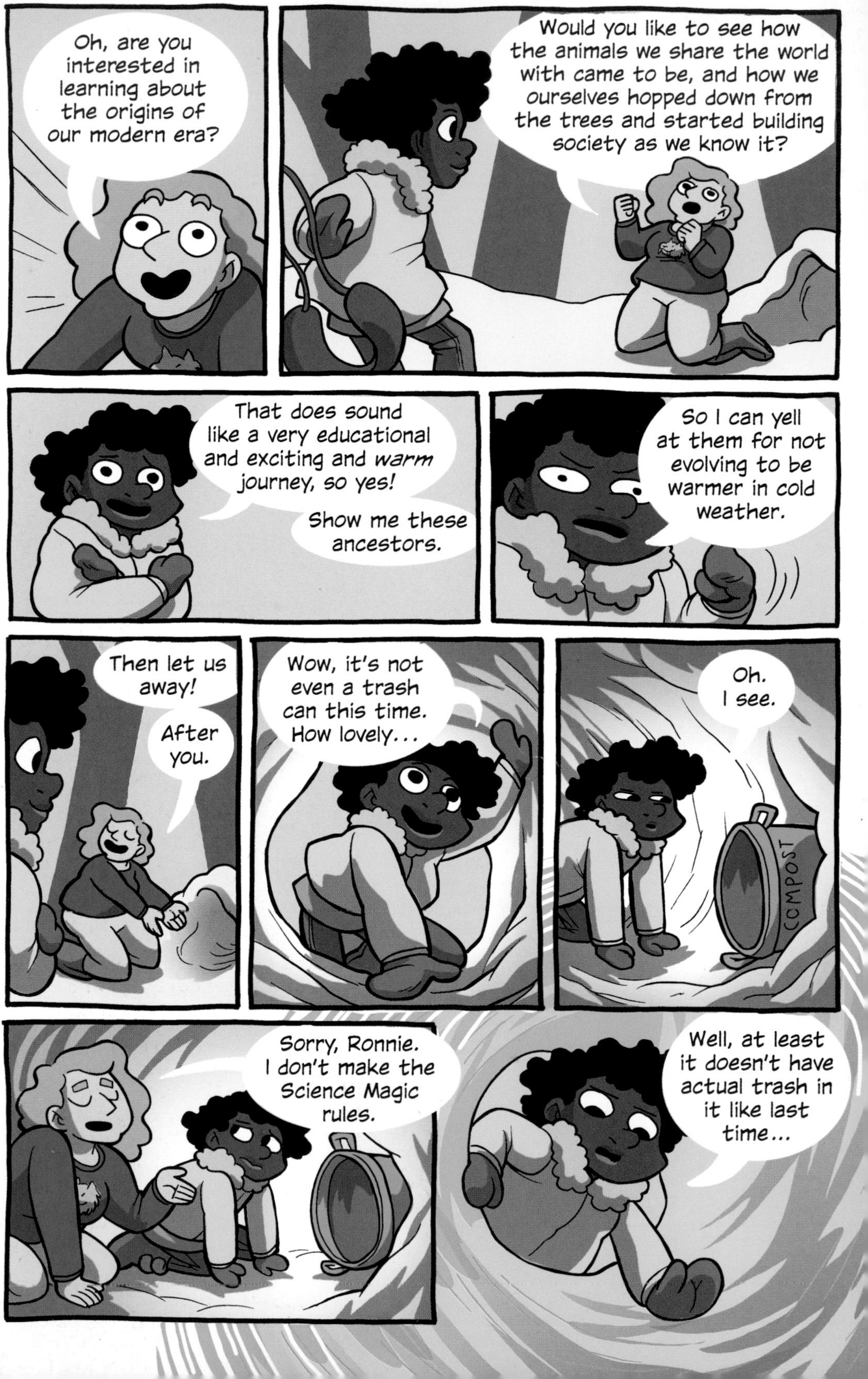

Oh, are you interested in learning about the origins of our modern era?
Would you like to see how the animals we share the world with came to be, and how we ourselves hopped down from the trees and started building society as we know it?
That does sound like a very educational and exciting and *warm* journey, so yes!
Show me these ancestors.
So I can yell at them for not evolving to be warmer in cold weather.
Then let us away!
After you.
Wow, it's not even a trash can this time. How lovely...
Oh. I see.
COMPOST
Sorry, Ronnie. I don't make the Science Magic rules.
Well, at least it doesn't have actual trash in it like last time...

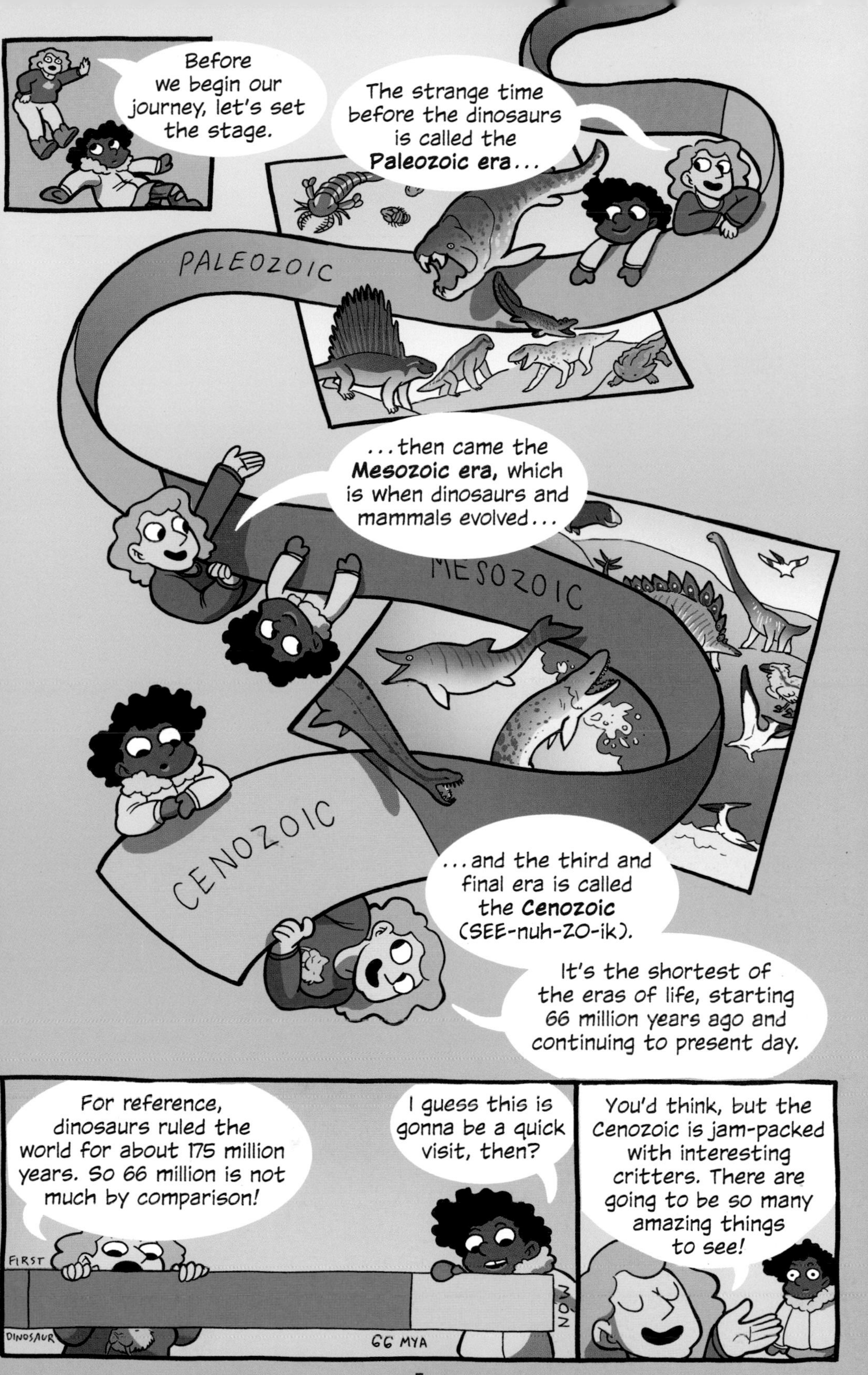
Before we begin our journey, let's set the stage.
The strange time before the dinosaurs is called the **Paleozoic era**...
PALEOZOIC
...then came the **Mesozoic era,** which is when dinosaurs and mammals evolved...
MESOZOIC
CENOZOIC
...and the third and final era is called the **Cenozoic** (SEE-nuh-ZO-ik).
It's the shortest of the eras of life, starting 66 million years ago and continuing to present day.
For reference, dinosaurs ruled the world for about 175 million years. So 66 million is not much by comparison!
FIRST
DINOSAUR
66 MYA
NOW
I guess this is gonna be a quick visit, then?
You'd think, but the Cenozoic is jam-packed with interesting critters. There are going to be so many amazing things to see!

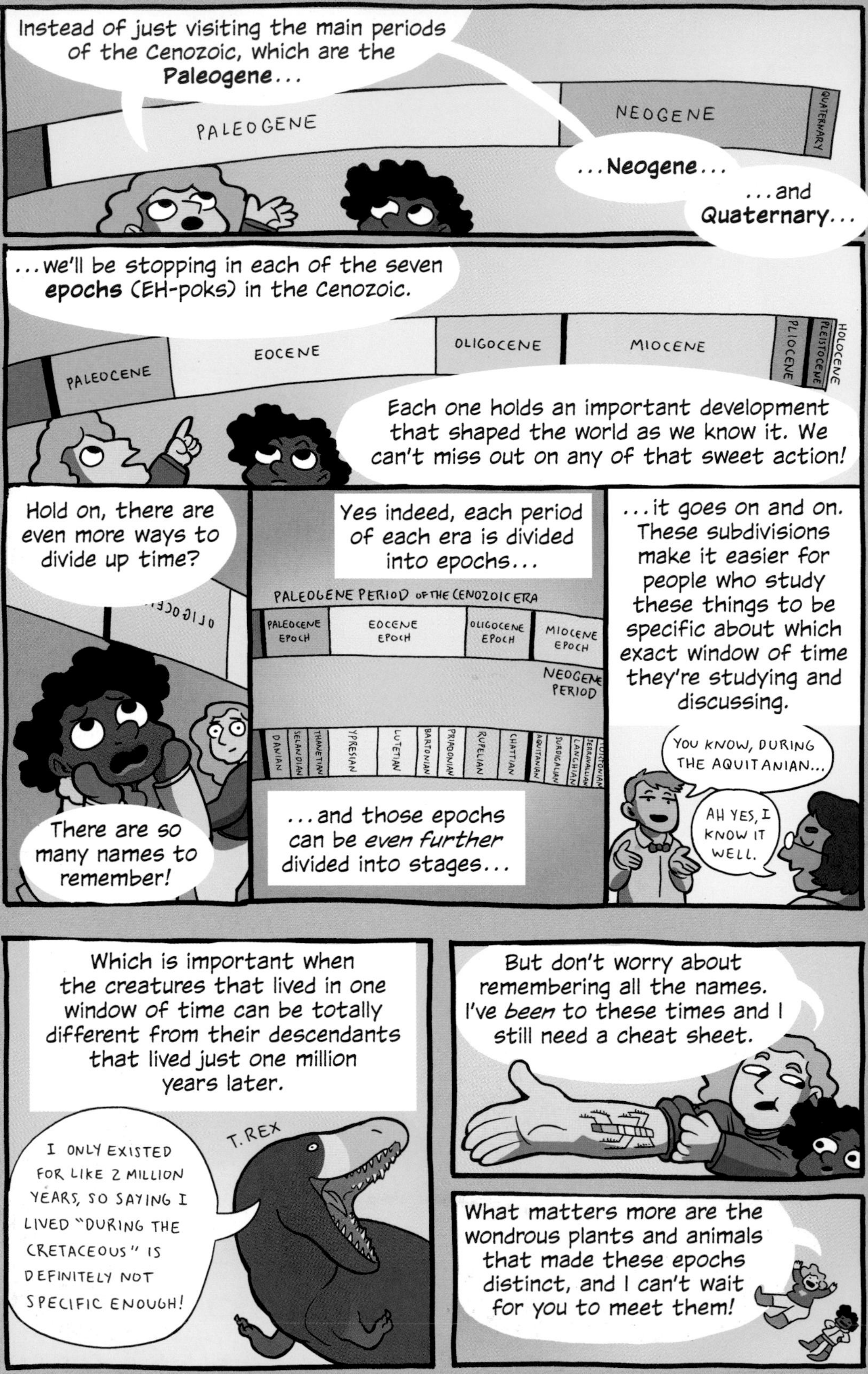
Instead of just visiting the main periods of the Cenozoic, which are the **Paleogene**...
PALEOGENE
NEOGENE
QUATERNARY
...**Neogene**...
...and **Quaternary**...
...we'll be stopping in each of the seven **epochs** (EH-poks) in the Cenozoic.
PALEOCENE
EOCENE
OLIGOCENE
MIOCENE
PLIOCENE
PLEISTOCENE
HOLOCENE
Each one holds an important development that shaped the world as we know it. We can't miss out on any of that sweet action!
Hold on, there are even more ways to divide up time?
There are so many names to remember!
Yes indeed, each period of each era is divided into epochs...
PALEOGENE PERIOD OF THE CENOZOIC ERA
PALEOCENE EPOCH
EOCENE EPOCH
OLIGOCENE EPOCH
MIOCENE EPOCH
NEOGENE PERIOD
DANIAN
SELANDIAN
THANETIAN
YPRESIAN
LUTETIAN
BARTONIAN
PRIABONIAN
RUPELIAN
CHATTIAN
AQUITANIAN
BURDIGALIAN
LANGHIAN
SERRAVALLIAN
TORTONIAN
...and those epochs can be *even further* divided into stages...
...it goes on and on. These subdivisions make it easier for people who study these things to be specific about which exact window of time they're studying and discussing.
YOU KNOW, DURING THE AQUITANIAN...
AH YES, I KNOW IT WELL.
Which is important when the creatures that lived in one window of time can be totally different from their descendants that lived just one million years later.
T. REX
I ONLY EXISTED FOR LIKE 2 MILLION YEARS, SO SAYING I LIVED "DURING THE CRETACEOUS" IS DEFINITELY NOT SPECIFIC ENOUGH!
But don't worry about remembering all the names. I've *been* to these times and I still need a cheat sheet.
What matters more are the wondrous plants and animals that made these epochs distinct, and I can't wait for you to meet them!

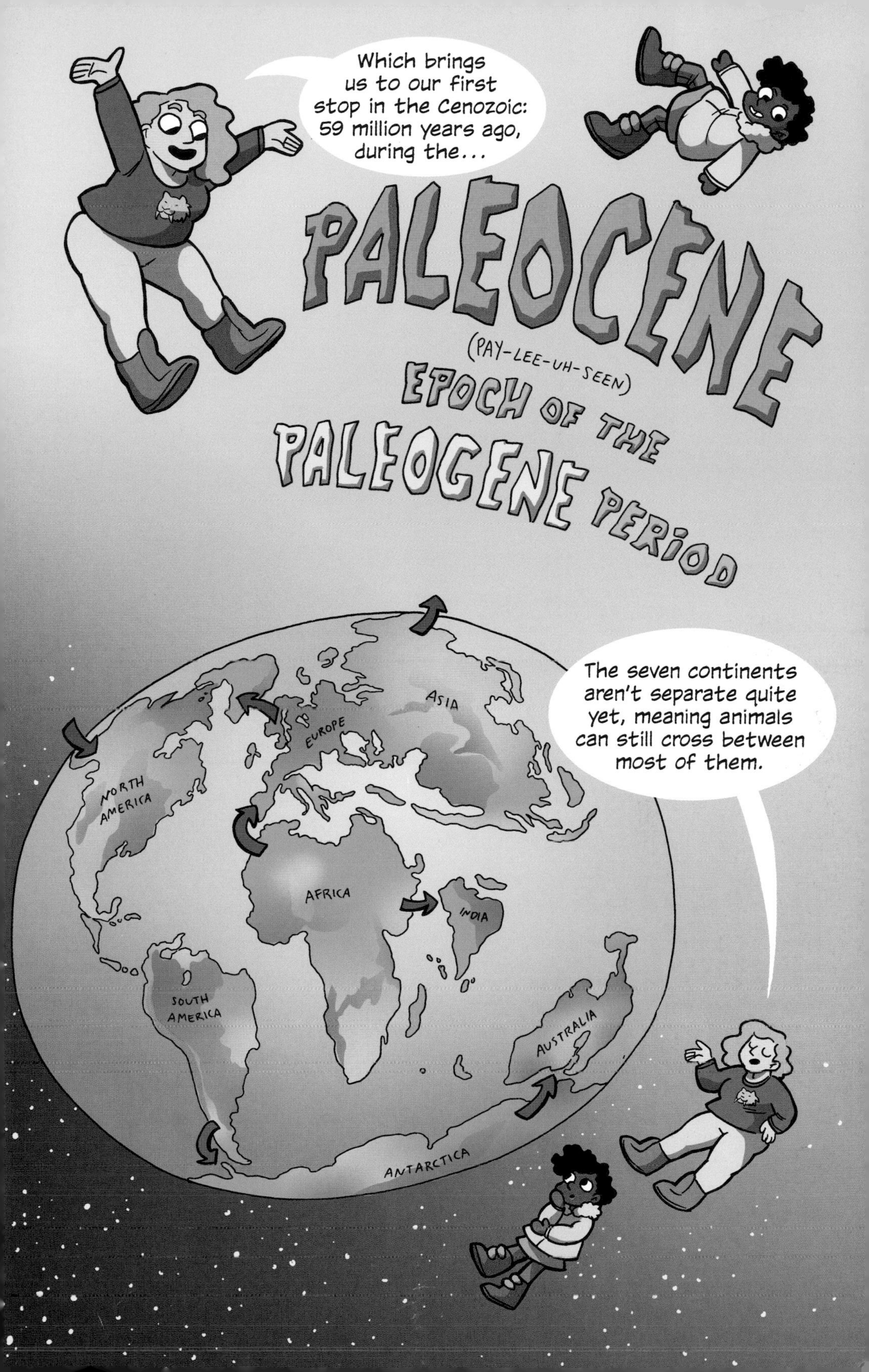

Which brings us to our first stop in the Cenozoic: 59 million years ago, during the...
PALEOCENE
(PAY-LEE-UH-SEEN)
EPOCH OF THE
PALEOGENE PERIOD
ASIA
EUROPE
NORTH AMERICA
AFRICA
INDIA
SOUTH AMERICA
AUSTRALIA
ANTARCTICA
The seven continents aren't separate quite yet, meaning animals can still cross between most of them.

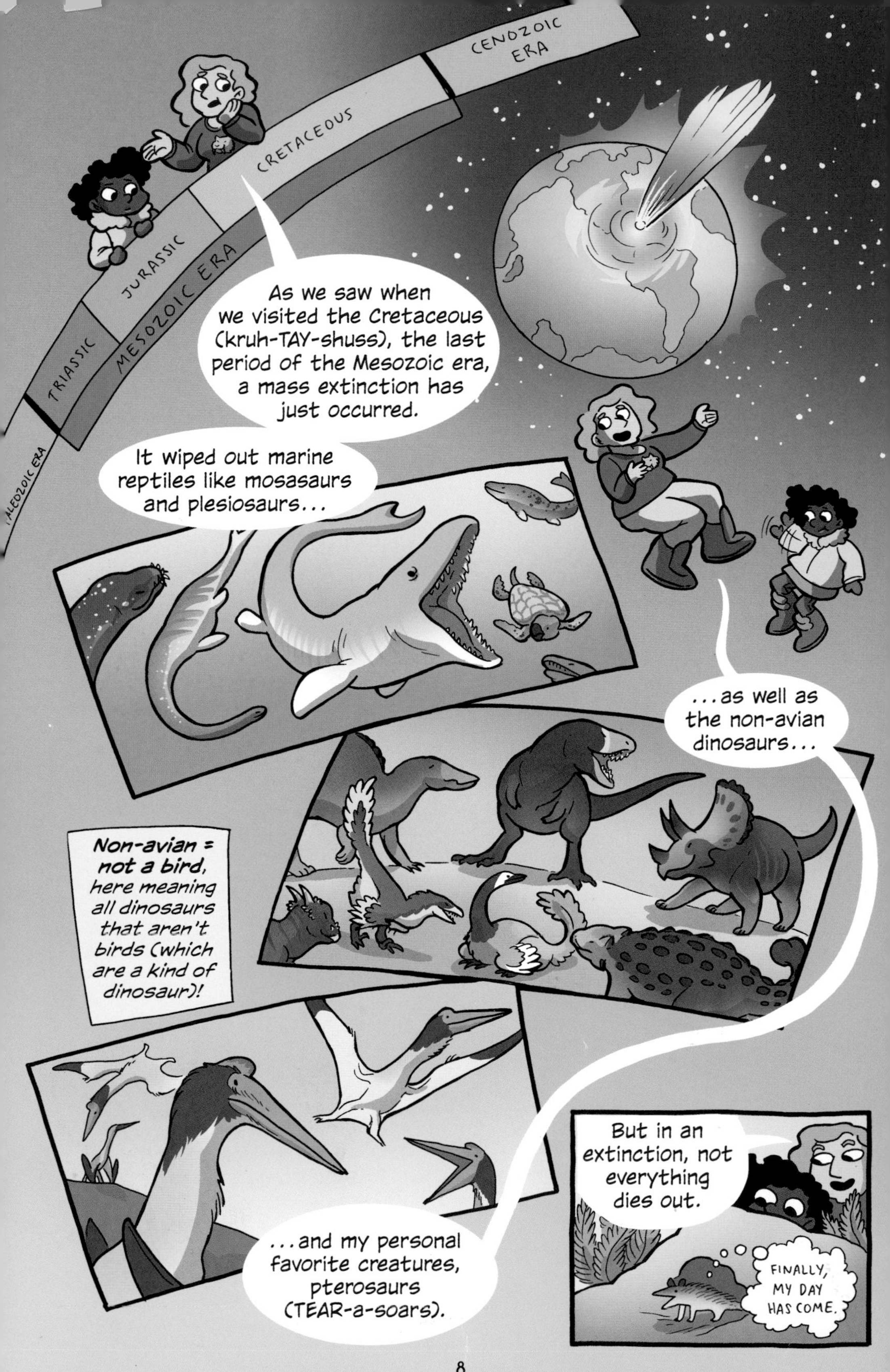
CENOZOIC ERA
CRETACEOUS
JURASSIC
TRIASSIC
MESOZOIC ERA
PALEOZOIC ERA
As we saw when we visited the Cretaceous (kruh-TAY-shuss), the last period of the Mesozoic era, a mass extinction has just occurred.
It wiped out marine reptiles like mosasaurs and plesiosaurs...
...as well as the non-avian dinosaurs...
Non-avian = not a bird, here meaning all dinosaurs that aren't birds (which are a kind of dinosaur)!
...and my personal favorite creatures, pterosaurs (TEAR-a-soars).
But in an extinction, not everything dies out.
FINALLY, MY DAY HAS COME.

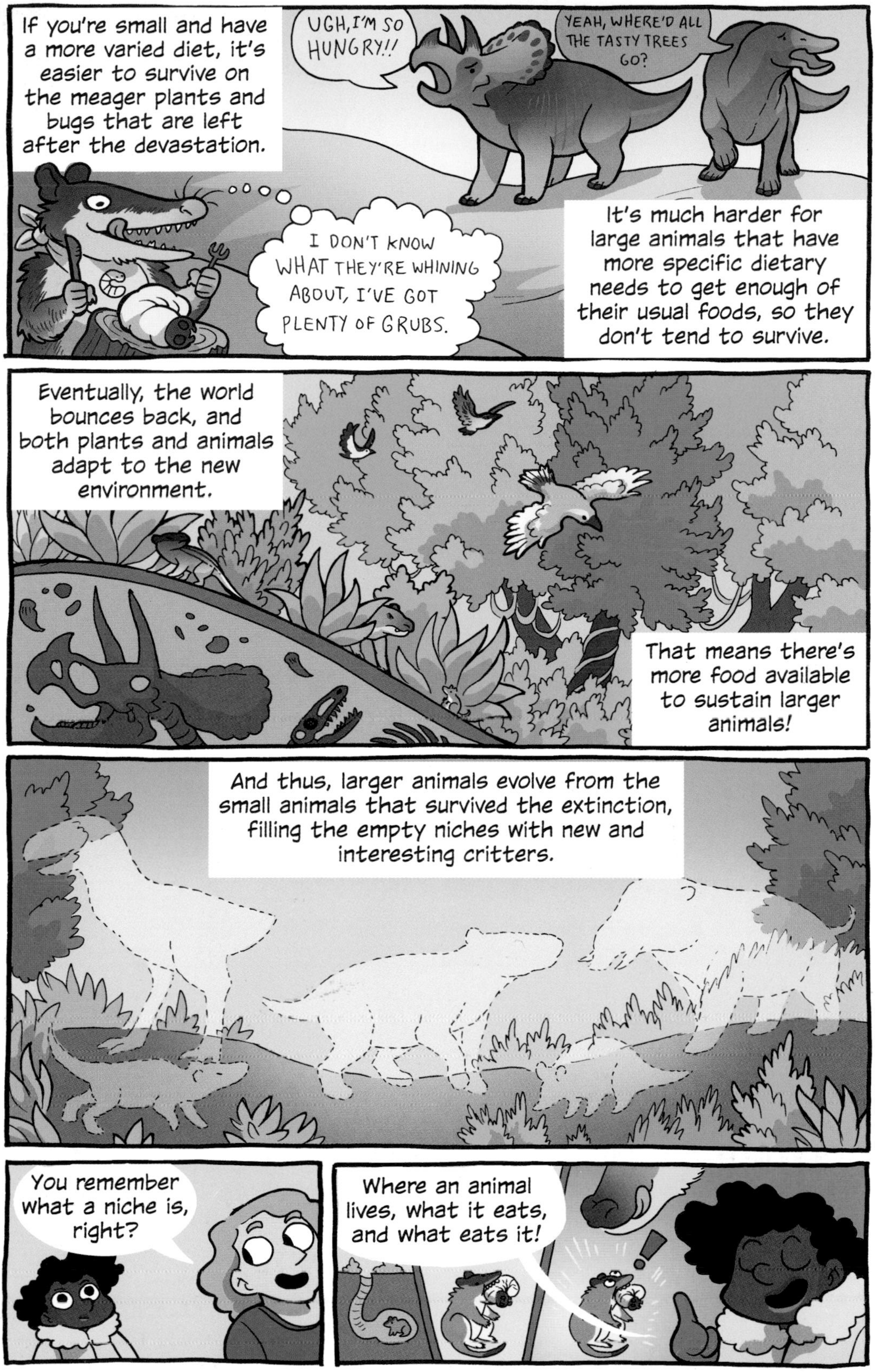

If you're small and have a more varied diet, it's easier to survive on the meager plants and bugs that are left after the devastation.
UGH, I'M SO HUNGRY!!
YEAH, WHERE'D ALL THE TASTY TREES GO?
I DON'T KNOW WHAT THEY'RE WHINING ABOUT, I'VE GOT PLENTY OF GRUBS.
It's much harder for large animals that have more specific dietary needs to get enough of their usual foods, so they don't tend to survive.
Eventually, the world bounces back, and both plants and animals adapt to the new environment.
That means there's more food available to sustain larger animals!
And thus, larger animals evolve from the small animals that survived the extinction, filling the empty niches with new and interesting critters.
You remember what a niche is, right?
Where an animal lives, what it eats, and what eats it!

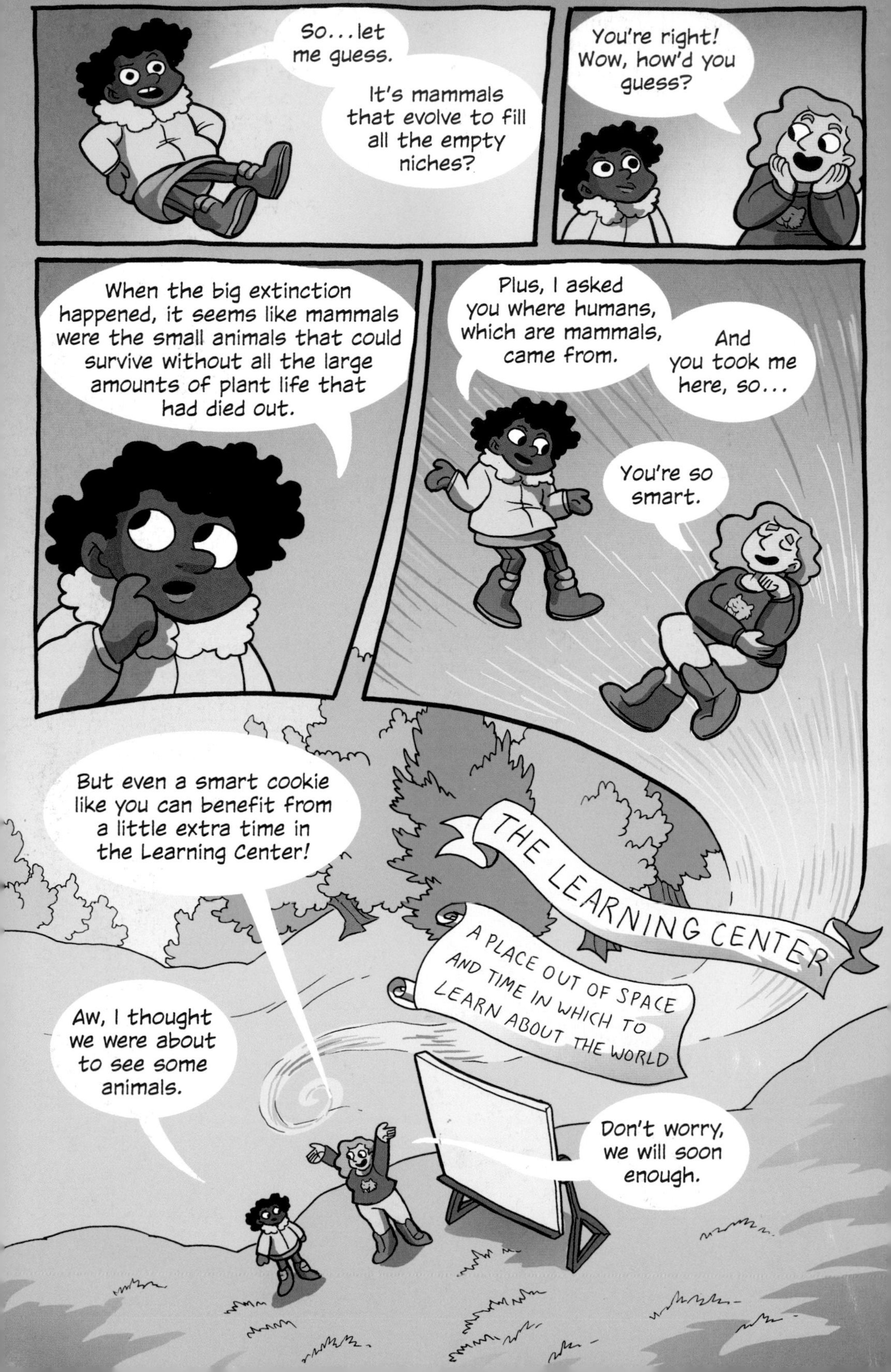
So... let me guess.
It's mammals that evolve to fill all the empty niches?
You're right! Wow, how'd you guess?
When the big extinction happened, it seems like mammals were the small animals that could survive without all the large amounts of plant life that had died out.
Plus, I asked you where humans, which are mammals, came from.
And you took me here, so...
You're so smart.
But even a smart cookie like you can benefit from a little extra time in the Learning Center!
THE LEARNING CENTER
A PLACE OUT OF SPACE AND TIME IN WHICH TO LEARN ABOUT THE WORLD
Aw, I thought we were about to see some animals.
Don't worry, we will soon enough.

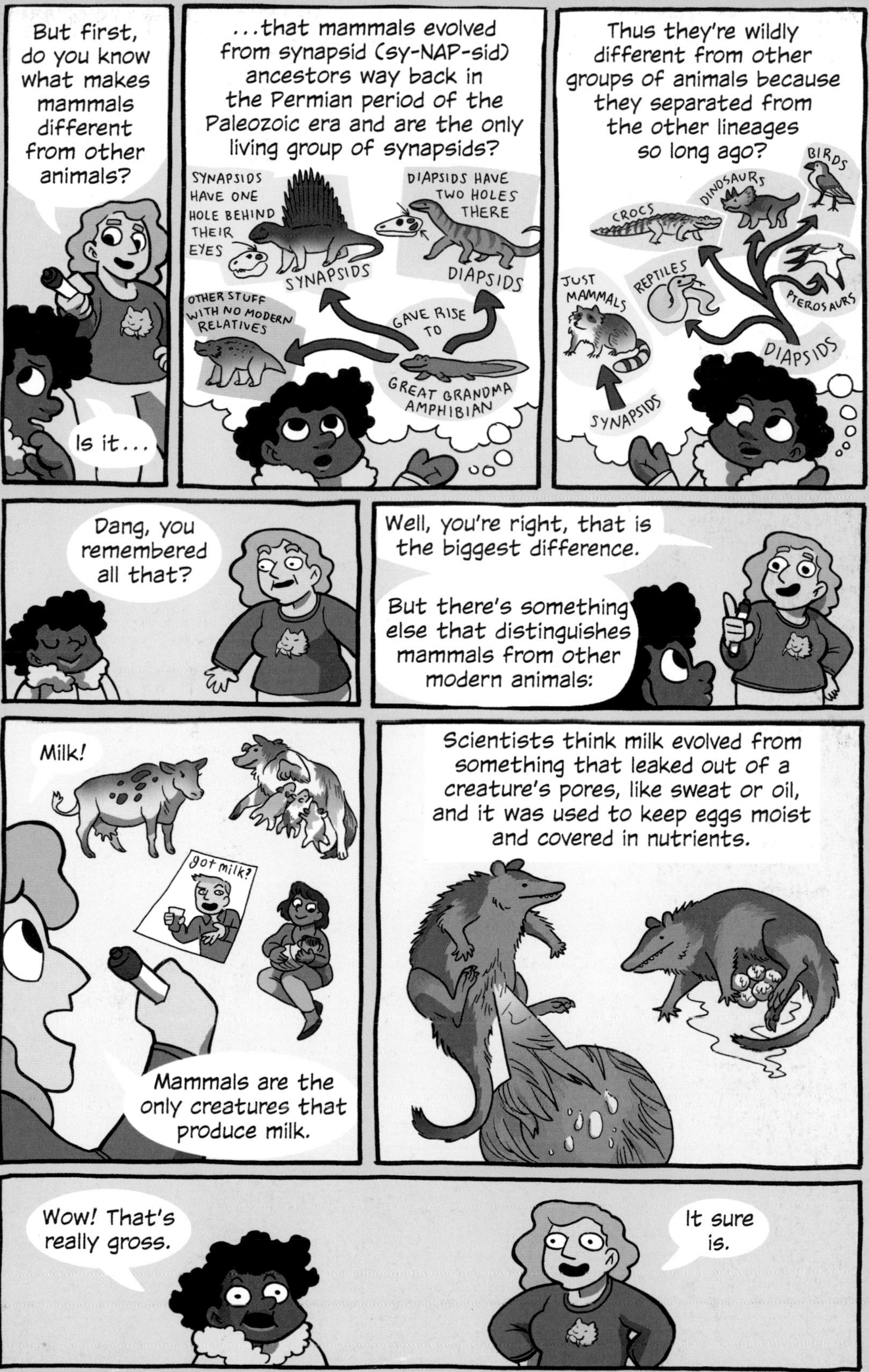
But first, do you know what makes mammals different from other animals?
Is it...
...that mammals evolved from synapsid (sy-NAP-sid) ancestors way back in the Permian period of the Paleozoic era and are the only living group of synapsids?
SYNAPSIDS HAVE ONE HOLE BEHIND THEIR EYES
DIAPSIDS HAVE TWO HOLES THERE
SYNAPSIDS
DIAPSIDS
OTHER STUFF WITH NO MODERN RELATIVES
GAVE RISE TO
GREAT GRANDMA AMPHIBIAN
Thus they're wildly different from other groups of animals because they separated from the other lineages so long ago?
BIRDS
DINOSAURS
CROCS
JUST MAMMALS
REPTILES
PTEROSAURS
DIAPSIDS
SYNAPSIDS
Dang, you remembered all that?
Well, you're right, that is the biggest difference.
But there's something else that distinguishes mammals from other modern animals:
Milk!
got milk?
Mammals are the only creatures that produce milk.
Scientists think milk evolved from something that leaked out of a creature's pores, like sweat or oil, and it was used to keep eggs moist and covered in nutrients.
Wow! That's really gross.
It sure is.

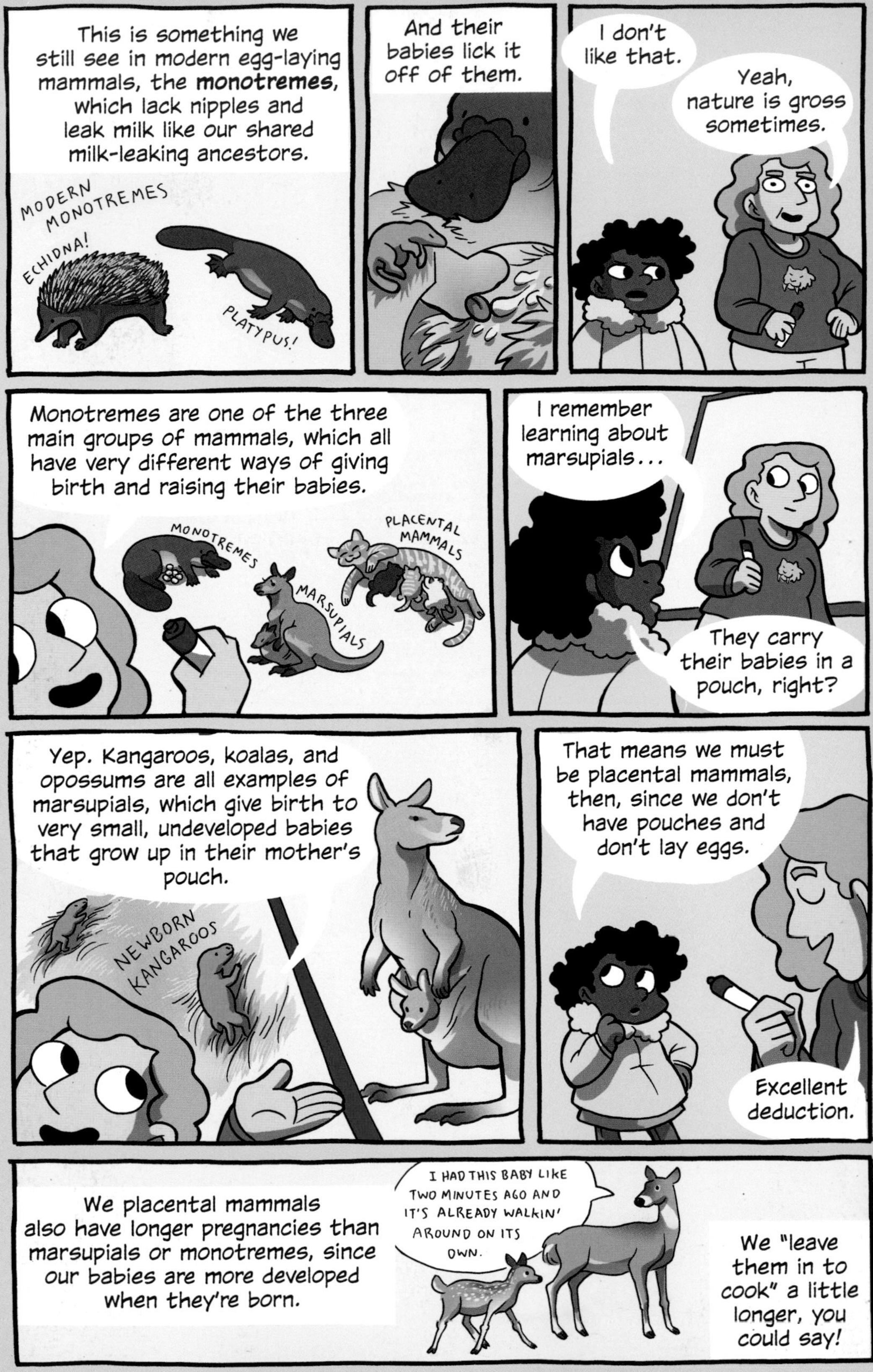
This is something we still see in modern egg-laying mammals, the **monotremes**, which lack nipples and leak milk like our shared milk-leaking ancestors.
MODERN MONOTREMES
ECHIDNA!
PLATYPUS!
And their babies lick it off of them.
I don't like that.
Yeah, nature is gross sometimes.
Monotremes are one of the three main groups of mammals, which all have very different ways of giving birth and raising their babies.
MONOTREMES
MARSUPIALS
PLACENTAL MAMMALS
I remember learning about marsupials...
They carry their babies in a pouch, right?
Yep. Kangaroos, koalas, and opossums are all examples of marsupials, which give birth to very small, undeveloped babies that grow up in their mother's pouch.
NEWBORN KANGAROOS
That means we must be placental mammals, then, since we don't have pouches and don't lay eggs.
Excellent deduction.
We placental mammals also have longer pregnancies than marsupials or monotremes, since our babies are more developed when they're born.
I HAD THIS BABY LIKE TWO MINUTES AGO AND IT'S ALREADY WALKIN' AROUND ON ITS OWN.
We "leave them in to cook" a little longer, you could say!

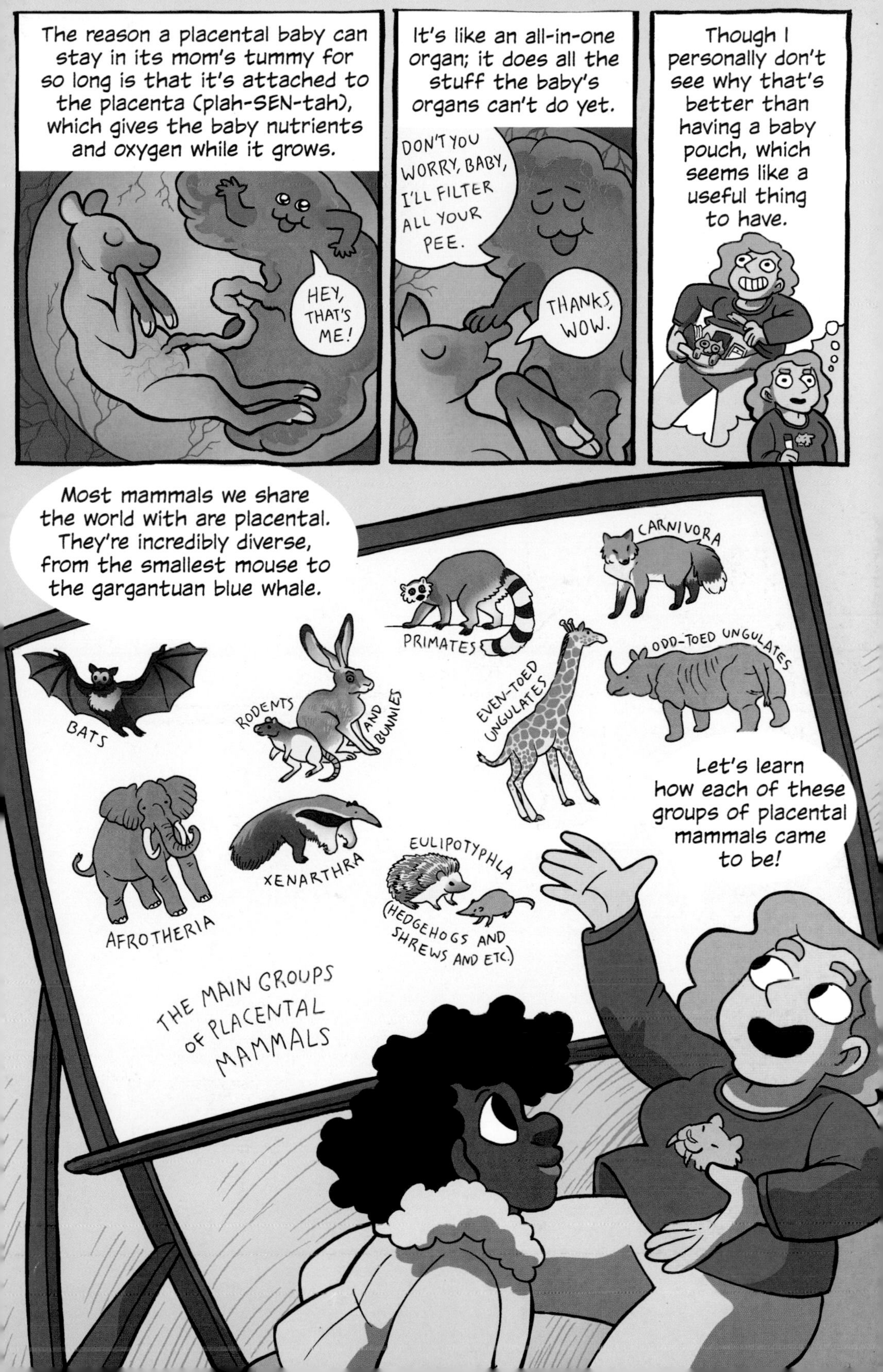

The reason a placental baby can stay in its mom's tummy for so long is that it's attached to the placenta (plah-SEN-tah), which gives the baby nutrients and oxygen while it grows.
HEY, THAT'S ME!
It's like an all-in-one organ; it does all the stuff the baby's organs can't do yet.
DON'T YOU WORRY, BABY, I'LL FILTER ALL YOUR PEE.
THANKS, WOW.
Though I personally don't see why that's better than having a baby pouch, which seems like a useful thing to have.
Most mammals we share the world with are placental. They're incredibly diverse, from the smallest mouse to the gargantuan blue whale.
CARNIVORA
PRIMATES
ODD-TOED UNGULATES
EVEN-TOED UNGULATES
BATS
RODENTS
AND BUNNIES
AFROTHERIA
XENARTHRA
EULIPOTYPHLA
(HEDGEHOGS AND SHREWS AND ETC.)
THE MAIN GROUPS OF PLACENTAL MAMMALS
Let's learn how each of these groups of placental mammals came to be!

Welcome to the Paleocene epoch of Eurasia, which is the joined continents of Europe and Asia.
You weren't kiddin' about the heat, yeesh.
So I know I said the Cenozoic is when mammals rule the world, but...
...the dinosaurs aren't done being on top quite yet.
BERRUORNIS (BEH-ROO-OR-NISS)
Whoa! That's a big bird! It could put my whole head in its mouth if it wanted to.
PRODINOCERAS (PRO-DI-NO-SEH-RASS)
Fortunately, it probably wouldn't try, because despite how large and scary Gastornis (gas-TOR-niss) is, it's an herbivore that most likely eats seeds and tough plants, not fifth-grade girls.
PACHYAENA
SINONYX (SY-NAW-NIKS)
Though I can't say the same for some of the mammals in this region, such as Pachyaena (PAH-kee-YEE-nah).
My jacket...

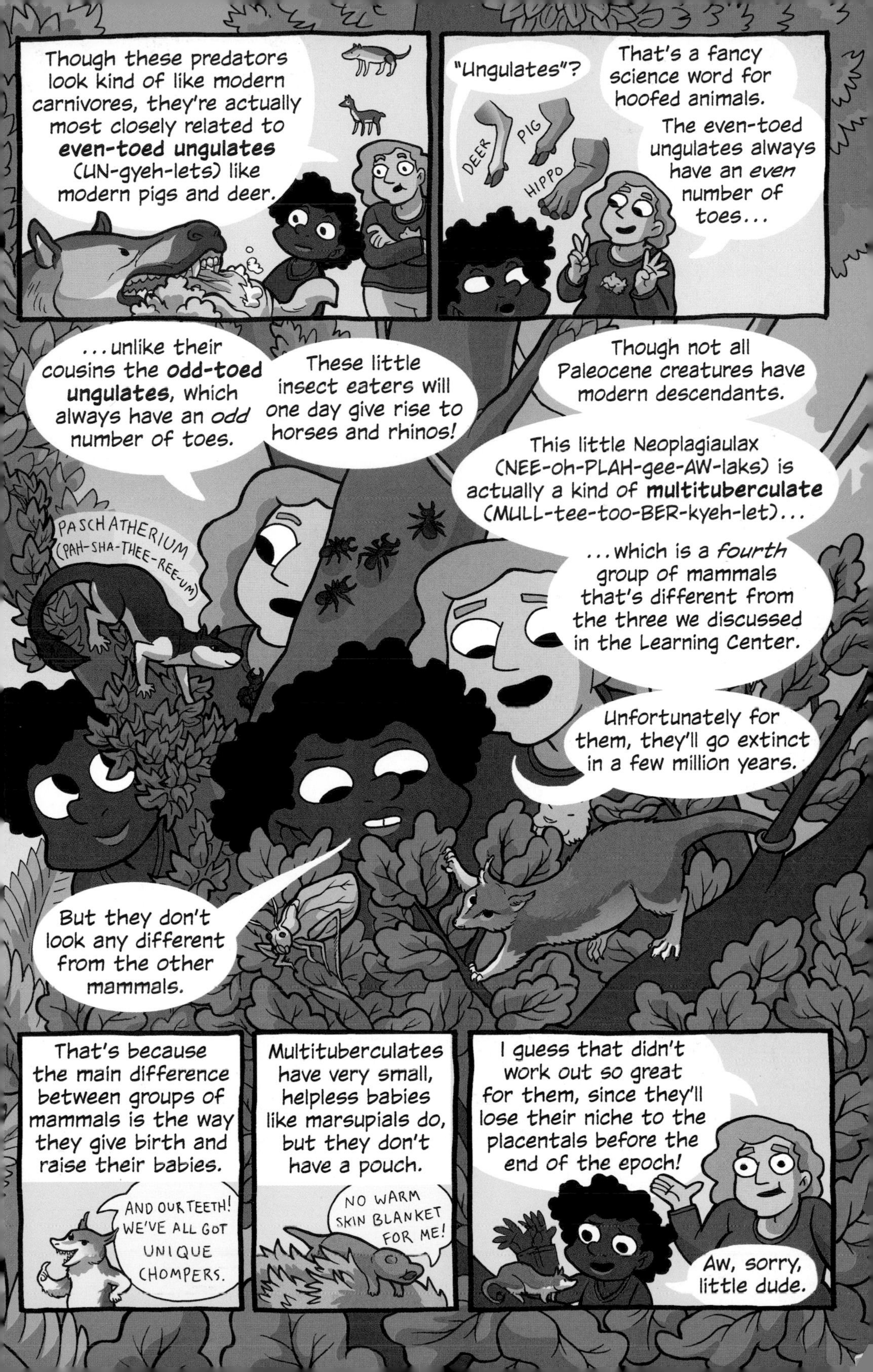
Though these predators look kind of like modern carnivores, they're actually most closely related to **even-toed ungulates** (UN-gyeh-lets) like modern pigs and deer.
"Ungulates"?
That's a fancy science word for hoofed animals.
DEER
PIG
HIPPO
The even-toed ungulates always have an *even* number of toes...
...unlike their cousins the **odd-toed ungulates**, which always have an *odd* number of toes.
These little insect eaters will one day give rise to horses and rhinos!
Though not all Paleocene creatures have modern descendants.
PASCHATHERIUM (PAH-SHA-THEE-REE-UM)
This little Neoplagiaulax (NEE-oh-PLAH-gee-AW-laks) is actually a kind of **multituberculate** (MULL-tee-too-BER-kyeh-let)...
...which is a *fourth* group of mammals that's different from the three we discussed in the Learning Center.
Unfortunately for them, they'll go extinct in a few million years.
But they don't look any different from the other mammals.
That's because the main difference between groups of mammals is the way they give birth and raise their babies.
AND OUR TEETH! WE'VE ALL GOT UNIQUE CHOMPERS.
Multituberculates have very small, helpless babies like marsupials do, but they don't have a pouch.
NO WARM SKIN BLANKET FOR ME!
I guess that didn't work out so great for them, since they'll lose their niche to the placentals before the end of the epoch!
Aw, sorry, little dude.

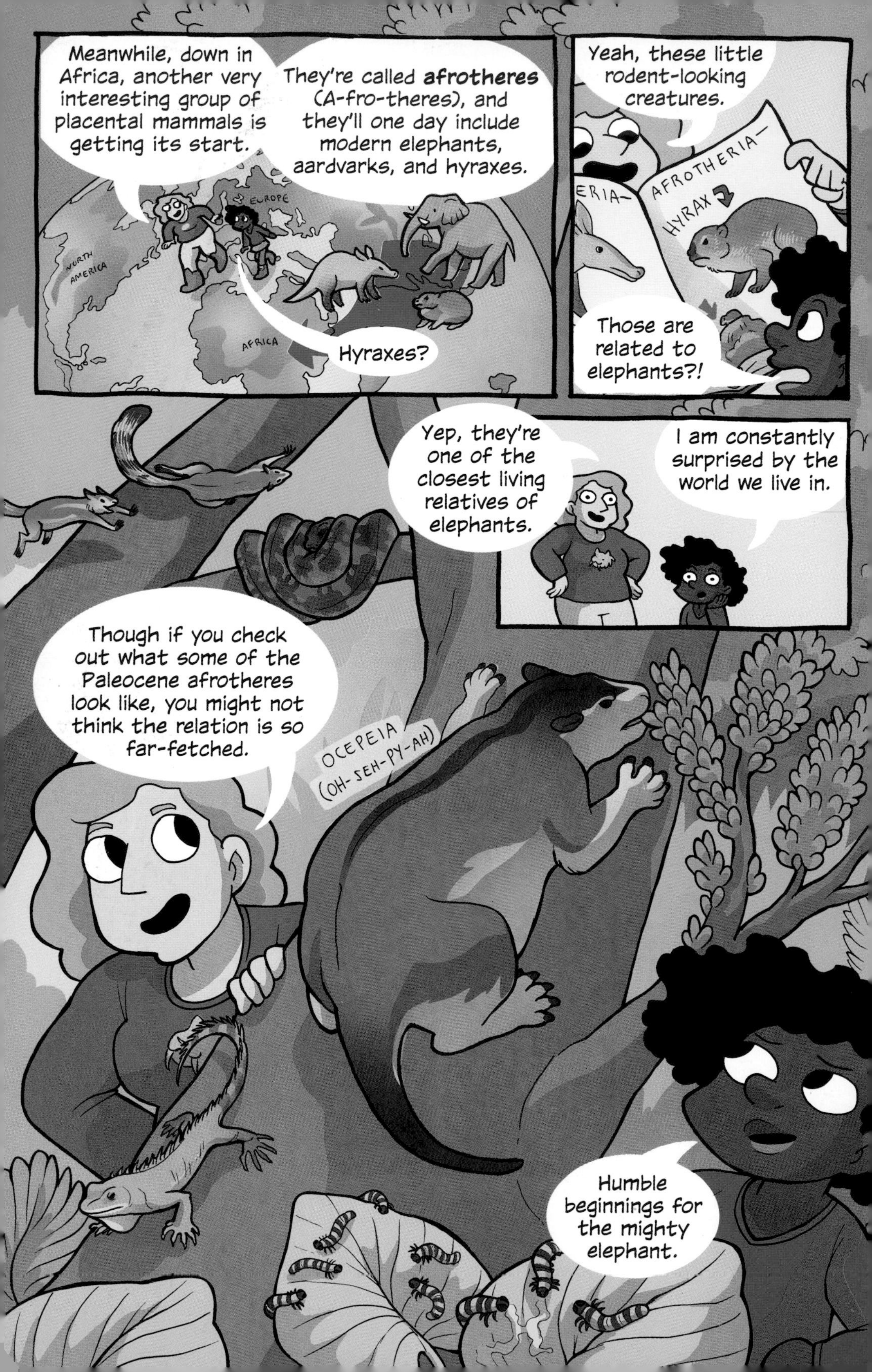
Meanwhile, down in Africa, another very interesting group of placental mammals is getting its start.
They're called **afrotheres** (A-fro-theres), and they'll one day include modern elephants, aardvarks, and hyraxes.
EUROPE
NORTH AMERICA
AFRICA
Hyraxes?
Yeah, these little rodent-looking creatures.
-ERIA-
-AFROTHERIA-
HYRAX
Those are related to elephants?!
Yep, they're one of the closest living relatives of elephants.
I am constantly surprised by the world we live in.
Though if you check out what some of the Paleocene afrotheres look like, you might not think the relation is so far-fetched.
OCEPEIA (OH-SEH-PY-AH)
Humble beginnings for the mighty elephant.

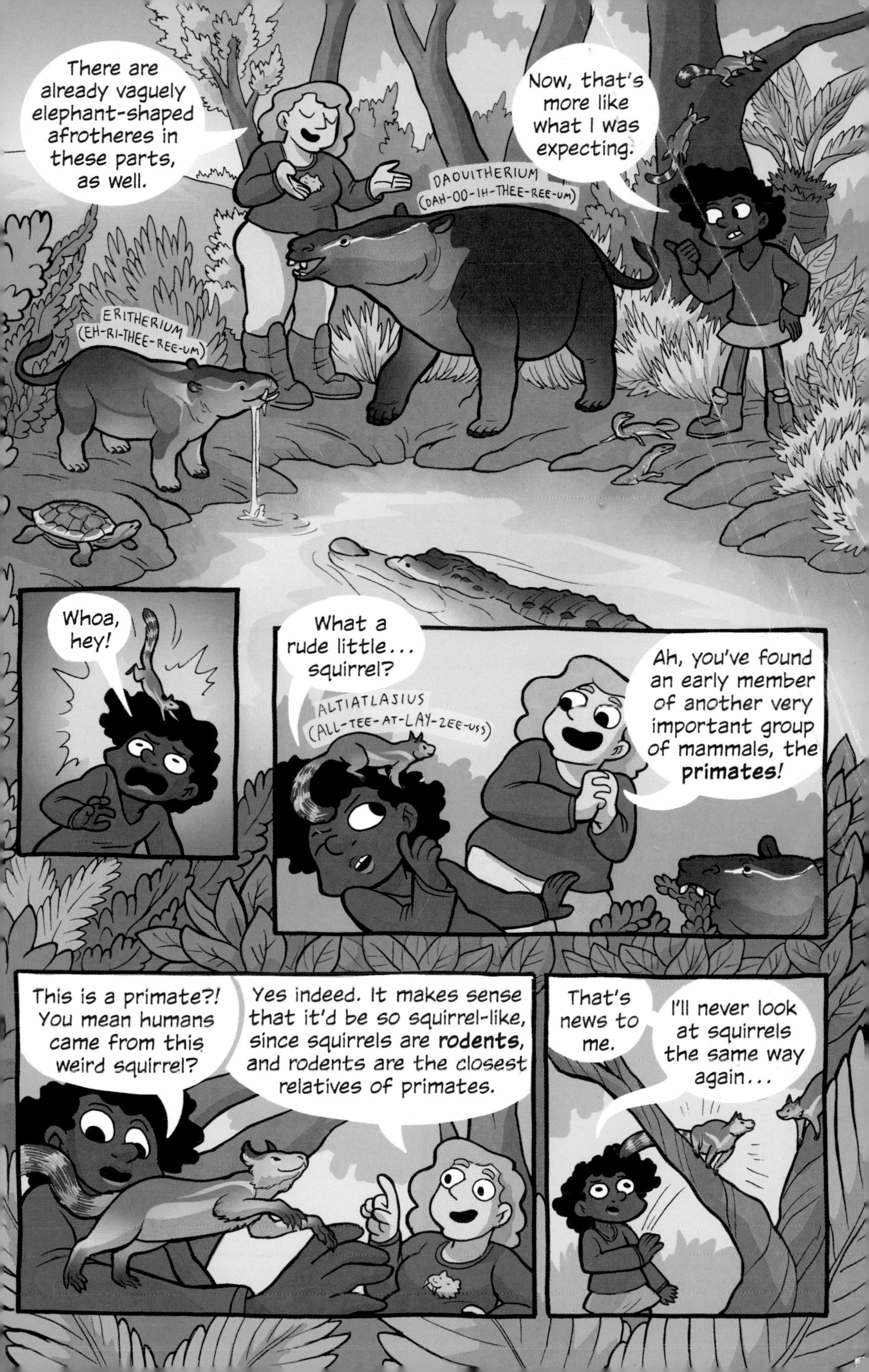
There are already vaguely elephant-shaped afrotheres in these parts, as well.
DAOUITHERIUM (DAH-OO-IH-THEE-REE-UM)
Now, that's more like what I was expecting.
ERITHERIUM (EH-RI-THEE-REE-UM)
Whoa, hey!
What a rude little... squirrel?
ALTIATLASIUS (ALL-TEE-AT-LAY-ZEE-USS)
Ah, you've found an early member of another very important group of mammals, the **primates**!
This is a primate?! You mean humans came from this weird squirrel?
Yes indeed. It makes sense that it'd be so squirrel-like, since squirrels are **rodents**, and rodents are the closest relatives of primates.
That's news to me.
I'll never look at squirrels the same way again...

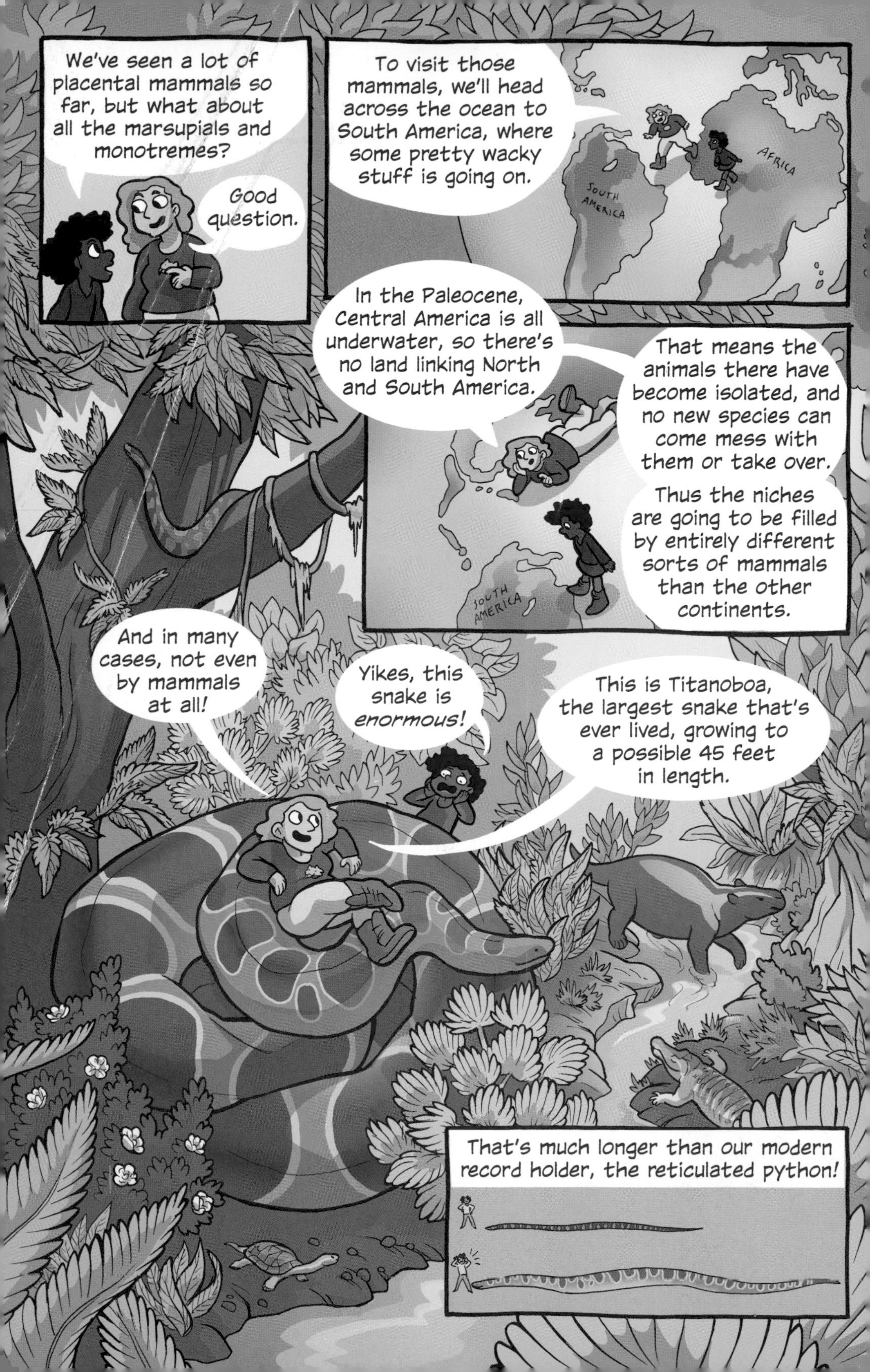
We've seen a lot of placental mammals so far, but what about all the marsupials and monotremes?
Good question.
To visit those mammals, we'll head across the ocean to South America, where some pretty wacky stuff is going on.
SOUTH AMERICA
AFRICA
In the Paleocene, Central America is all underwater, so there's no land linking North and South America.
That means the animals there have become isolated, and no new species can come mess with them or take over.
Thus the niches are going to be filled by entirely different sorts of mammals than the other continents.
SOUTH AMERICA
And in many cases, not even by mammals at all!
Yikes, this snake is *enormous*!
This is Titanoboa, the largest snake that's ever lived, growing to a possible 45 feet in length.
That's much longer than our modern record holder, the reticulated python!

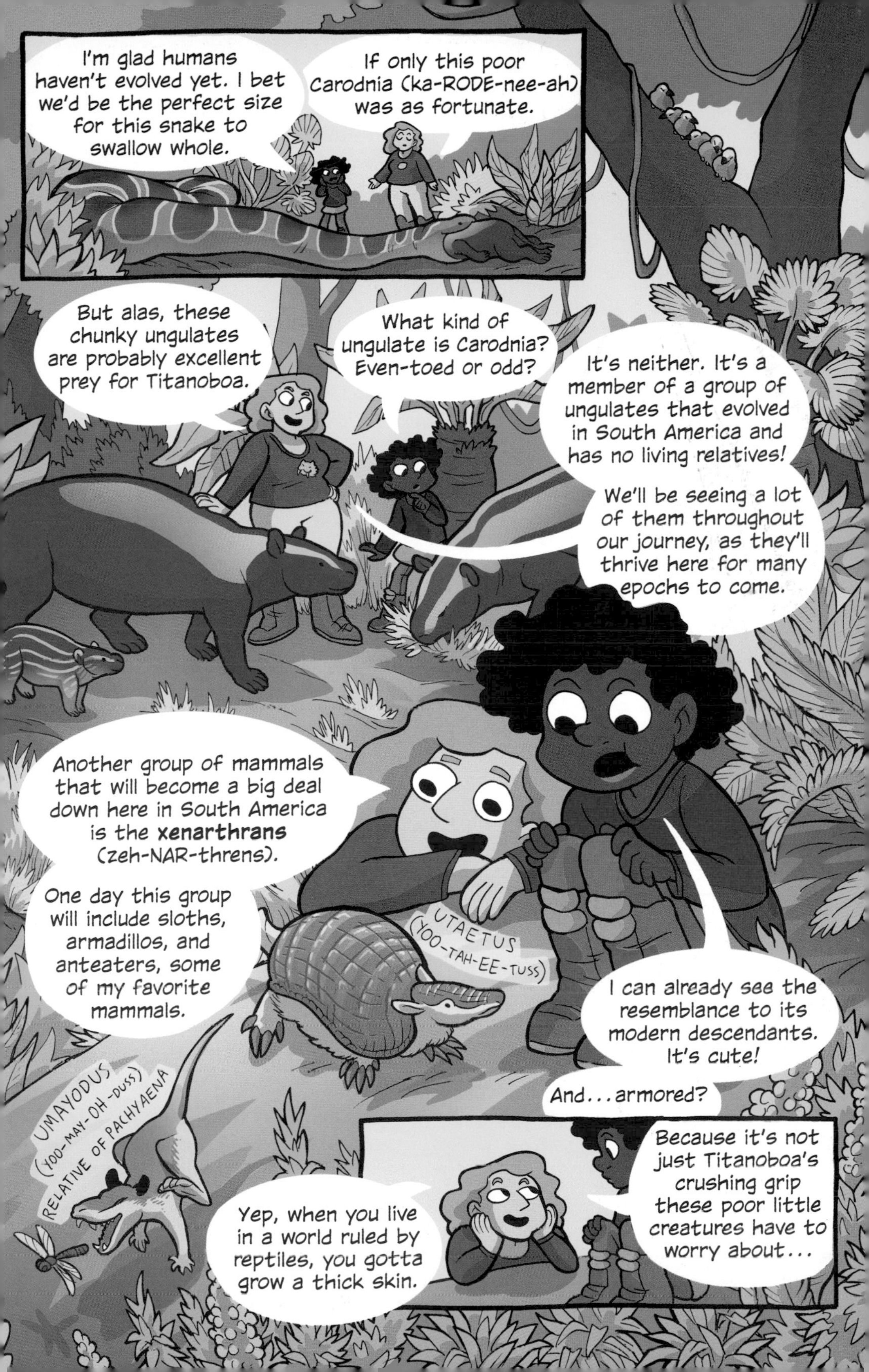

I'm glad humans haven't evolved yet. I bet we'd be the perfect size for this snake to swallow whole.
If only this poor Carodnia (ka-RODE-nee-ah) was as fortunate.
But alas, these chunky ungulates are probably excellent prey for Titanoboa.
What kind of ungulate is Carodnia? Even-toed or odd?
It's neither. It's a member of a group of ungulates that evolved in South America and has no living relatives!
We'll be seeing a lot of them throughout our journey, as they'll thrive here for many epochs to come.
Another group of mammals that will become a big deal down here in South America is the **xenarthrans** (zeh-NAR-threns).
One day this group will include sloths, armadillos, and anteaters, some of my favorite mammals.
UTAETUS (YOO-TAH-EE-TUSS)
I can already see the resemblance to its modern descendants. It's cute!
And...armored?
UMAYODUS (YOO-MAY-OH-DUSS) RELATIVE OF PACHYAENA
Yep, when you live in a world ruled by reptiles, you gotta grow a thick skin.
Because it's not just Titanoboa's crushing grip these poor little creatures have to worry about...

...It's also the jaws of crocs such as Bretesuchus (BREH-teh-SOO-kuss), one of the largest predators in Paleocene South America.
CARREJONISUCHUS (KA-RAY-HO-NEE-SOO-KUSS)
And don't think you're safe in the water, either, because its cousin Acherontisuchus (AH-ker-ON-tee-SOO-kuss) rules the waterways alongside another ferocious reptile...
...the giant freshwater turtle Carbonemys (KAR-bo-NEH-miss).
A turtle that eats meat? Aren't turtles supposed to be gentle vegetarians?
Some of them are, but some, such as snapping turtles and softshell turtles, are definitely not.
Turtles that eat meat can be quite vicious, so no doubt Carbonemys was a formidable creature!

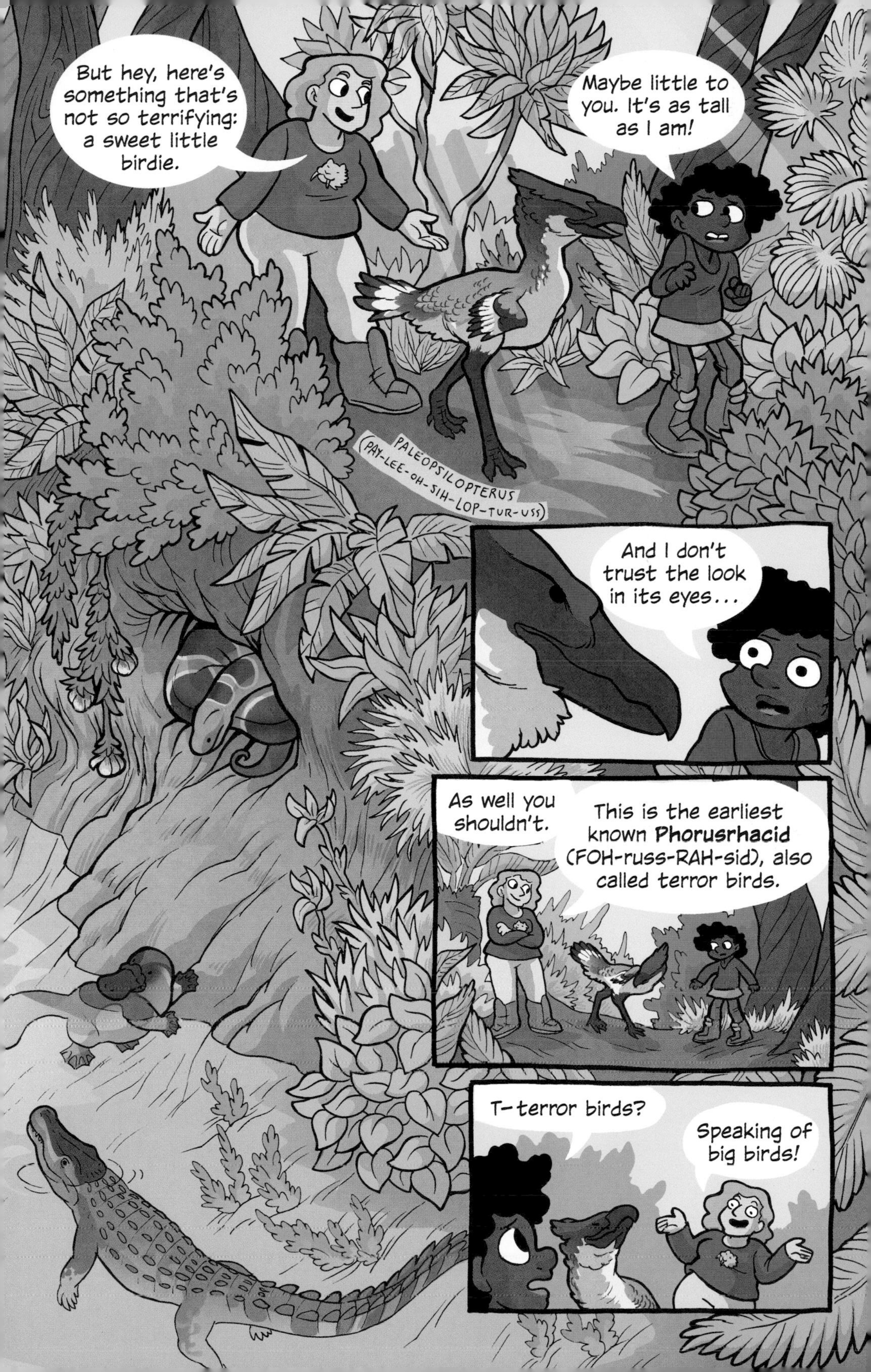
But hey, here's something that's not so terrifying: a sweet little birdie.
Maybe little to you. It's as tall as I am!
PALEOPSILOPTERUS (PAY-LEE-OH-SIH-LOP-TUR-USS)
And I don't trust the look in its eyes...
As well you shouldn't.
This is the earliest known **Phorusrhacid** (FOH-russ-RAH-sid), also called terror birds.
T-terror birds?
Speaking of big birds!

There are penguins now!
WAIMANU (WY-MAH-NOO)
Are we... still in South America?
Nope, we're in Australia now, a haven for monotremes and marsupials.
Such as Obdurodon (ob-DUR-o-don), a very large relative of modern platypus that thrived both here and in parts of South America.
How'd they get all the way over to South America?!

Through Antarctica, of course!
You're not telling me *this* is Antarctica? This place that's covered in trees and animals?
I am telling you that, yes. Antarctica only became a barren wasteland when the world got much colder.
For now, and for many millions of years to come, it's a continent full of life, though we know very little about its animals compared to how much we know about other continents.
Why is the life here so mysterious?
Because in our time, it's extremely cold and uninhabitable (meaning no people can live there), so Antarctic paleontology digs are pretty rare.
COLD.
That must mean there are a lot of undiscovered fossils in Antarctica...
That's exciting! Who knows what neat things once lived here.
It's a wonderful mystery, and I hope one day we can find out.

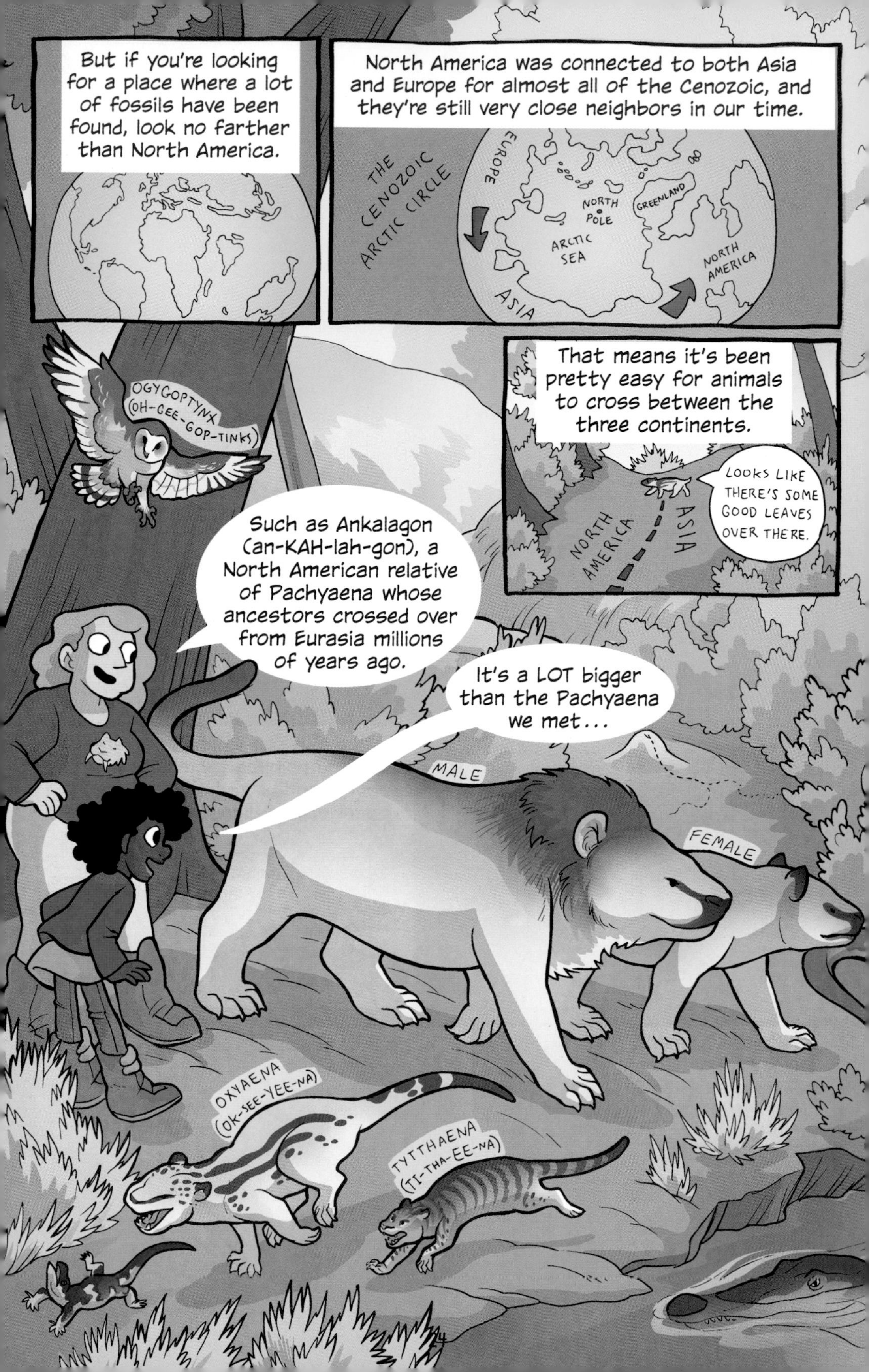

But if you're looking for a place where a lot of fossils have been found, look no farther than North America.
North America was connected to both Asia and Europe for almost all of the Cenozoic, and they're still very close neighbors in our time.
THE CENOZOIC ARCTIC CIRCLE
EUROPE
NORTH POLE
GREENLAND
ARCTIC SEA
NORTH AMERICA
ASIA
That means it's been pretty easy for animals to cross between the three continents.
LOOKS LIKE THERE'S SOME GOOD LEAVES OVER THERE.
NORTH AMERICA
ASIA
OGYGOPTYNX (OH-GEE-GOP-TINKS)
Such as Ankalagon (an-KAH-lah-gon), a North American relative of Pachyaena whose ancestors crossed over from Eurasia millions of years ago.
It's a LOT bigger than the Pachyaena we met...
MALE
FEMALE
OXYAENA (OK-SEE-YEE-NA)
TYTTHAENA (TI-THA-EE-NA)

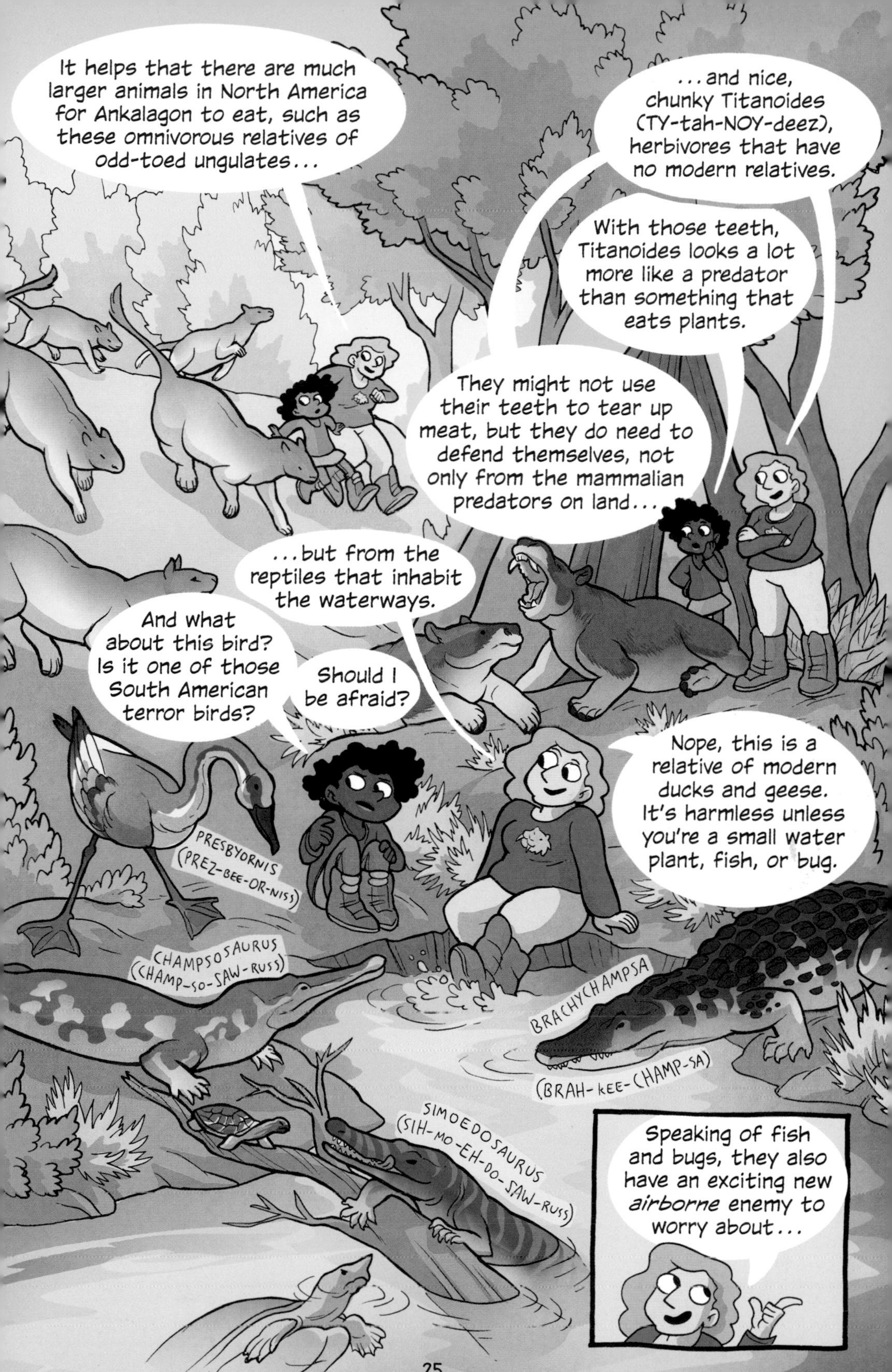

It helps that there are much larger animals in North America for Ankalagon to eat, such as these omnivorous relatives of odd-toed ungulates...
...and nice, chunky Titanoides (TY-tah-NOY-deez), herbivores that have no modern relatives.
With those teeth, Titanoides looks a lot more like a predator than something that eats plants.
They might not use their teeth to tear up meat, but they do need to defend themselves, not only from the mammalian predators on land...
...but from the reptiles that inhabit the waterways.
And what about this bird? Is it one of those South American terror birds?
Should I be afraid?
Nope, this is a relative of modern ducks and geese. It's harmless unless you're a small water plant, fish, or bug.
PRESBYORNIS (PREZ-BEE-OR-NISS)
CHAMPSOSAURUS (CHAMP-SO-SAW-RUSS)
BRACHYCHAMPSA (BRAH-KEE-CHAMP-SA)
SIMOEDOSAURUS (SIH-MO-EH-DO-SAW-RUSS)
Speaking of fish and bugs, they also have an exciting new *airborne* enemy to worry about...

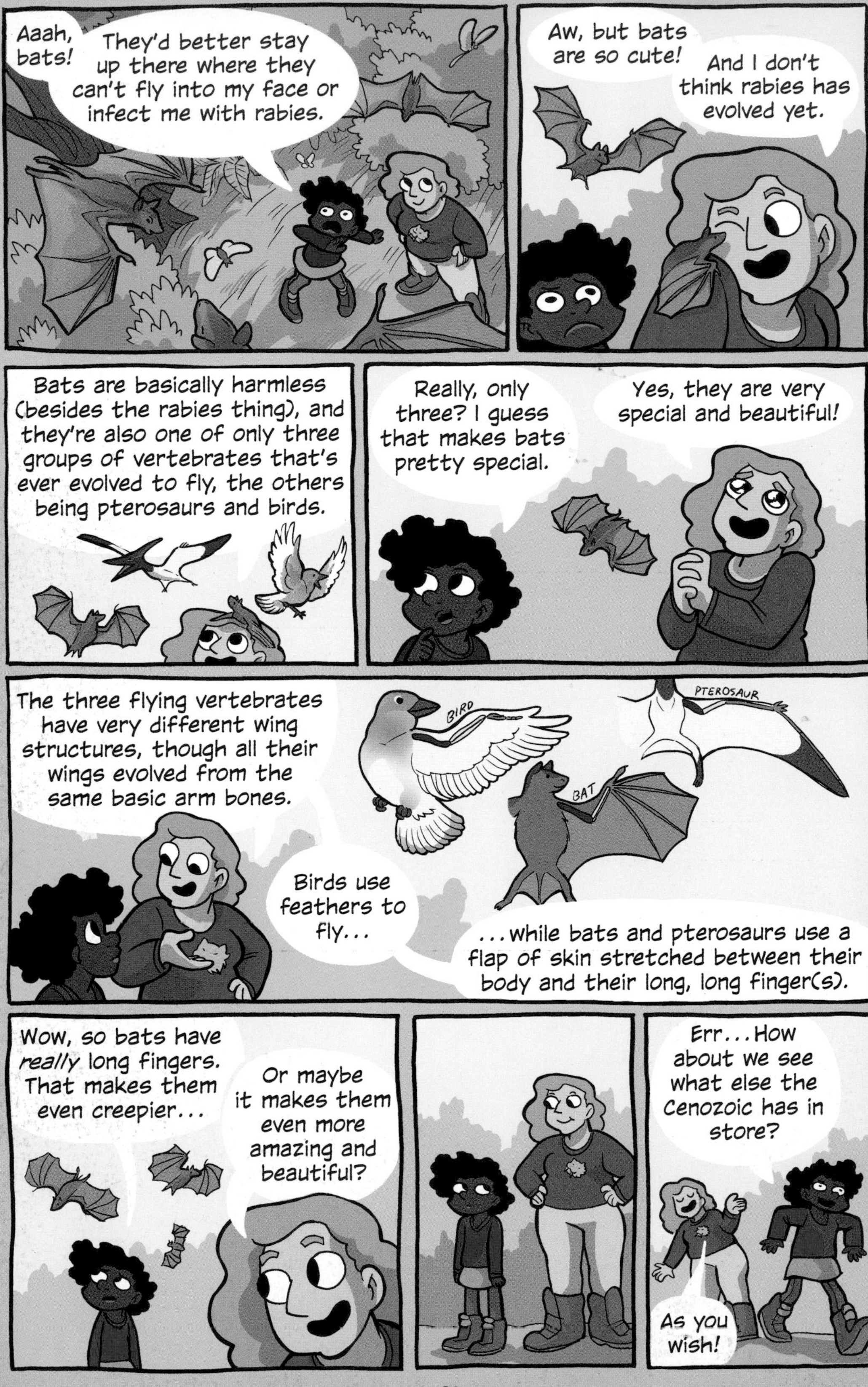

Aaah, bats!
They'd better stay up there where they can't fly into my face or infect me with rabies.
Aw, but bats are so cute!
And I don't think rabies has evolved yet.
Bats are basically harmless (besides the rabies thing), and they're also one of only three groups of vertebrates that's ever evolved to fly, the others being pterosaurs and birds.
Really, only three? I guess that makes bats pretty special.
Yes, they are very special and beautiful!
The three flying vertebrates have very different wing structures, though all their wings evolved from the same basic arm bones.
BIRD
PTEROSAUR
BAT
Birds use feathers to fly...
...while bats and pterosaurs use a flap of skin stretched between their body and their long, long finger(s).
Wow, so bats have *really* long fingers. That makes them even creepier...
Or maybe it makes them even more amazing and beautiful?
Err...How about we see what else the Cenozoic has in store?
As you wish!

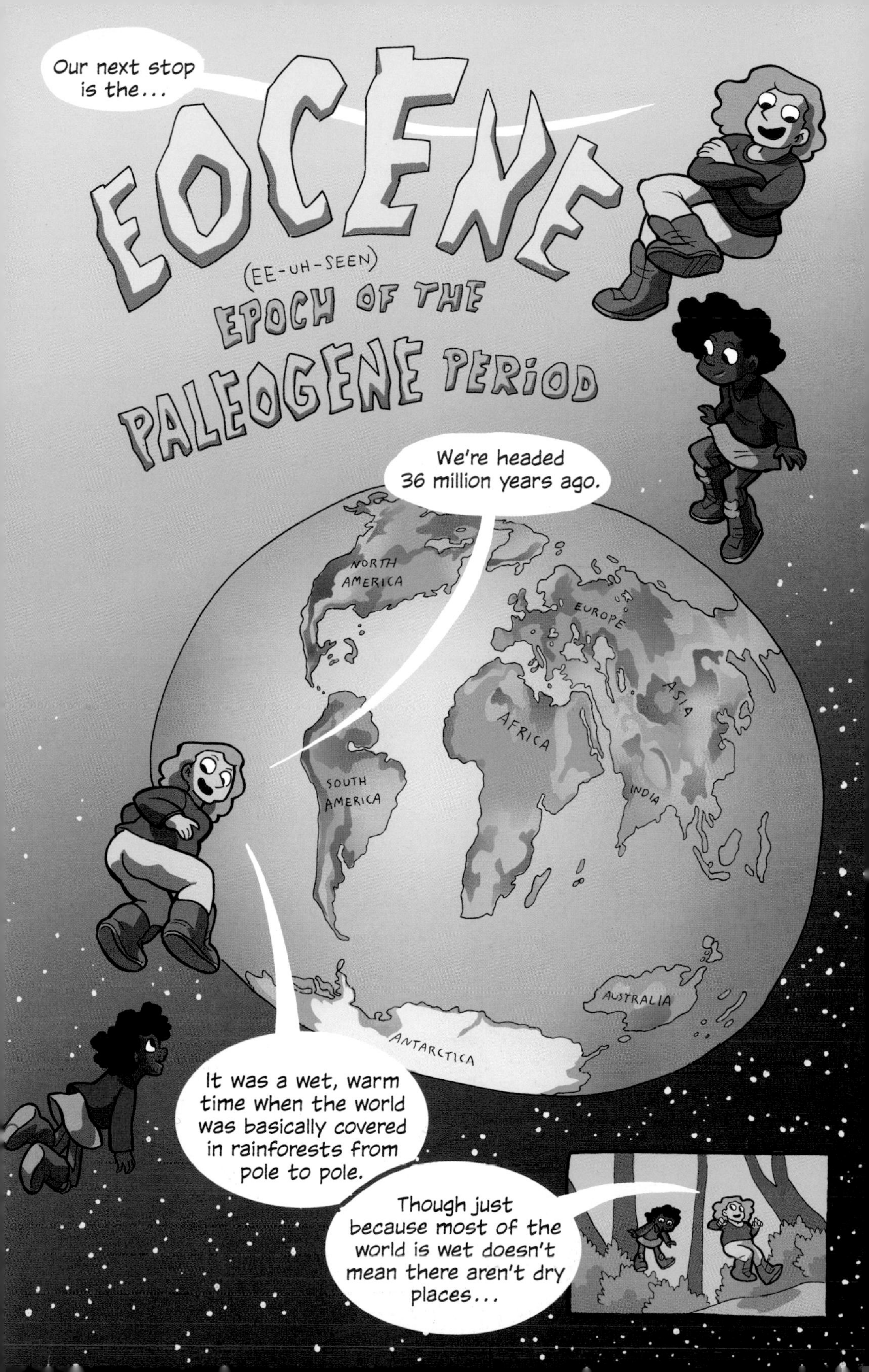
Our next stop is the...
EOCENE
(EE-UH-SEEN)
EPOCH OF THE
PALEOGENE PERIOD
We're headed 36 million years ago.
NORTH AMERICA
EUROPE
ASIA
AFRICA
SOUTH AMERICA
INDIA
AUSTRALIA
ANTARCTICA
It was a wet, warm time when the world was basically covered in rainforests from pole to pole.
Though just because most of the world is wet doesn't mean there aren't dry places...

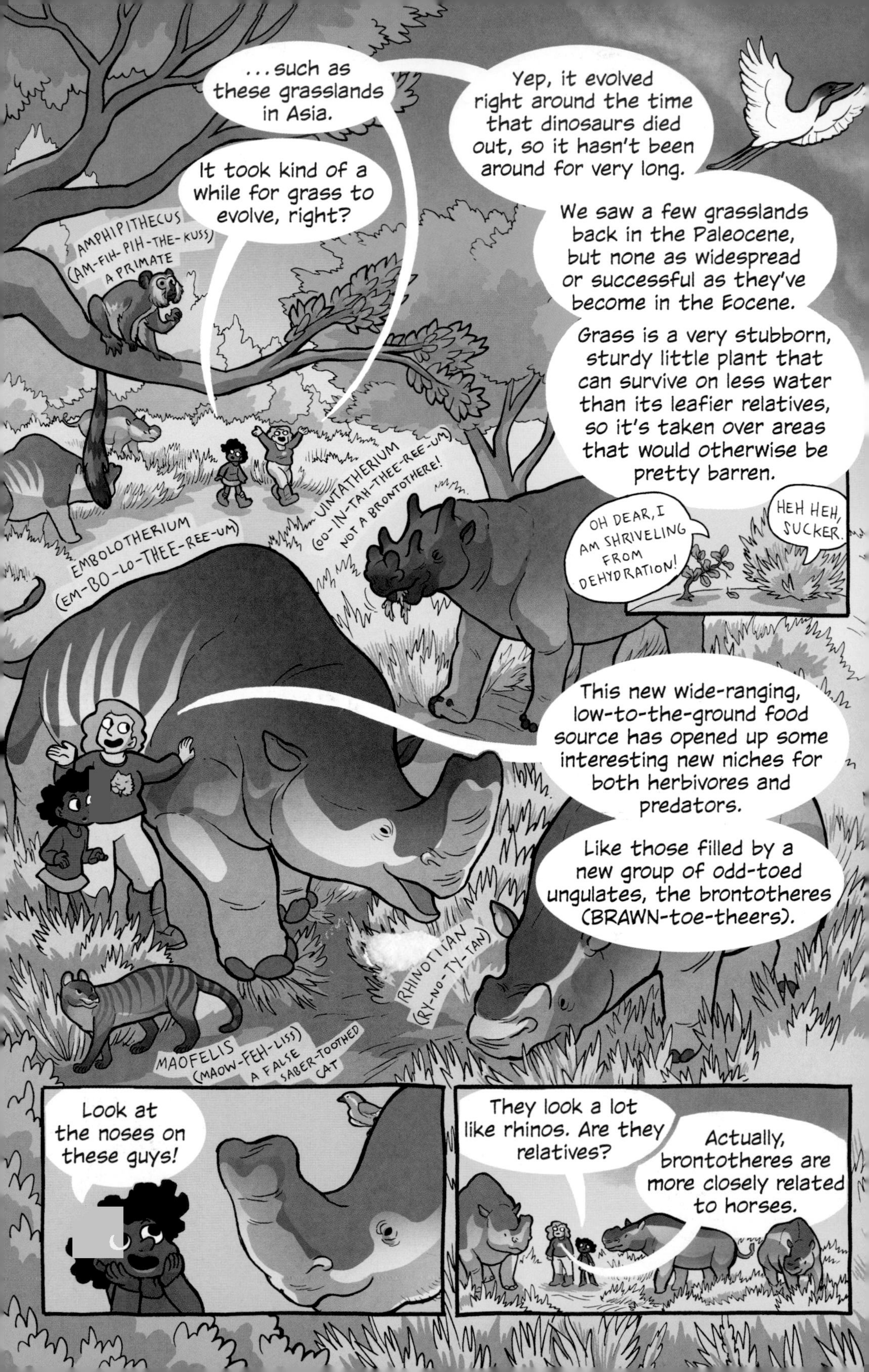

...such as these grasslands in Asia.
Yep, it evolved right around the time that dinosaurs died out, so it hasn't been around for very long.
It took kind of a while for grass to evolve, right?
We saw a few grasslands back in the Paleocene, but none as widespread or successful as they've become in the Eocene.
AMPHIPITHECUS (AM-FIH-PIH-THE-KUSS) A PRIMATE
Grass is a very stubborn, sturdy little plant that can survive on less water than its leafier relatives, so it's taken over areas that would otherwise be pretty barren.
OH DEAR, I AM SHRIVELING FROM DEHYDRATION!
HEH HEH, SUCKER.
UINTATHERIUM (OO-IN-TAH-THEE-REE-UM) NOT A BRONTOTHERE!
EMBOLOTHERIUM (EM-BO-LO-THEE-REE-UM)
This new wide-ranging, low-to-the-ground food source has opened up some interesting new niches for both herbivores and predators.
Like those filled by a new group of odd-toed ungulates, the brontotheres (BRAWN-toe-theers).
RHINOTITAN (RY-NO-TY-TAN)
MAOFELIS (MAOW-FEH-LISS) A FALSE SABER-TOOTHED CAT
Look at the noses on these guys!
They look a lot like rhinos. Are they relatives?
Actually, brontotheres are more closely related to horses.

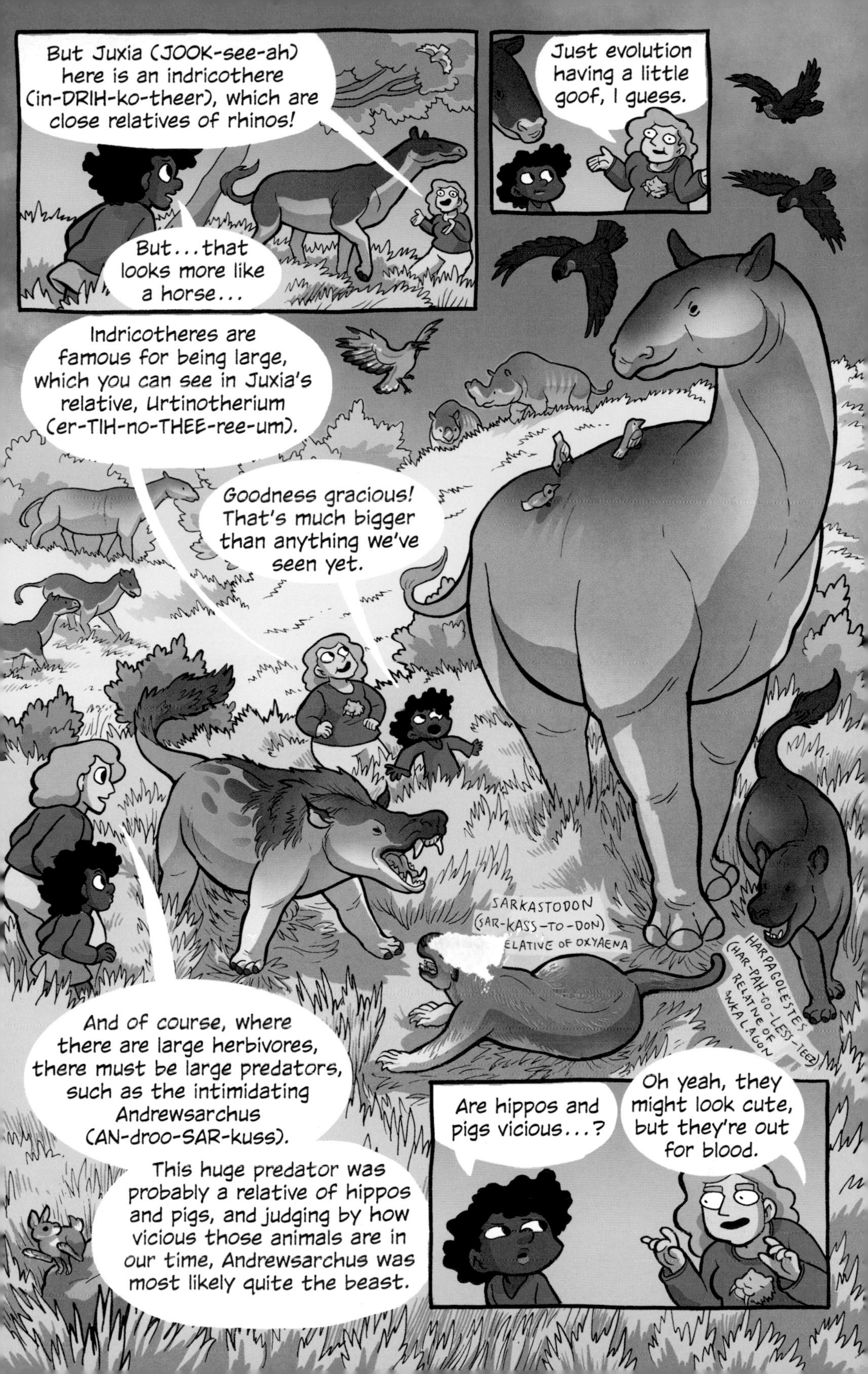
But Juxia (JOOK-see-ah) here is an indricothere (in-DRIH-ko-theer), which are close relatives of rhinos!
But...that looks more like a horse...
Just evolution having a little goof, I guess.
Indricotheres are famous for being large, which you can see in Juxia's relative, Urtinotherium (er-TIH-no-THEE-ree-um).
Goodness gracious! That's much bigger than anything we've seen yet.
SARKASTODON
(SAR-KASS-TO-DON)
ELATIVE OF OXYAENA
HARPAGOLESTES
(HAR-PAH-GO-LESS-TEEZ)
RELATIVE OF
KALAGON
And of course, where there are large herbivores, there must be large predators, such as the intimidating Andrewsarchus (AN-droo-SAR-kuss).
This huge predator was probably a relative of hippos and pigs, and judging by how vicious those animals are in our time, Andrewsarchus was most likely quite the beast.
Are hippos and pigs vicious...?
Oh yeah, they might look cute, but they're out for blood.

Andrewsarchus isn't the only relative of hippos prowling the Eurasian landscape.
Farther west, we meet the fearsome Entelodon (en-TEH-lo-don), a member of an omnivorous group of even-toed ungulates called entelodonts.
Yikes, those teeth...
HYAENODON GIGAS
There are also some strict meat eaters in these parts, from the tremendous Hyaenodon gigas (hi-YEE-no-don GIH-gass)...
...to little Miacis (my-AH-siss), which is one of the earliest relatives of modern-day carnivores.
MIACIS
But doesn't carnivore just mean "meat eater"? Aren't these all carnivores?
Yes, but there's also a group of mammals called the **carnivores**.
This group includes cats, dogs, weasels, bears ...Basically anything from our time that eats meat is a member of this group!
KITTIES
HYENAS
WEASELS
DOGGIES
SEALS
BEARS
CARNIVORA
RACCOONS
HYAENODON
ENTELODON
And they're all descendants of this cute little carnivore, while the other groups of meat eaters we've met have no living descendants.

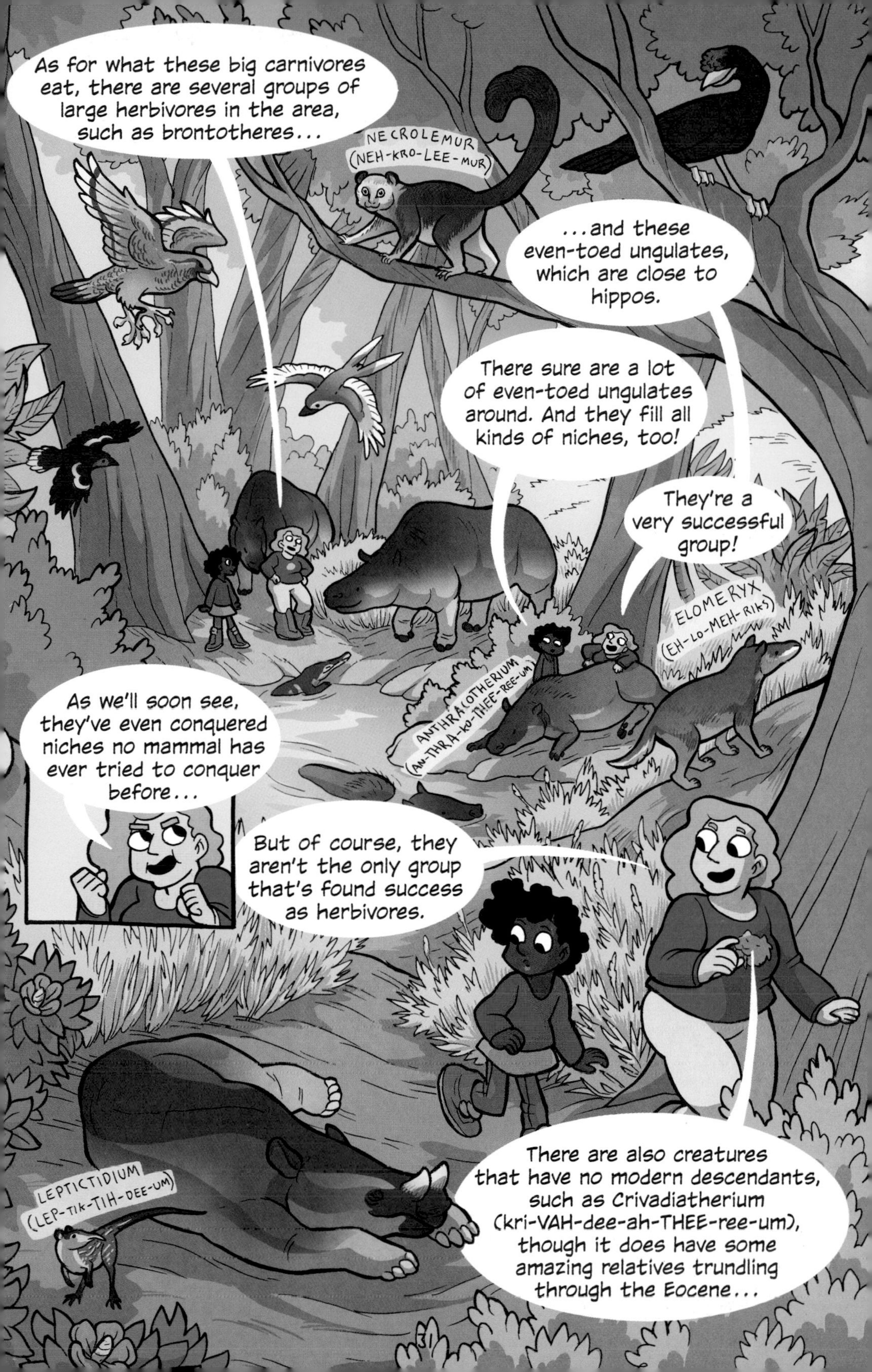
As for what these big carnivores eat, there are several groups of large herbivores in the area, such as brontotheres...
NECROLEMUR (NEH-KRO-LEE-MUR)
...and these even-toed ungulates, which are close to hippos.
There sure are a lot of even-toed ungulates around. And they fill all kinds of niches, too!
They're a very successful group!
ELOMERYX (EH-LO-MEH-RIKS)
ANTHRACOTHERIUM (AN-THRA-KO-THEE-REE-UM)
As we'll soon see, they've even conquered niches no mammal has ever tried to conquer before...
But of course, they aren't the only group that's found success as herbivores.
There are also creatures that have no modern descendants, such as Crivadiatherium (kri-VAH-dee-ah-THEE-ree-um), though it does have some amazing relatives trundling through the Eocene...
LEPTICTIDIUM (LEP-TIK-TIH-DEE-UM)

...such as the African two-horned Arsinoitherium (AR-sih-NO-ih-THEE-ree-um), one of the most impressive herbivores of its time.
Though Africa is quickly becoming elephant country, as the small relatives of elephants we met in the Paleocene have begun to evolve into strange and interesting forms.
Wow, like this guy! What's up with its mouth?
This lovely Phiomia (fy-OH-mee-ah) is a kind of shovel-mouthed proboscidean (PRO-baw-SIH-dee-an), which is a group of creatures that will one day include modern elephants.
PALAEOMASTODON (PAY-LEE-OH-MASS-TO-DON) A PROBOSCIDEAN
BARYTHERIUM (BARE-EE-THEE-REE-UM) A PROBOSCIDEAN
RELATIVE OF HYAENODON
MOERITHERIUM (MOW-AIR-IH-THEE-REE-UM) A PROBOSCIDEAN
DILAMBDOGALE (DY-LAM-DO-GAYL) AN AFROTHERE

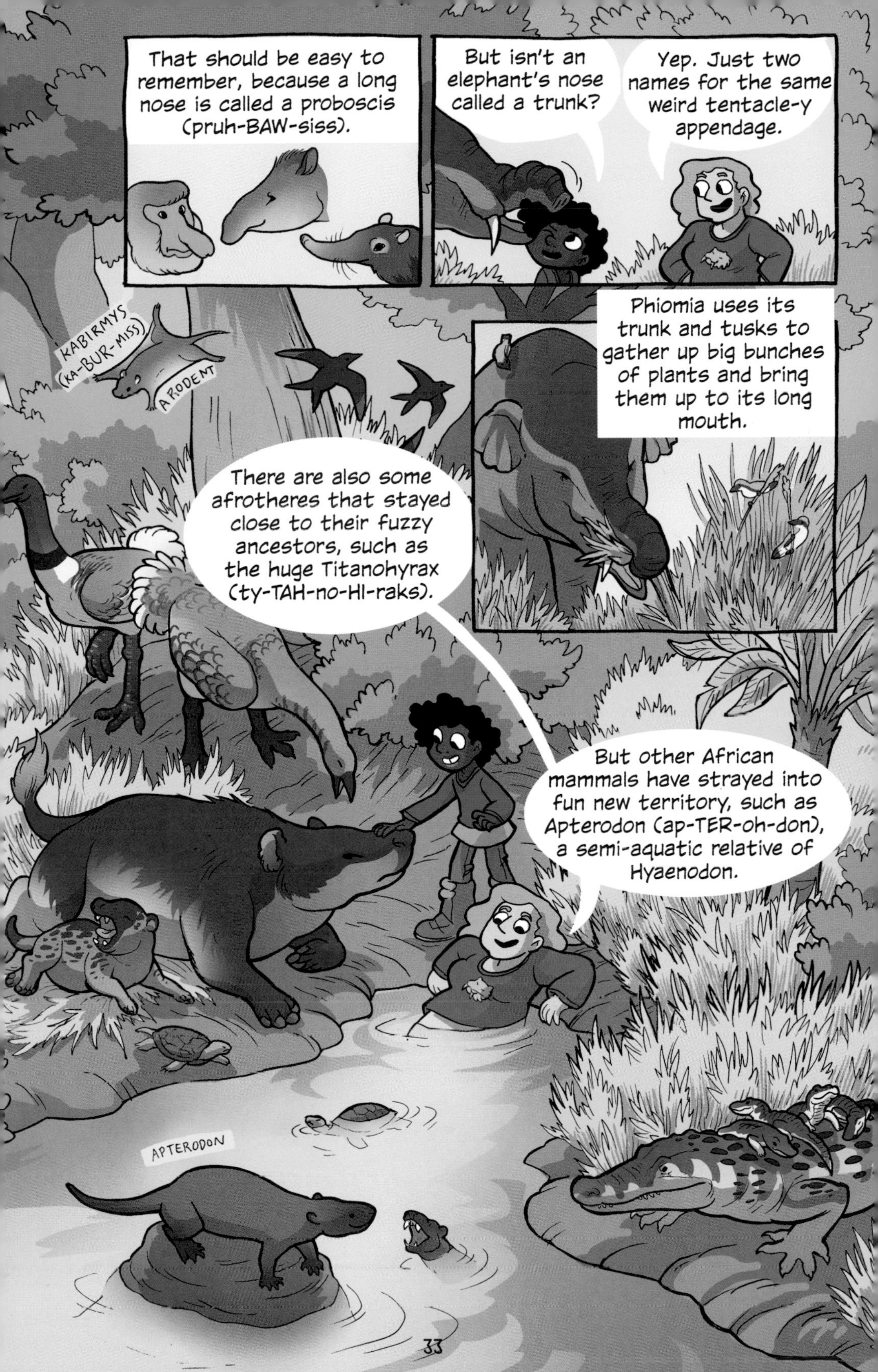
That should be easy to remember, because a long nose is called a proboscis (pruh-BAW-siss).
But isn't an elephant's nose called a trunk?
Yep. Just two names for the same weird tentacle-y appendage.
KABIRMYS (KA-BUR-MISS)
A RODENT
Phiomia uses its trunk and tusks to gather up big bunches of plants and bring them up to its long mouth.
There are also some afrotheres that stayed close to their fuzzy ancestors, such as the huge Titanohyrax (ty-TAH-no-HI-raks).
But other African mammals have strayed into fun new territory, such as Apterodon (ap-TER-oh-don), a semi-aquatic relative of Hyaenodon.
APTERODON

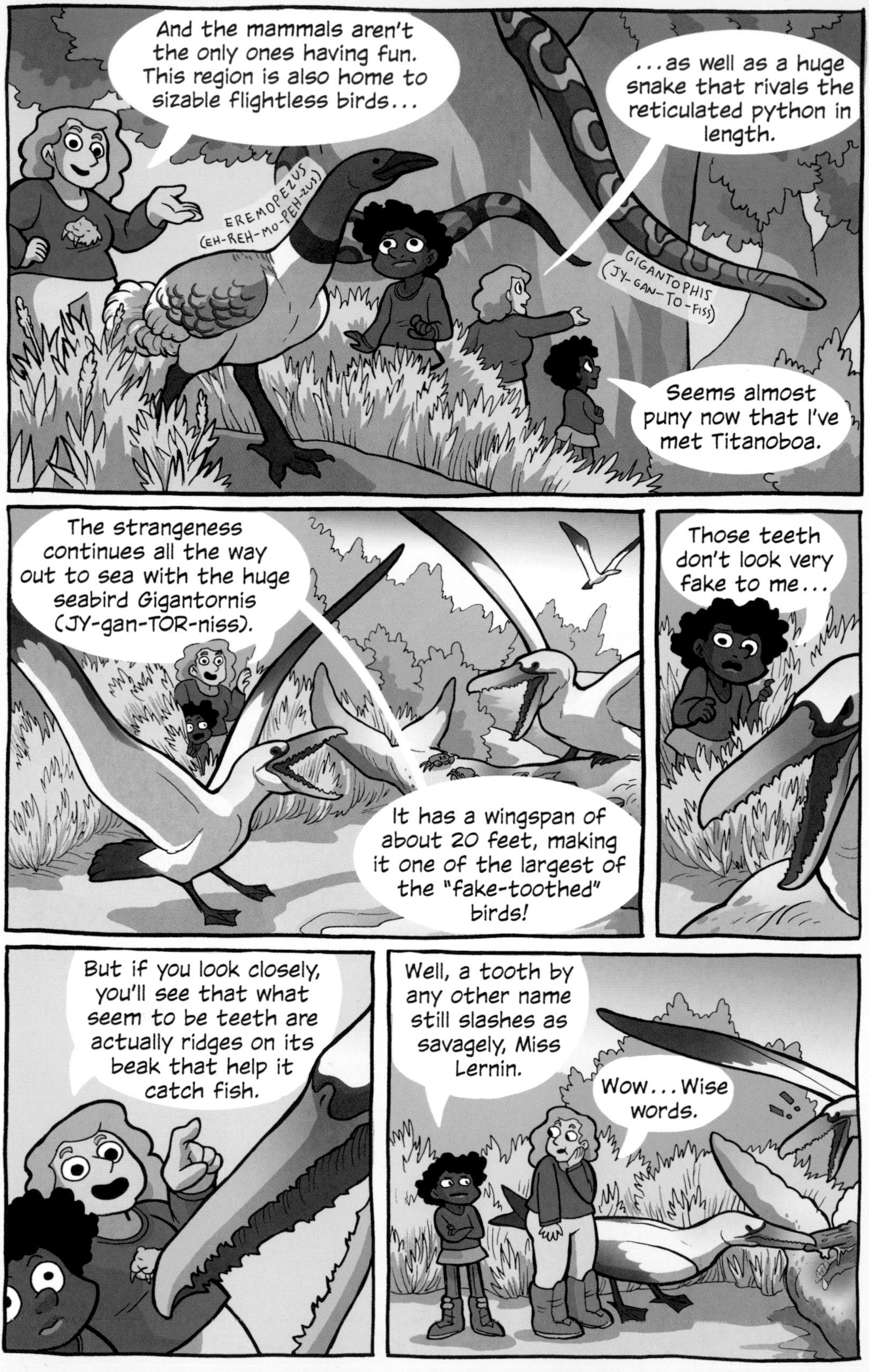
And the mammals aren't the only ones having fun. This region is also home to sizable flightless birds...
EREMOPEZUS (EH-REH-MO-PEH-ZUS)
...as well as a huge snake that rivals the reticulated python in length.
GIGANTOPHIS (JY-GAN-TO-FISS)
Seems almost puny now that I've met Titanoboa.
The strangeness continues all the way out to sea with the huge seabird Gigantornis (JY-gan-TOR-niss).
It has a wingspan of about 20 feet, making it one of the largest of the "fake-toothed" birds!
Those teeth don't look very fake to me...
But if you look closely, you'll see that what seem to be teeth are actually ridges on its beak that help it catch fish.
Well, a tooth by any other name still slashes as savagely, Miss Lernin.
Wow... Wise words.

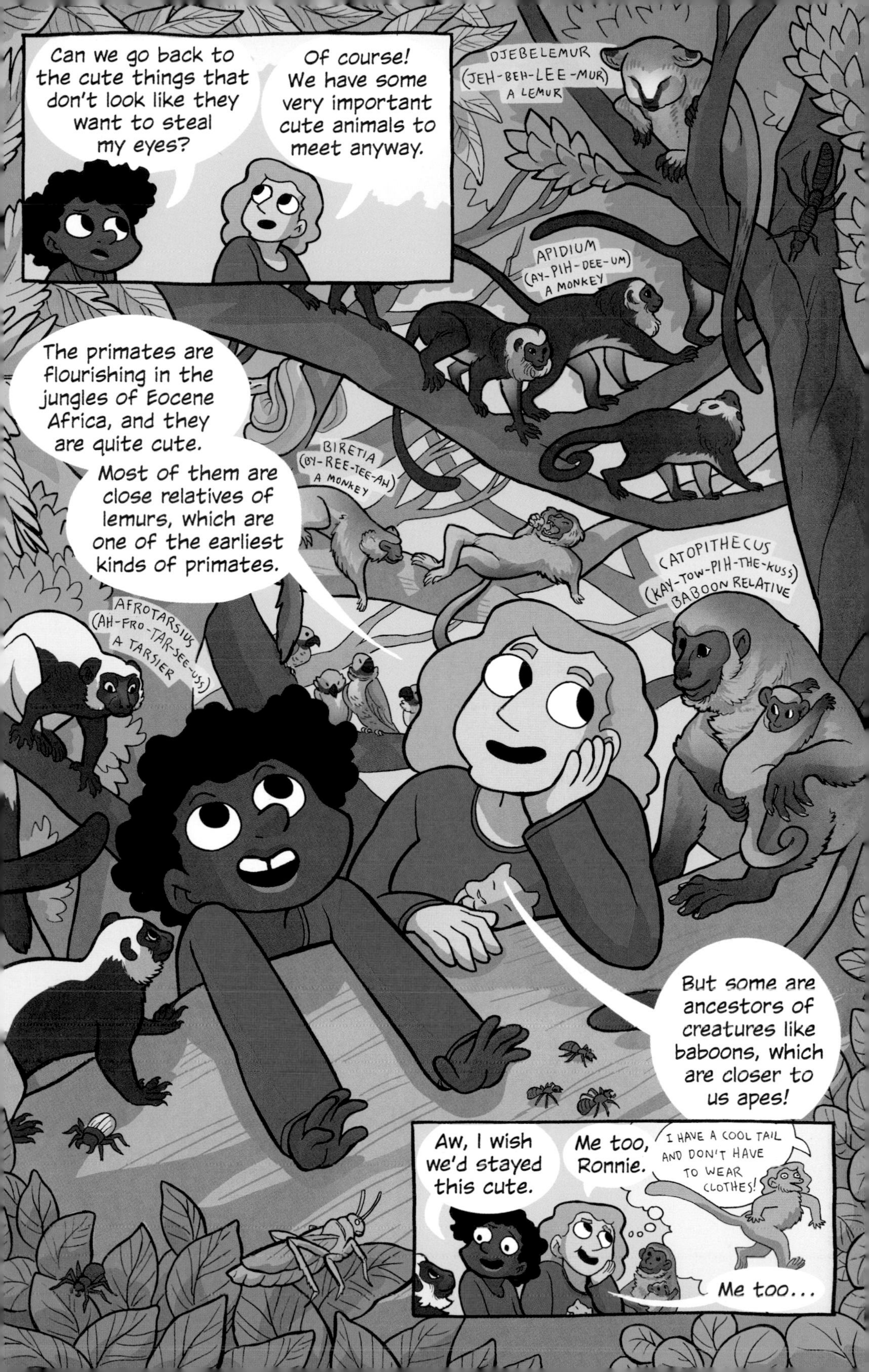

Can we go back to the cute things that don't look like they want to steal my eyes?
Of course! We have some very important cute animals to meet anyway.
DJEBELEMUR (JEH-BEH-LEE-MUR) A LEMUR
APIDIUM (AY-PIH-DEE-UM) A MONKEY
The primates are flourishing in the jungles of Eocene Africa, and they are quite cute.
Most of them are close relatives of lemurs, which are one of the earliest kinds of primates.
BIRETIA (BY-REE-TEE-AH) A MONKEY
CATOPITHECUS (KAY-TOW-PIH-THE-KUSS) BABOON RELATIVE
AFROTARSIUS (AH-FRO-TAR-SEE-USS) A TARSIER
But some are ancestors of creatures like baboons, which are closer to us apes!
Aw, I wish we'd stayed this cute.
Me too, Ronnie.
I HAVE A COOL TAIL AND DON'T HAVE TO WEAR CLOTHES!
Me too...

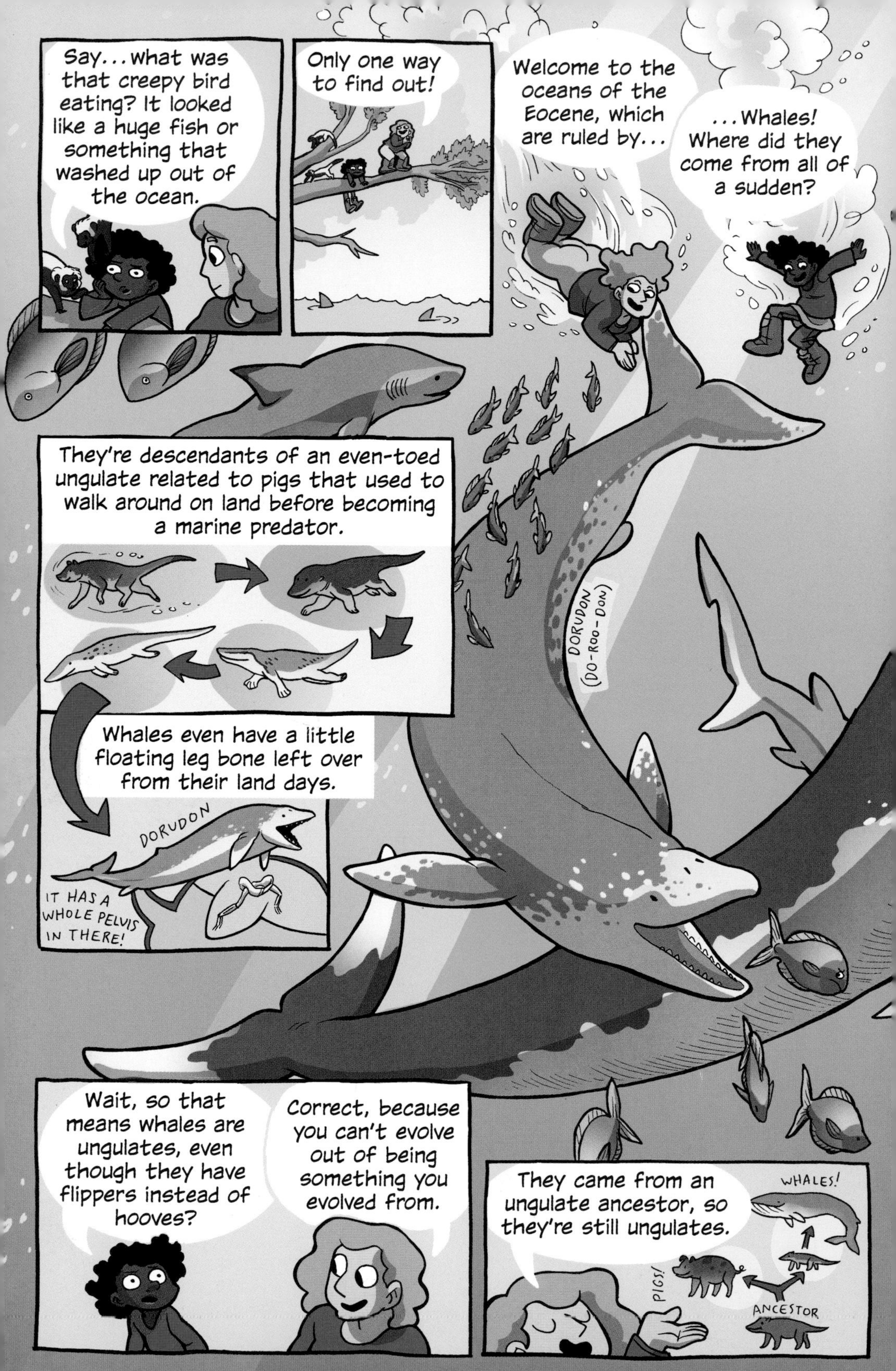

Say...what was that creepy bird eating? It looked like a huge fish or something that washed up out of the ocean.
Only one way to find out!
Welcome to the oceans of the Eocene, which are ruled by...
...Whales! Where did they come from all of a sudden?
They're descendants of an even-toed ungulate related to pigs that used to walk around on land before becoming a marine predator.
DORUDON (DO-ROO-DON)
Whales even have a little floating leg bone left over from their land days.
DORUDON
IT HAS A WHOLE PELVIS IN THERE!
Wait, so that means whales are ungulates, even though they have flippers instead of hooves?
Correct, because you can't evolve out of being something you evolved from.
They came from an ungulate ancestor, so they're still ungulates.
WHALES!
PIGS!
ANCESTOR

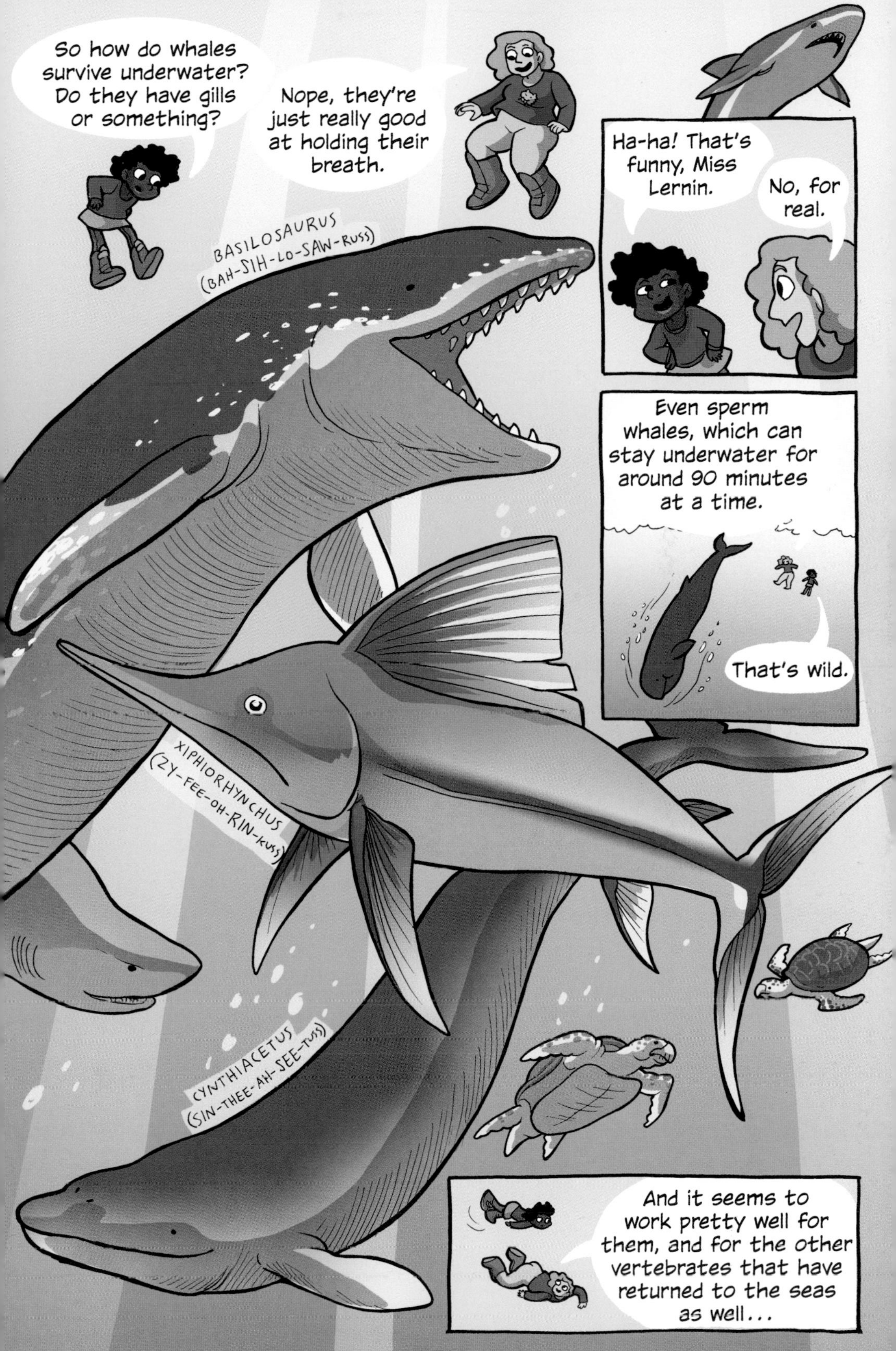

So how do whales survive underwater? Do they have gills or something?
Nope, they're just really good at holding their breath.
BASILOSAURUS (BAH-SIH-LO-SAW-RUSS)
Ha-ha! That's funny, Miss Lernin.
No, for real.
Even sperm whales, which can stay underwater for around 90 minutes at a time.
That's wild.
XIPHIORHYNCHUS (ZY-FEE-OH-RIN-KUSS)
CYNTHIACETUS (SIN-THEE-AH-SEE-TUSS)
And it seems to work pretty well for them, and for the other vertebrates that have returned to the seas as well...

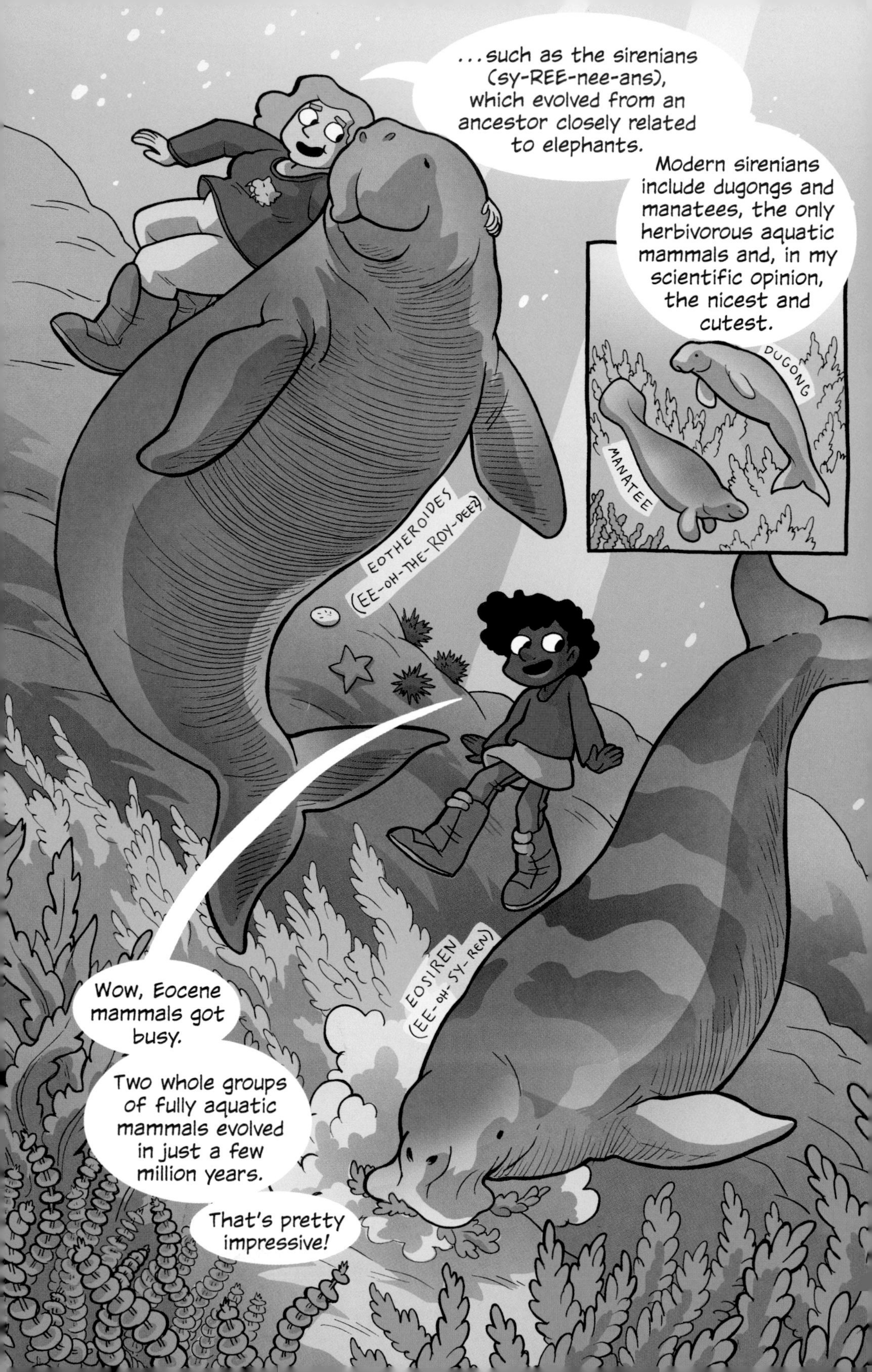

...such as the sirenians (sy-REE-nee-ans), which evolved from an ancestor closely related to elephants.
Modern sirenians include dugongs and manatees, the only herbivorous aquatic mammals and, in my scientific opinion, the nicest and cutest.
DUGONG
MANATEE
EOTHEROIDES (EE-OH-THE-ROY-DEEZ)
EOSIREN (EE-OH-SY-REN)
Wow, Eocene mammals got busy.
Two whole groups of fully aquatic mammals evolved in just a few million years.
That's pretty impressive!

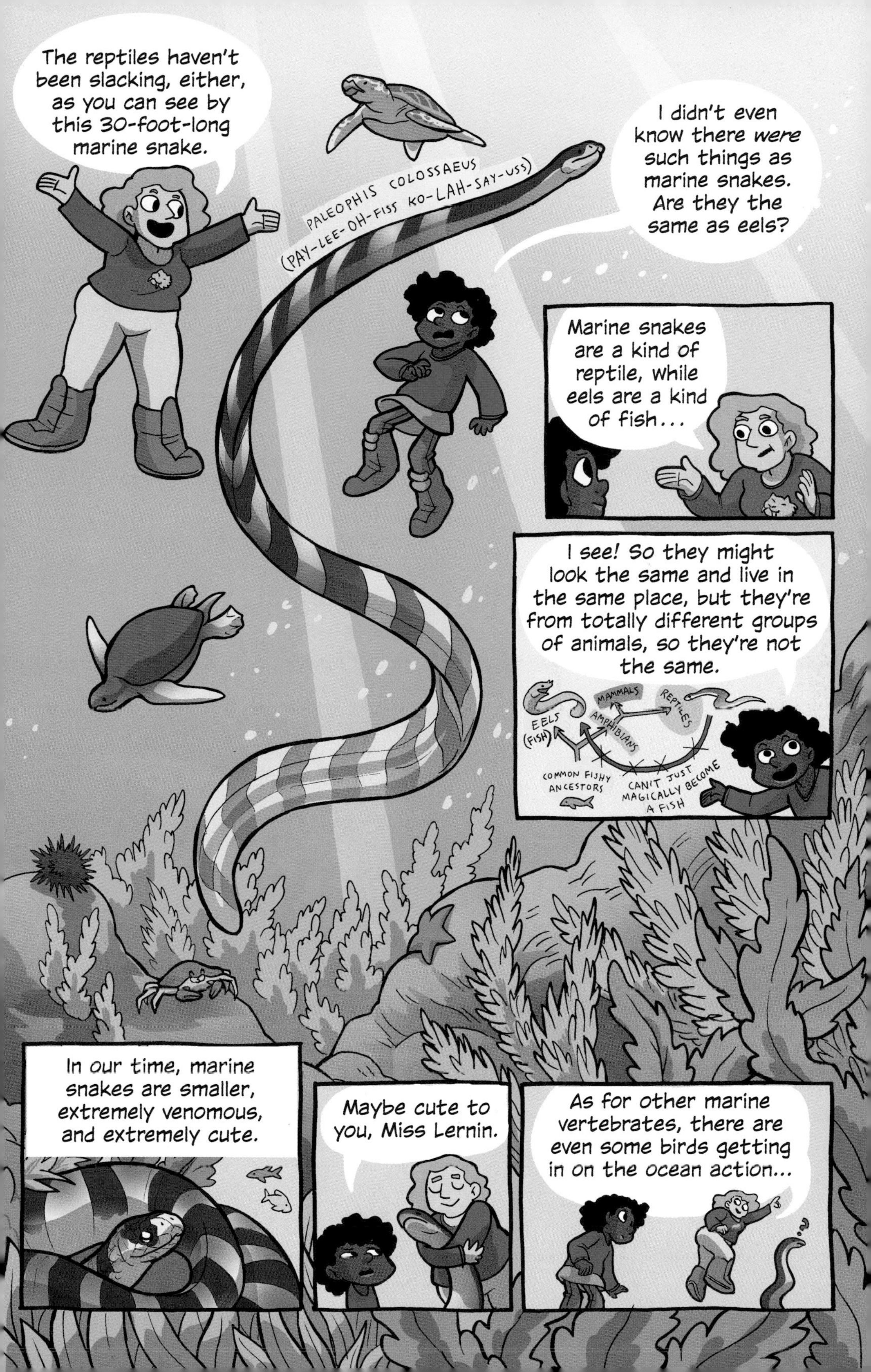
The reptiles haven't been slacking, either, as you can see by this 30-foot-long marine snake.
PALEOPHIS COLOSSAEUS
(PAY-LEE-OH-FISS KO-LAH-SAY-USS)
I didn't even know there *were* such things as marine snakes. Are they the same as eels?
Marine snakes are a kind of reptile, while eels are a kind of fish...
I see! So they might look the same and live in the same place, but they're from totally different groups of animals, so they're not the same.
EELS (FISH)
MAMMALS
AMPHIBIANS
REPTILES
COMMON FISHY ANCESTORS
CAN'T JUST MAGICALLY BECOME A FISH
In our time, marine snakes are smaller, extremely venomous, and extremely cute.
Maybe cute to you, Miss Lernin.
As for other marine vertebrates, there are even some birds getting in on the ocean action...

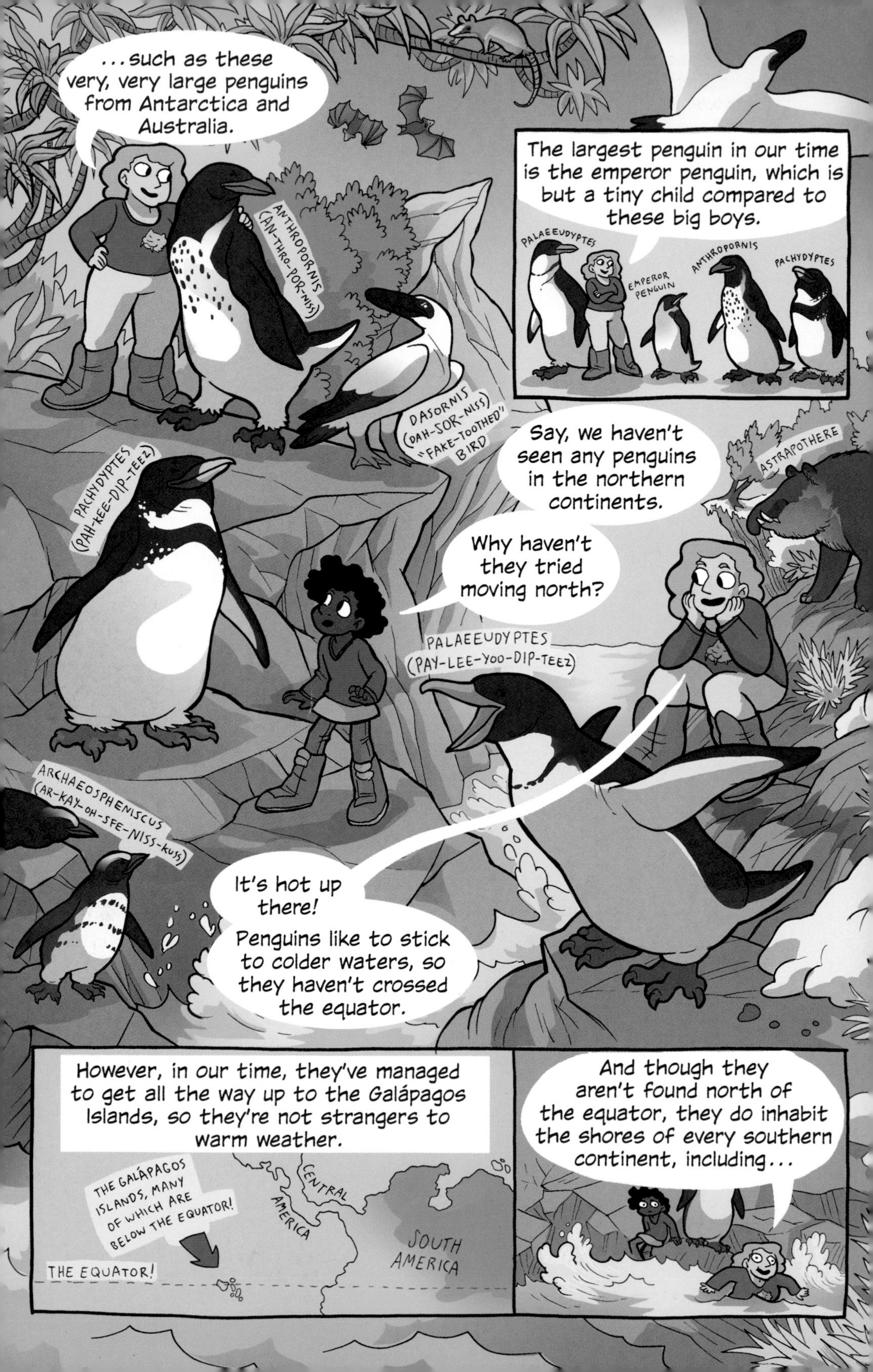
...such as these very, very large penguins from Antarctica and Australia.
ANTHROPORNIS (AN-THRO-POR-NISS)
The largest penguin in our time is the emperor penguin, which is but a tiny child compared to these big boys.
PALAEEUDYPTES
EMPEROR PENGUIN
ANTHROPORNIS
PACHYDYPTES
DASORNIS (DAH-SOR-NISS) "FAKE-TOOTHED" BIRD
PACHYDYPTES (PAH-KEE-DIP-TEEZ)
Say, we haven't seen any penguins in the northern continents.
ASTRAPOTHERE
Why haven't they tried moving north?
PALAEEUDYPTES (PAY-LEE-YOO-DIP-TEEZ)
ARCHAEOSPHENISCUS (AR-KAY-OH-SFE-NISS-KUSS)
It's hot up there!
Penguins like to stick to colder waters, so they haven't crossed the equator.
However, in our time, they've managed to get all the way up to the Galápagos Islands, so they're not strangers to warm weather.
THE GALÁPAGOS ISLANDS, MANY OF WHICH ARE BELOW THE EQUATOR!
CENTRAL AMERICA
SOUTH AMERICA
THE EQUATOR!
And though they aren't found north of the equator, they do inhabit the shores of every southern continent, including...

...South America, which has its own share of Eocene penguins.
ICADYPTES (IH-KAH-DIP-TEEZ)
Ooo, and more of those land crocs!
Yep, South America is still run by reptiles. The top predators are crocs like these that hunt exclusively on land, unlike their water-dwelling cousins.
ELAPHROCNEMUS (EH-LAH-FROK-NEH-MUSS)
SEBECUS (SEH-BEH-KUSS)
BARINASUCHUS (BAH-RIH-NAH-SOO-KUSS)
This isn't related to elephants, right?
I've been fooled by these South American mammals before, but the tusks and trunk are so similar to afrotheres...
COLOMBITHERIUM (KO-LOM-BEE-THEE-REE-UM) SOUTH AMERICAN UNGULATE
XENARTHRAN
NOTOSTYLOPS (NO-TO-STY-LOPS) A SOUTH AMERICAN UNGULATE
Indeed, Astraponotus (ah-STRAH-po-NO-tuss) is not an afrothere, but a kind of South American ungulate. Like the Carodnia we met back in the Paleocene.

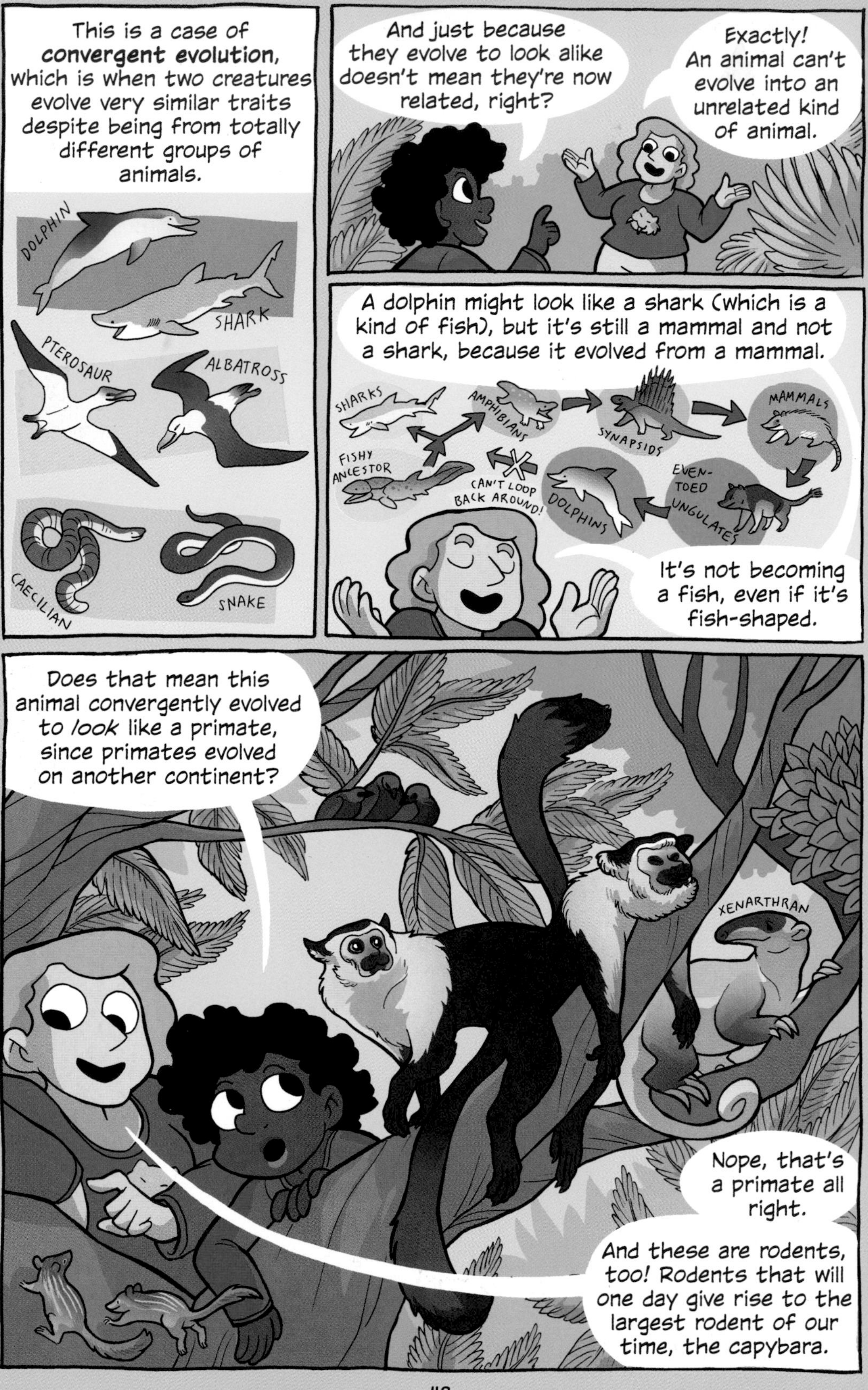
This is a case of **convergent evolution**, which is when two creatures evolve very similar traits despite being from totally different groups of animals.
DOLPHIN
SHARK
PTEROSAUR
ALBATROSS
CAECILIAN
SNAKE
And just because they evolve to look alike doesn't mean they're now related, right?
Exactly! An animal can't evolve into an unrelated kind of animal.
A dolphin might look like a shark (which is a kind of fish), but it's still a mammal and not a shark, because it evolved from a mammal.
SHARKS
AMPHIBIANS
SYNAPSIDS
MAMMALS
FISHY ANCESTOR
CAN'T LOOP BACK AROUND!
DOLPHINS
EVEN-TOED UNGULATES
It's not becoming a fish, even if it's fish-shaped.
Does that mean this animal convergently evolved to *look* like a primate, since primates evolved on another continent?
XENARTHRAN
Nope, that's a primate all right.
And these are rodents, too! Rodents that will one day give rise to the largest rodent of our time, the capybara.

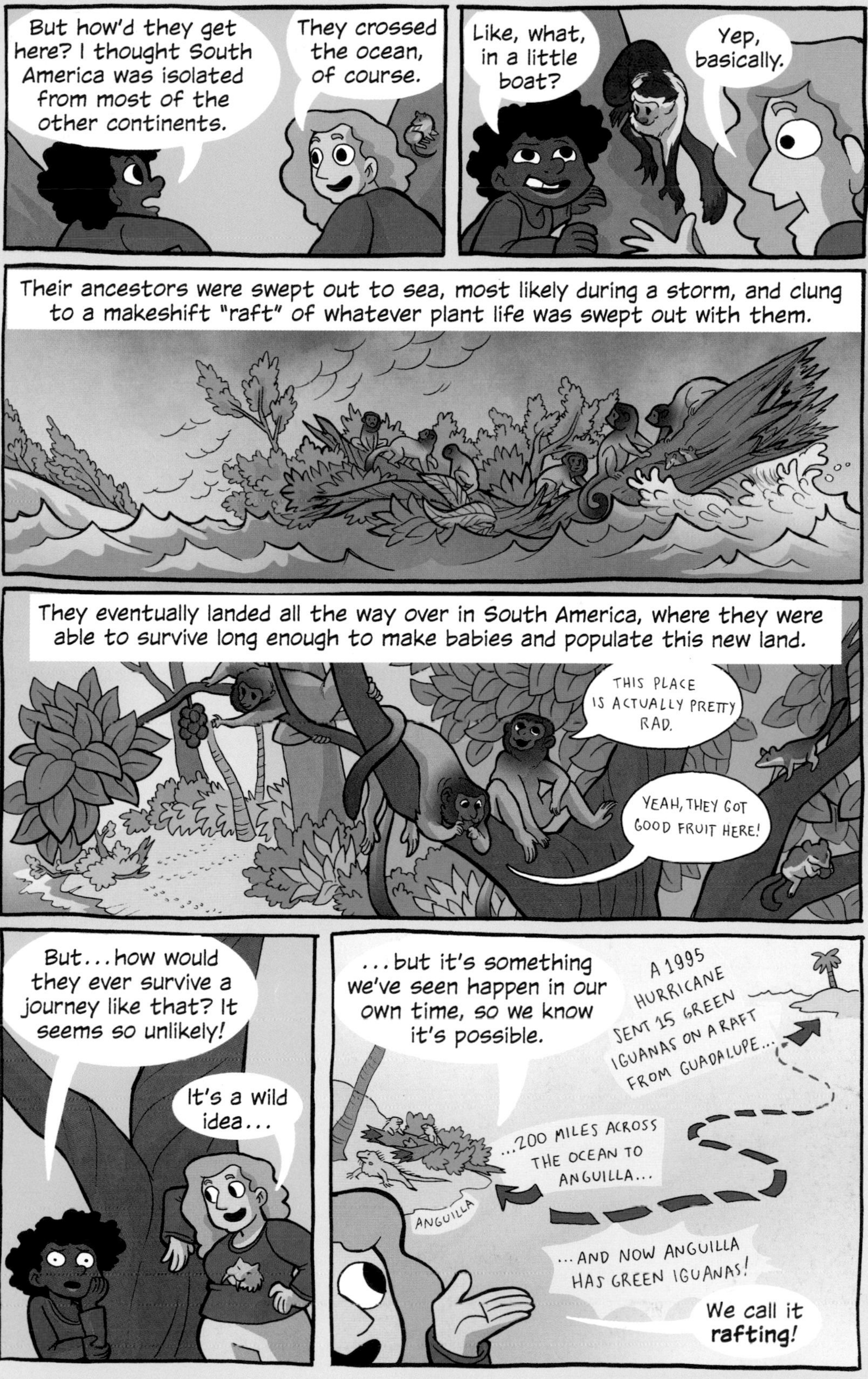
But how'd they get here? I thought South America was isolated from most of the other continents.
They crossed the ocean, of course.
Like, what, in a little boat?
Yep, basically.
Their ancestors were swept out to sea, most likely during a storm, and clung to a makeshift "raft" of whatever plant life was swept out with them.
They eventually landed all the way over in South America, where they were able to survive long enough to make babies and populate this new land.
THIS PLACE IS ACTUALLY PRETTY RAD.
YEAH, THEY GOT GOOD FRUIT HERE!
But... how would they ever survive a journey like that? It seems so unlikely!
It's a wild idea...
...but it's something we've seen happen in our own time, so we know it's possible.
A 1995 HURRICANE SENT 15 GREEN IGUANAS ON A RAFT FROM GUADALUPE...
...200 MILES ACROSS THE OCEAN TO ANGUILLA...
ANGUILLA
...AND NOW ANGUILLA HAS GREEN IGUANAS!
We call it **rafting!**

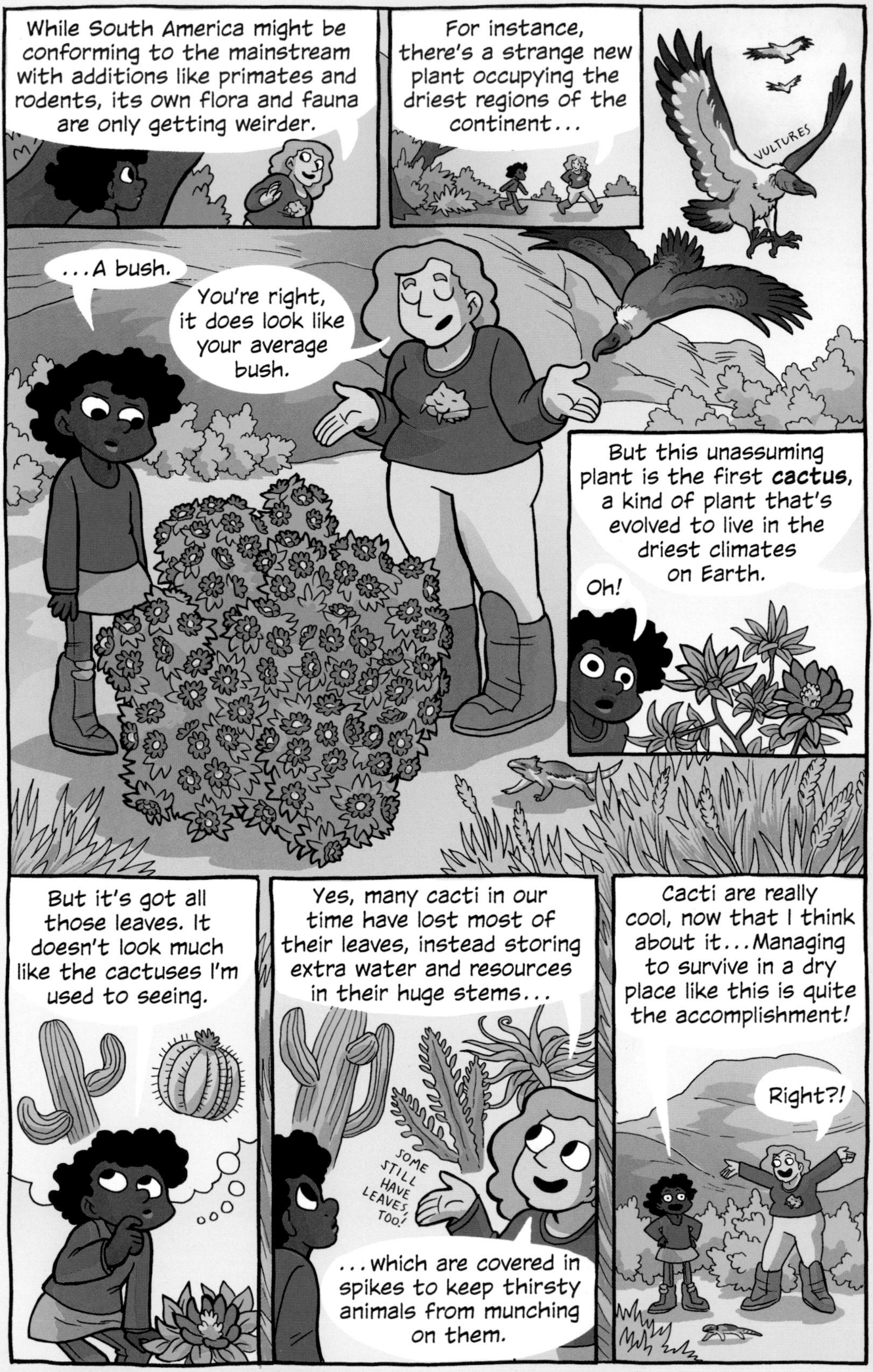
While South America might be conforming to the mainstream with additions like primates and rodents, its own flora and fauna are only getting weirder.
For instance, there's a strange new plant occupying the driest regions of the continent...
VULTURES
...A bush.
You're right, it does look like your average bush.
But this unassuming plant is the first **cactus**, a kind of plant that's evolved to live in the driest climates on Earth.
Oh!
But it's got all those leaves. It doesn't look much like the cactuses I'm used to seeing.
Yes, many cacti in our time have lost most of their leaves, instead storing extra water and resources in their huge stems...
SOME STILL HAVE LEAVES, TOO!
...which are covered in spikes to keep thirsty animals from munching on them.
Cacti are really cool, now that I think about it...Managing to survive in a dry place like this is quite the accomplishment!
Right?!

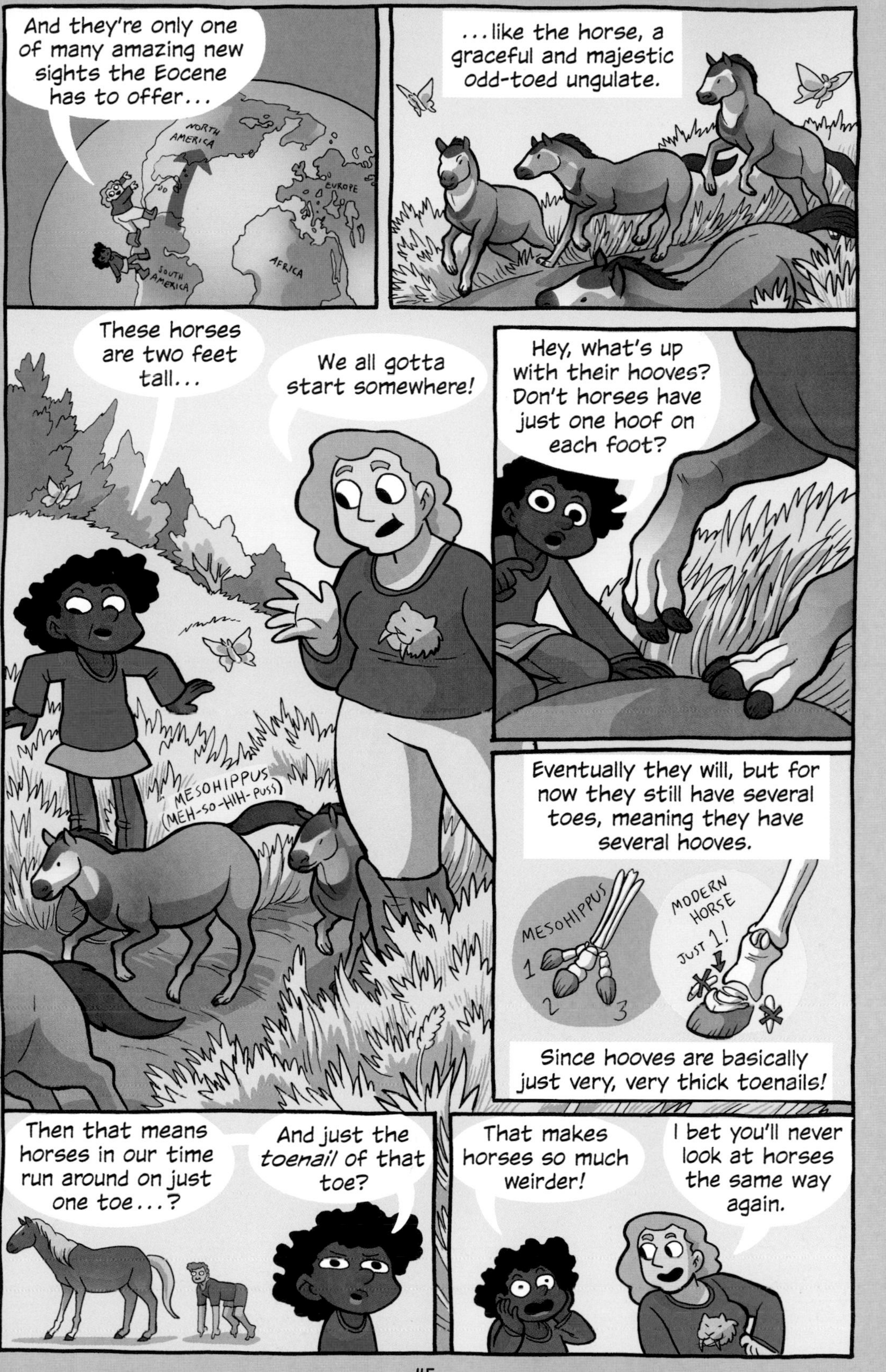

And they're only one of many amazing new sights the Eocene has to offer...
NORTH AMERICA
EUROPE
SOUTH AMERICA
AFRICA
...like the horse, a graceful and majestic odd-toed ungulate.
These horses are two feet tall...
We all gotta start somewhere!
MESOHIPPUS (MEH-SO-HIH-PUSS)
Hey, what's up with their hooves? Don't horses have just one hoof on each foot?
Eventually they will, but for now they still have several toes, meaning they have several hooves.
MESOHIPPUS
1
2
3
MODERN HORSE
JUST 1!
Since hooves are basically just very, very thick toenails!
Then that means horses in our time run around on just one toe...?
And just the *toenail* of that toe?
That makes horses so much weirder!
I bet you'll never look at horses the same way again.

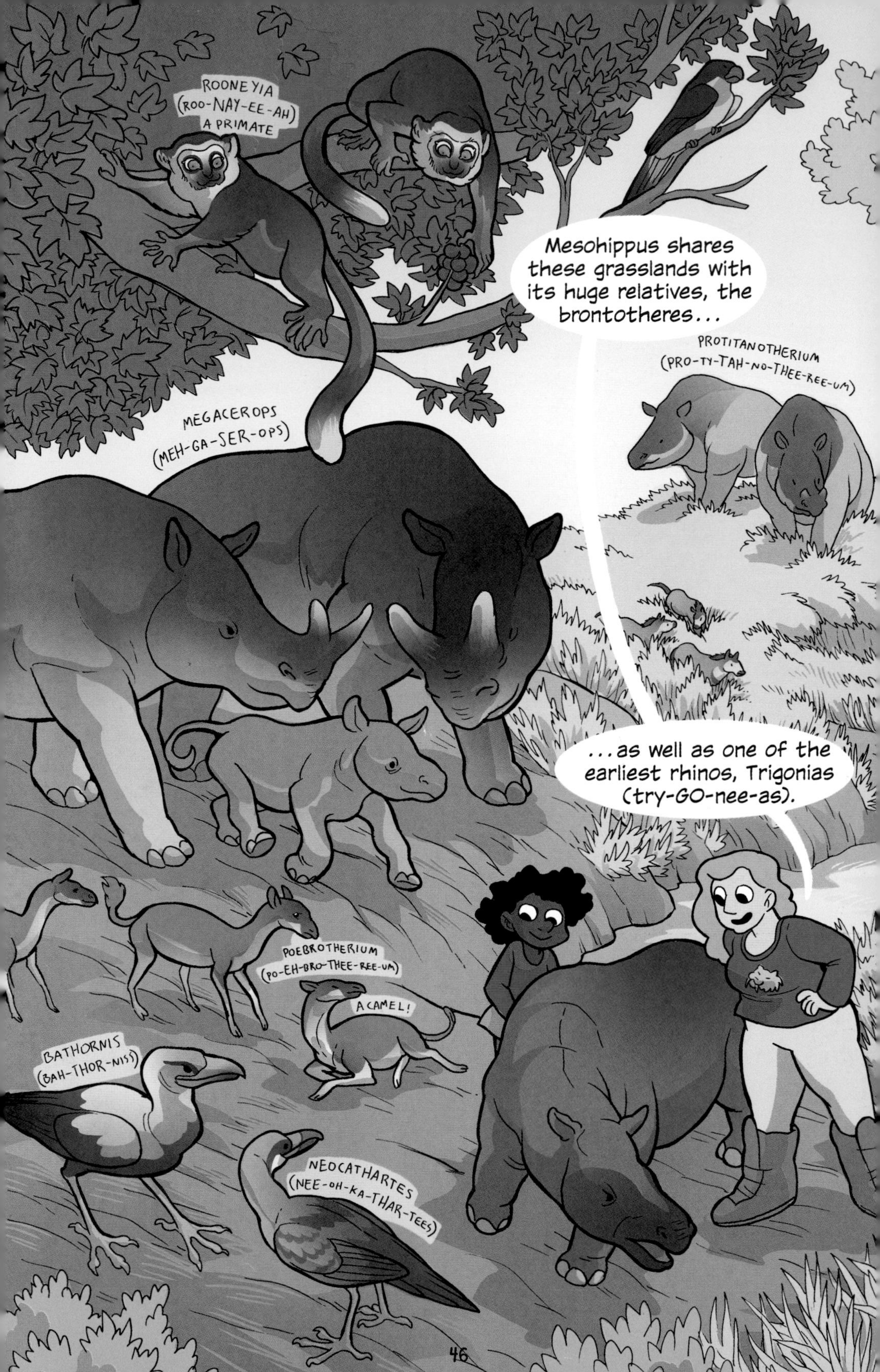
ROONEYIA (ROO-NAY-EE-AH) A PRIMATE
Mesohippus shares these grasslands with its huge relatives, the brontotheres...
PROTITANOTHERIUM (PRO-TY-TAH-NO-THEE-REE-UM)
MEGACEROPS (MEH-GA-SER-OPS)
...as well as one of the earliest rhinos, Trigonias (try-GO-nee-as).
POEBROTHERIUM (PO-EH-BRO-THEE-REE-UM)
A CAMEL!
BATHORNIS (BAH-THOR-NISS)
NEOCATHARTES (NEE-OH-KA-THAR-TEES)

This looks like one of those omnivores we met in Eurasia. You know, the big scary ones.
Yep, Archaeotherium (ar-KAY-oh-THEE-ree-um) here is a member of the entelodont group of even-toed ungulates.
Like its fellow entelodonts, Archaeotherium eats both meat and plants.
SYNOPLONOTHERIUM (SY-NO-PLO-NO-THEE-REE-UM) A PREDATORY UNGULATE
HOPLOPHONEUS (HAWP-LO-FO-NEE-USS) A FALSE SABER-TOOTHED CAT
BOREALOSUCHUS (BO-REE-AH-LO-SOO-KUSS)
HYAENODON HORRIDUS
HYAENODON MICRODON (THE SMALLEST SPECIES)
Yikes, look at the chompers on that thing! Entelodonts are definitely the scariest meat eaters we've met.
But pretty amazing, you have to admit! As are the smaller, fuzzier carnivores that prowl the North American landscape...

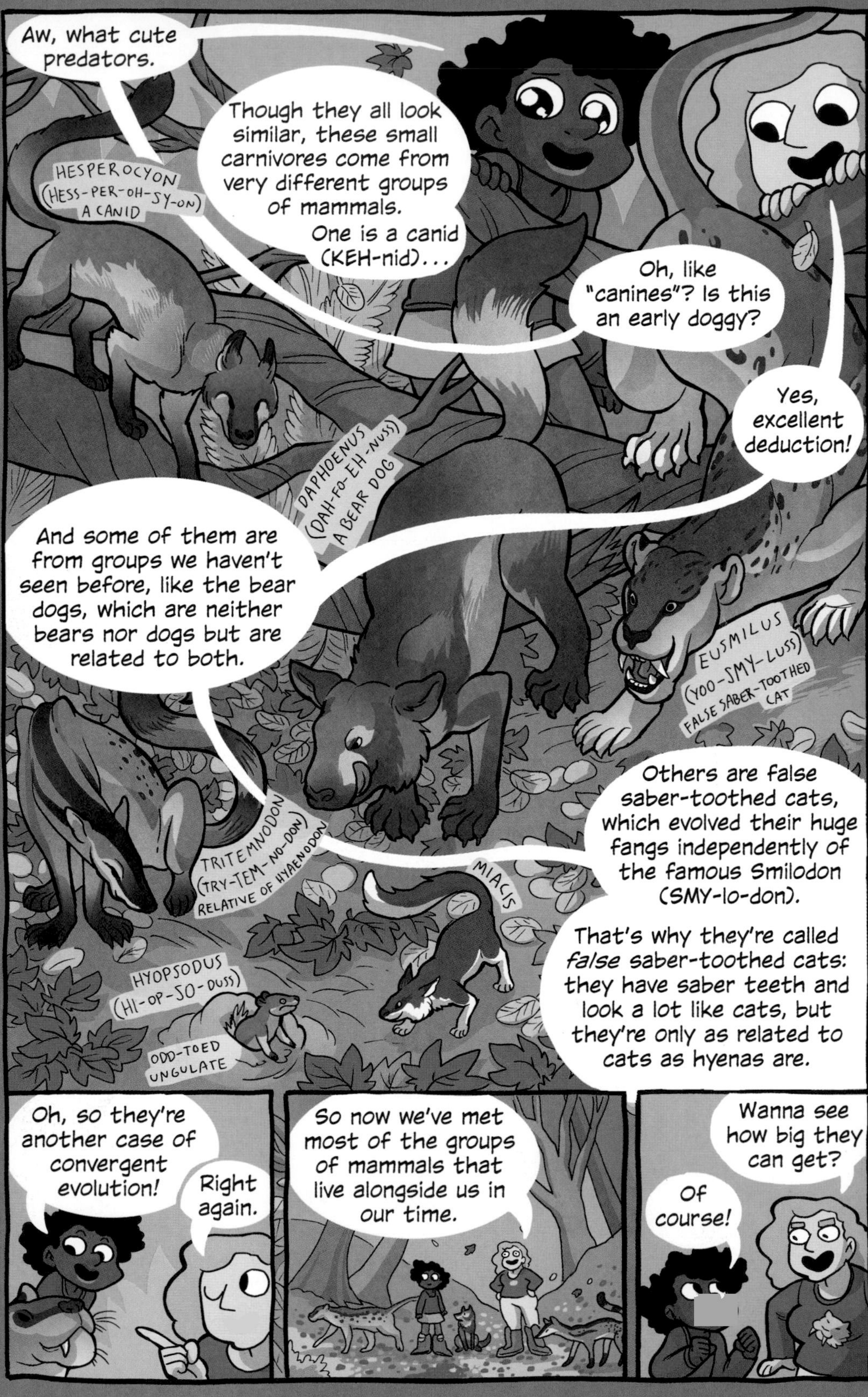

Aw, what cute predators.
Though they all look similar, these small carnivores come from very different groups of mammals.
One is a canid (KEH-nid). . .
HESPEROCYON (HESS-PER-OH-SY-ON) A CANID
Oh, like "canines"? Is this an early doggy?
Yes, excellent deduction!
DAPHOENUS (DAH-FO-EH-NUSS) A BEAR DOG
And some of them are from groups we haven't seen before, like the bear dogs, which are neither bears nor dogs but are related to both.
EUSMILUS (YOO-SMY-LUSS) FALSE SABER-TOOTHED CAT
TRITEMNODON (TRY-TEM-NO-DON) RELATIVE OF HYAENODON
MIACIS
HYOPSODUS (HI-OP-SO-DUSS) ODD-TOED UNGULATE
Others are false saber-toothed cats, which evolved their huge fangs independently of the famous Smilodon (SMY-lo-don).
That's why they're called *false* saber-toothed cats: they have saber teeth and look a lot like cats, but they're only as related to cats as hyenas are.
Oh, so they're another case of convergent evolution!
Right again.
So now we've met most of the groups of mammals that live alongside us in our time.
Wanna see how big they can get?
Of course!

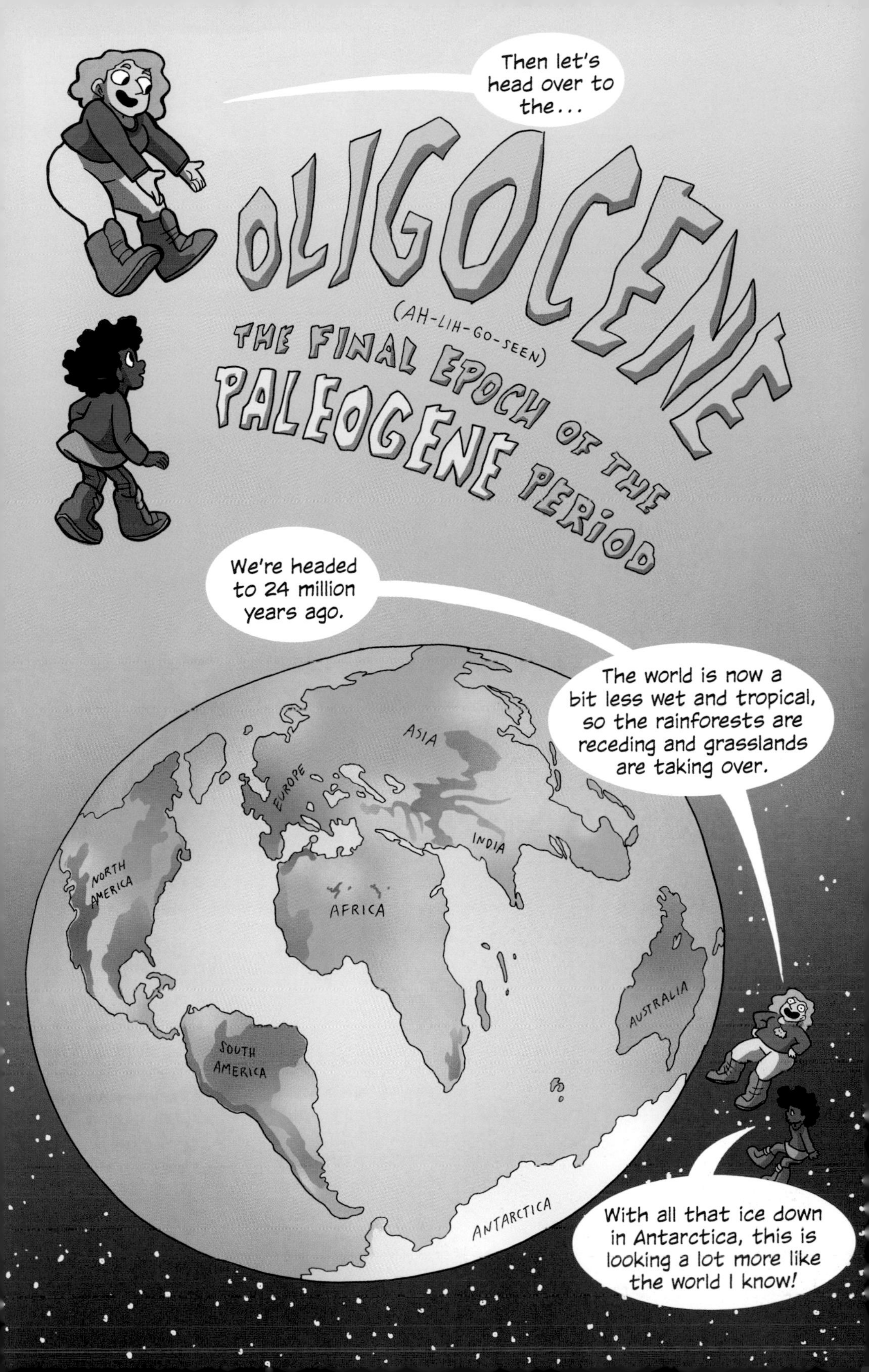

Then let's head over to the...
OLIGOCENE
(AH-LIH-GO-SEEN)
THE FINAL EPOCH OF THE PALEOGENE PERIOD
We're headed to 24 million years ago.
The world is now a bit less wet and tropical, so the rainforests are receding and grasslands are taking over.
ASIA
EUROPE
INDIA
NORTH AMERICA
AFRICA
AUSTRALIA
SOUTH AMERICA
ANTARCTICA
With all that ice down in Antarctica, this is looking a lot more like the world I know!

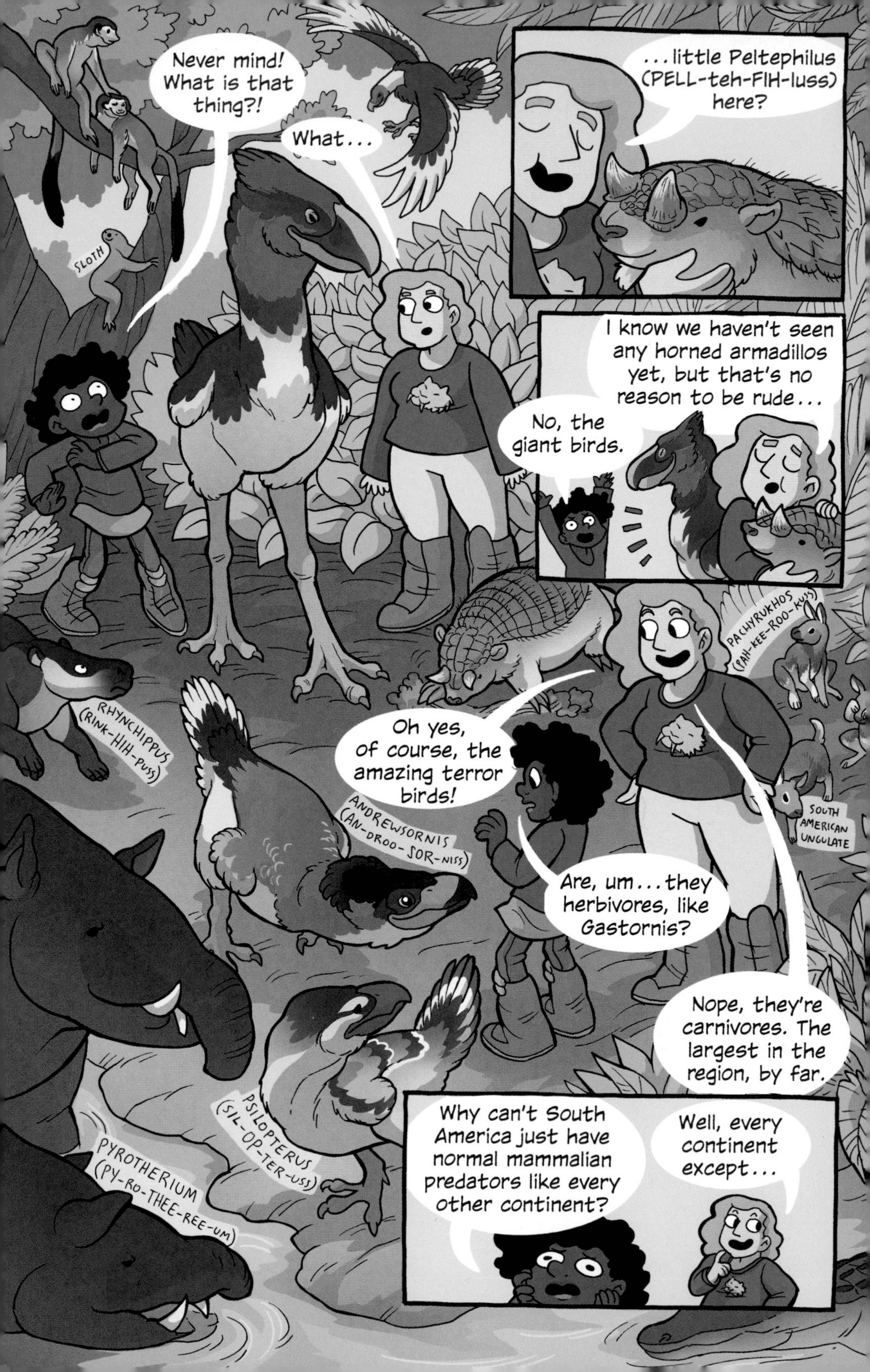
Never mind! What is that thing?!
What...
...little Peltephilus (PELL-teh-FIH-luss) here?
SLOTH
I know we haven't seen any horned armadillos yet, but that's no reason to be rude...
No, the giant birds.
PACHYRUKHOS (PAH-KEE-ROO-KUSS)
RHYNCHIPPUS (RINK-HIH-PUSS)
Oh yes, of course, the amazing terror birds!
ANDREWSORNIS (AN-DROO-SOR-NISS)
SOUTH AMERICAN UNGULATE
Are, um... they herbivores, like Gastornis?
Nope, they're carnivores. The largest in the region, by far.
PSILOPTERUS (SIL-OP-TER-USS)
PYROTHERIUM (PY-RO-THEE-REE-UM)
Why can't South America just have normal mammalian predators like every other continent?
Well, every continent except...

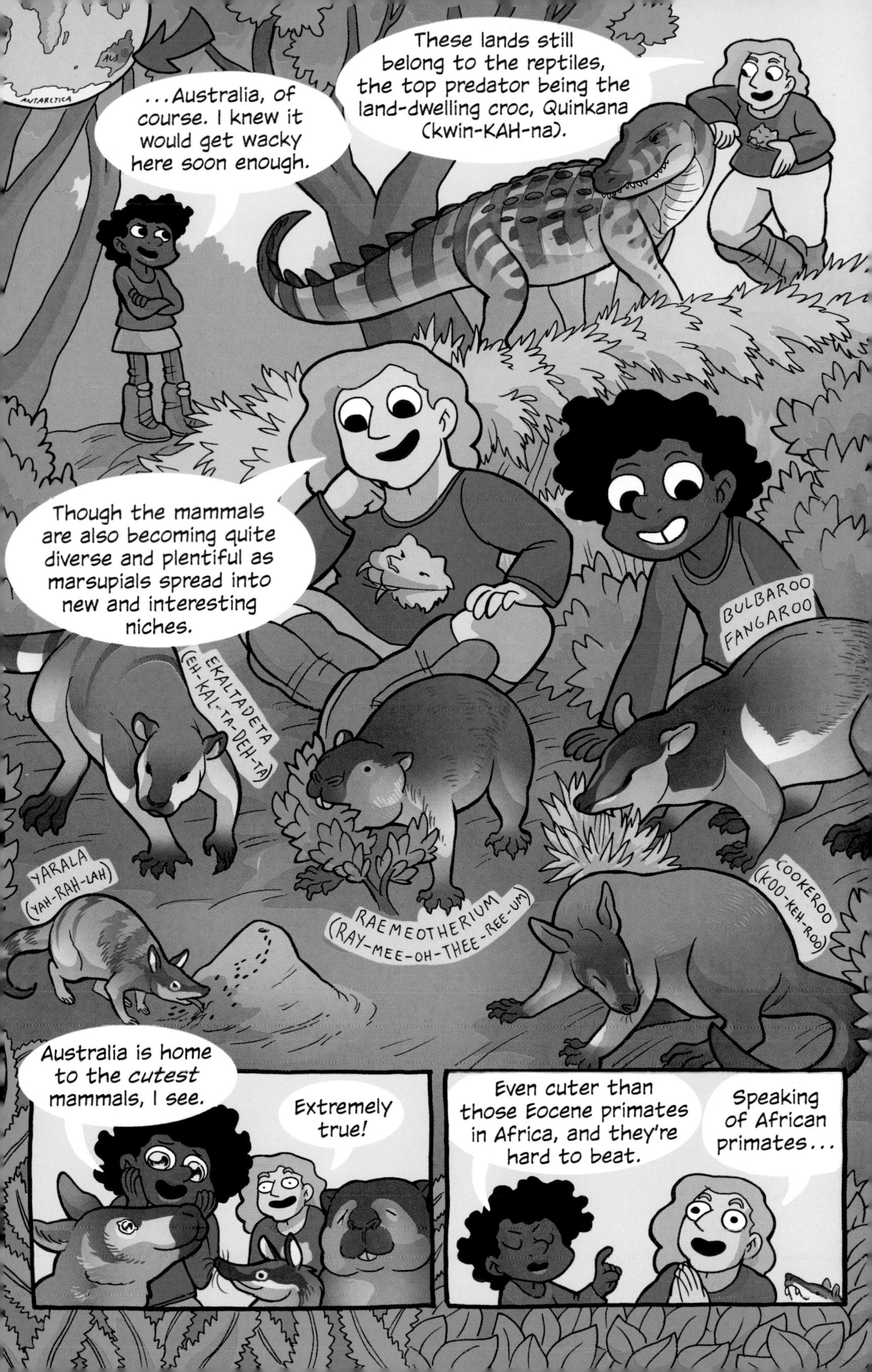

AUS
ANTARCTICA
. . . Australia, of course. I knew it would get wacky here soon enough.
These lands still belong to the reptiles, the top predator being the land-dwelling croc, Quinkana (kwin-KAH-na).
Though the mammals are also becoming quite diverse and plentiful as marsupials spread into new and interesting niches.
EKALTADETA (EH-KAL-TA-DEH-TA)
BULBAROO FANGAROO
YARALA (YAH-RAH-LAH)
RAEMEOTHERIUM (RAY-MEE-OH-THEE-REE-UM)
COOKEROO (KOO-KEH-ROO)
Australia is home to the *cutest* mammals, I see.
Extremely true!
Even cuter than those Eocene primates in Africa, and they're hard to beat.
Speaking of African primates . . .

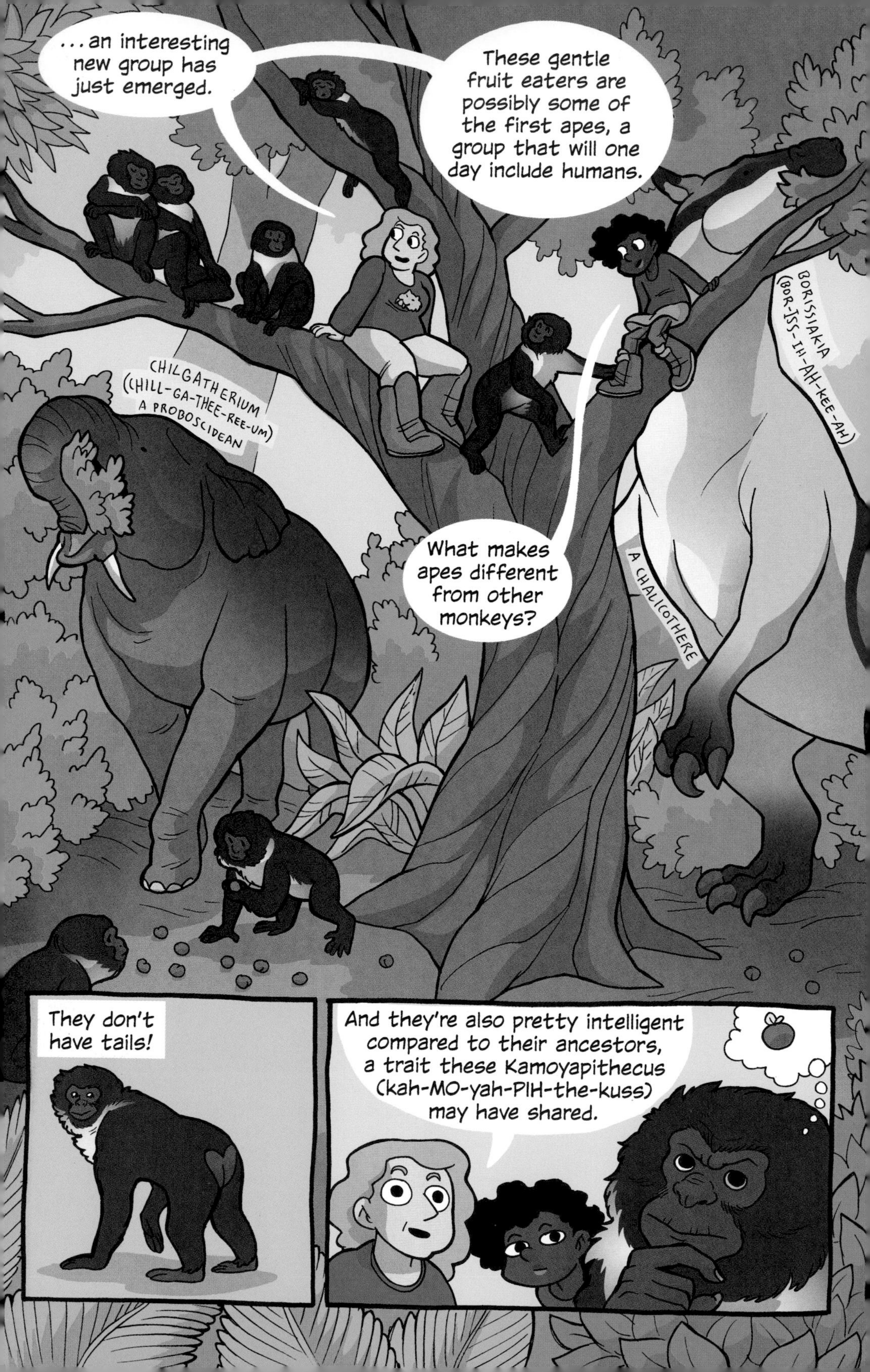
...an interesting new group has just emerged.
These gentle fruit eaters are possibly some of the first apes, a group that will one day include humans.
CHILGATHERIUM (CHILL-GA-THEE-REE-UM) A PROBOSCIDEAN
BORISSIAKIA (BOR-ISS-IH-AH-KEE-AH)
A CHALICOTHERE
What makes apes different from other monkeys?
They don't have tails!
And they're also pretty intelligent compared to their ancestors, a trait these Kamoyapithecus (kah-MO-yah-PIH-the-kuss) may have shared.

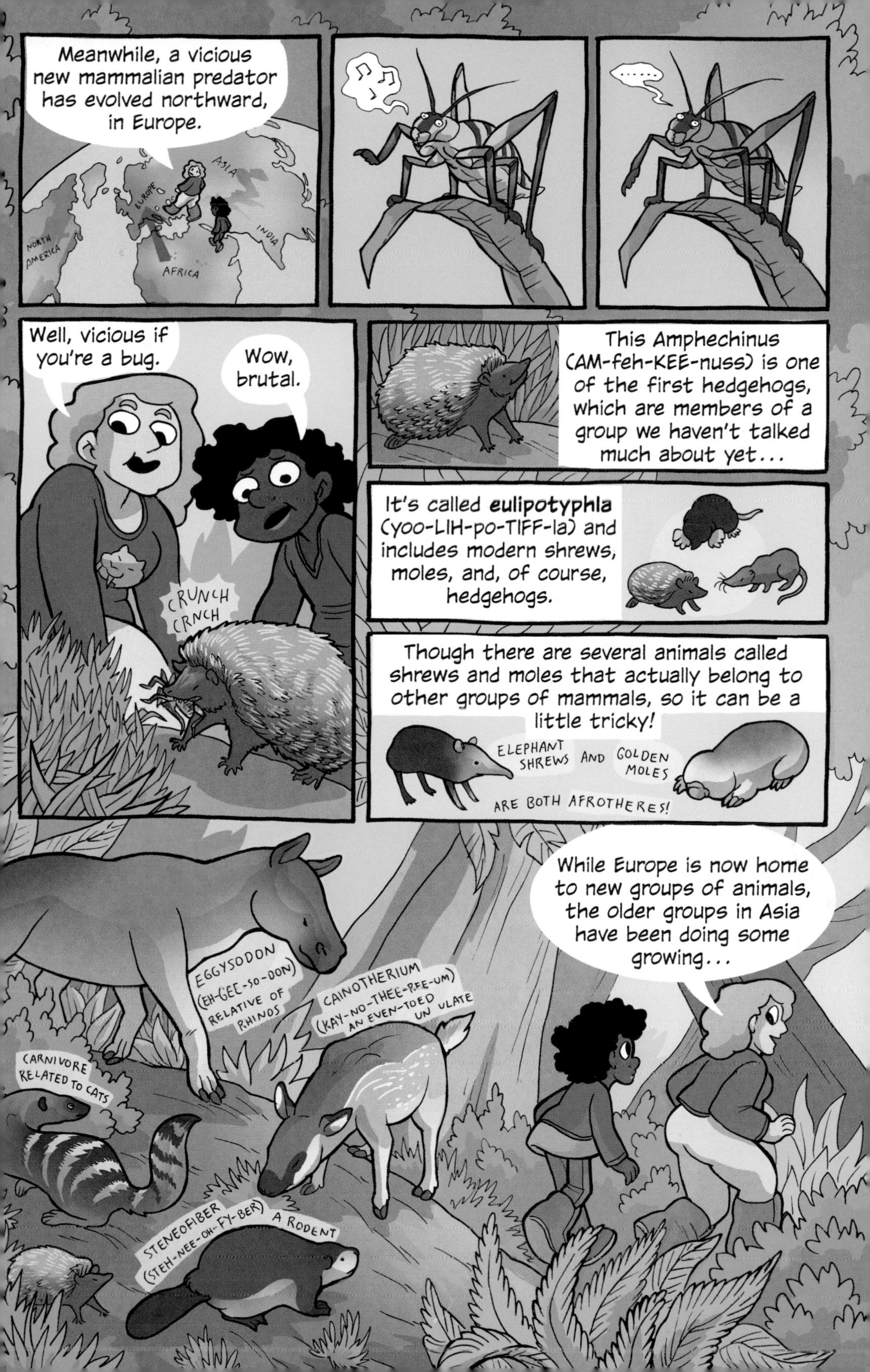
Meanwhile, a vicious new mammalian predator has evolved northward, in Europe.
EUROPE
ASIA
NORTH AMERICA
AFRICA
INDIA
......
Well, vicious if you're a bug.
Wow, brutal.
CRUNCH CRNCH
This Amphechinus (AM-feh-KEE-nuss) is one of the first hedgehogs, which are members of a group we haven't talked much about yet...
It's called **eulipotyphla** (yoo-LIH-po-TIFF-la) and includes modern shrews, moles, and, of course, hedgehogs.
Though there are several animals called shrews and moles that actually belong to other groups of mammals, so it can be a little tricky!
ELEPHANT SHREWS AND GOLDEN MOLES ARE BOTH AFROTHERES!
While Europe is now home to new groups of animals, the older groups in Asia have been doing some growing...
EGGYSODON (EH-GEE-SO-DON) RELATIVE OF RHINOS
CAINOTHERIUM (KAY-NO-THEE-REE-UM) AN EVEN-TOED UN ULATE
CARNIVORE RELATED TO CATS
STENEOFIBER (STEH-NEE-OH-FY-BER) A RODENT

Holy moly, you weren't kidding!
This Paraceratherium (PAH-rah-SEH-rah-THEE-ree-um) is the largest indricothere, and possibly the largest mammal that's ever walked the Earth.
Do you remember what indricotheres are?
Yeah, they're those relatives of rhinos that look like horses.
This one does look more rhino-like, though.
Yep, it's a much chunkier animal than the other indricotheres we met. Gotta have a lot of muscle to move all those big bones around!
SAADANIUS (SA-DAH-NEE-USS) A PRIMATE

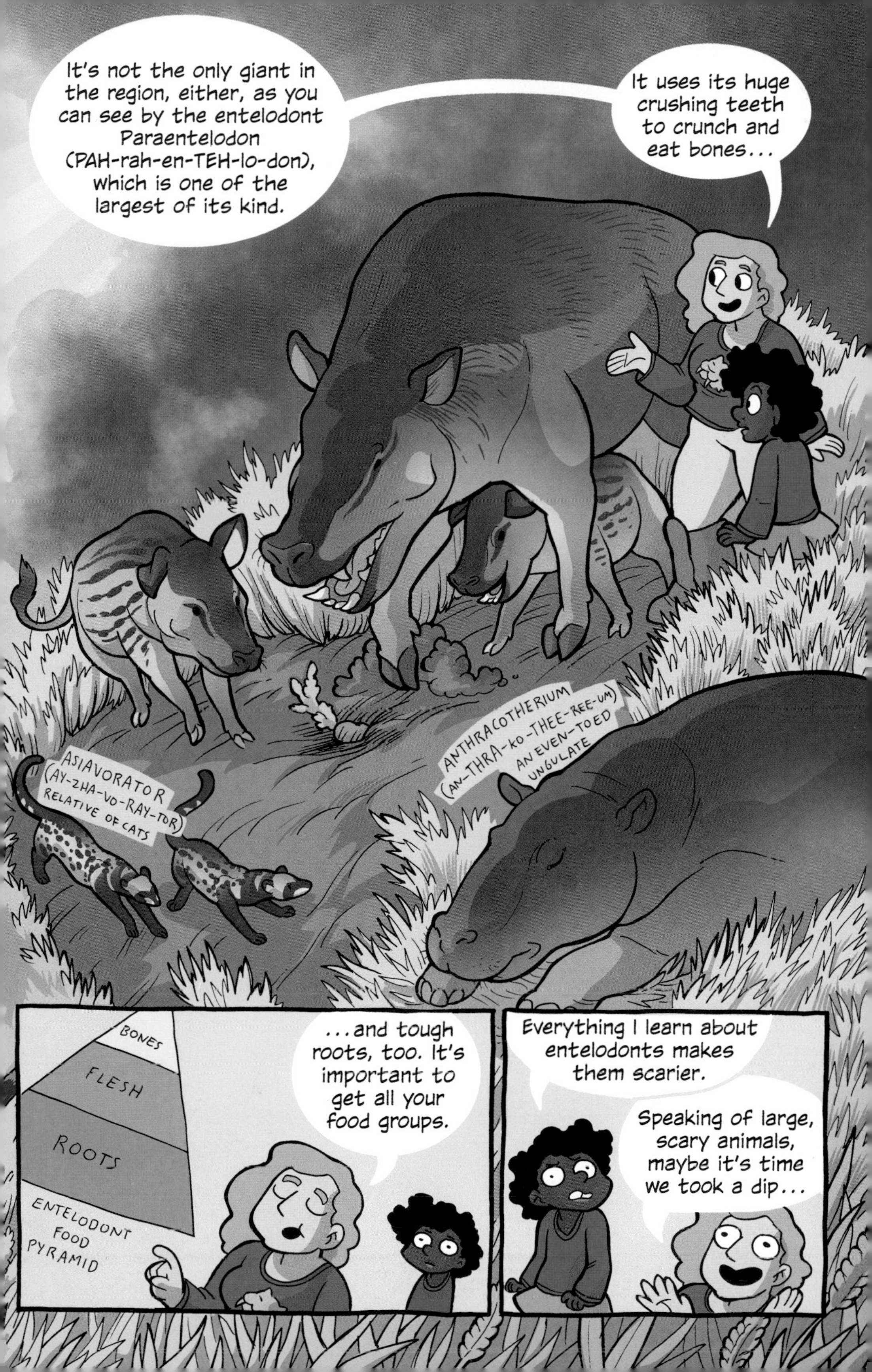
It's not the only giant in the region, either, as you can see by the entelodont Paraentelodon (PAH-rah-en-TEH-lo-don), which is one of the largest of its kind.
It uses its huge crushing teeth to crunch and eat bones...
ASIAVORATOR (AY-ZHA-VO-RAY-TOR) RELATIVE OF CATS
ANTHRACOTHERIUM (AN-THRA-KO-THEE-REE-UM) AN EVEN-TOED UNGULATE
BONES
FLESH
ROOTS
ENTELODONT FOOD PYRAMID
...and tough roots, too. It's important to get all your food groups.
Everything I learn about entelodonts makes them scarier.
Speaking of large, scary animals, maybe it's time we took a dip...

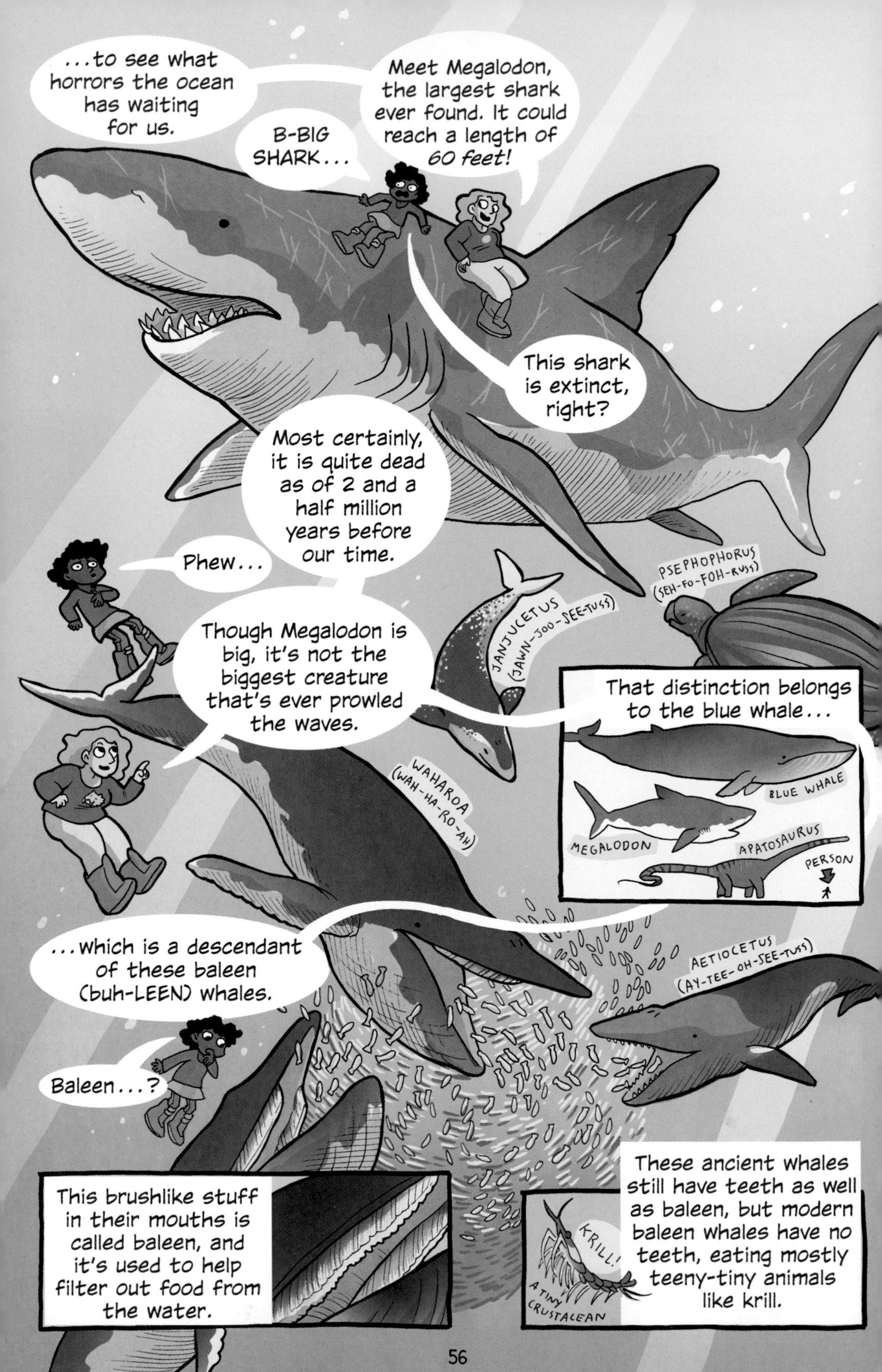

...to see what horrors the ocean has waiting for us.
Meet Megalodon, the largest shark ever found. It could reach a length of *60 feet!*
B-BIG SHARK...
This shark is extinct, right?
Most certainly, it is quite dead as of 2 and a half million years before our time.
Phew...
PSEPHOPHORUS (SEH-FO-FOH-RUSS)
JANJUCETUS (JAWN-JOO-SEE-TUSS)
Though Megalodon is big, it's not the biggest creature that's ever prowled the waves.
That distinction belongs to the blue whale...
BLUE WHALE
MEGALODON
APATOSAURUS
PERSON
WAHAROA (WAH-HA-RO-AH)
...which is a descendant of these baleen (buh-LEEN) whales.
AETIOCETUS (AY-TEE-OH-SEE-TUSS)
Baleen...?
This brushlike stuff in their mouths is called baleen, and it's used to help filter out food from the water.
KRILL!
A TINY CRUSTACEAN
These ancient whales still have teeth as well as baleen, but modern baleen whales have no teeth, eating mostly teeny-tiny animals like krill.

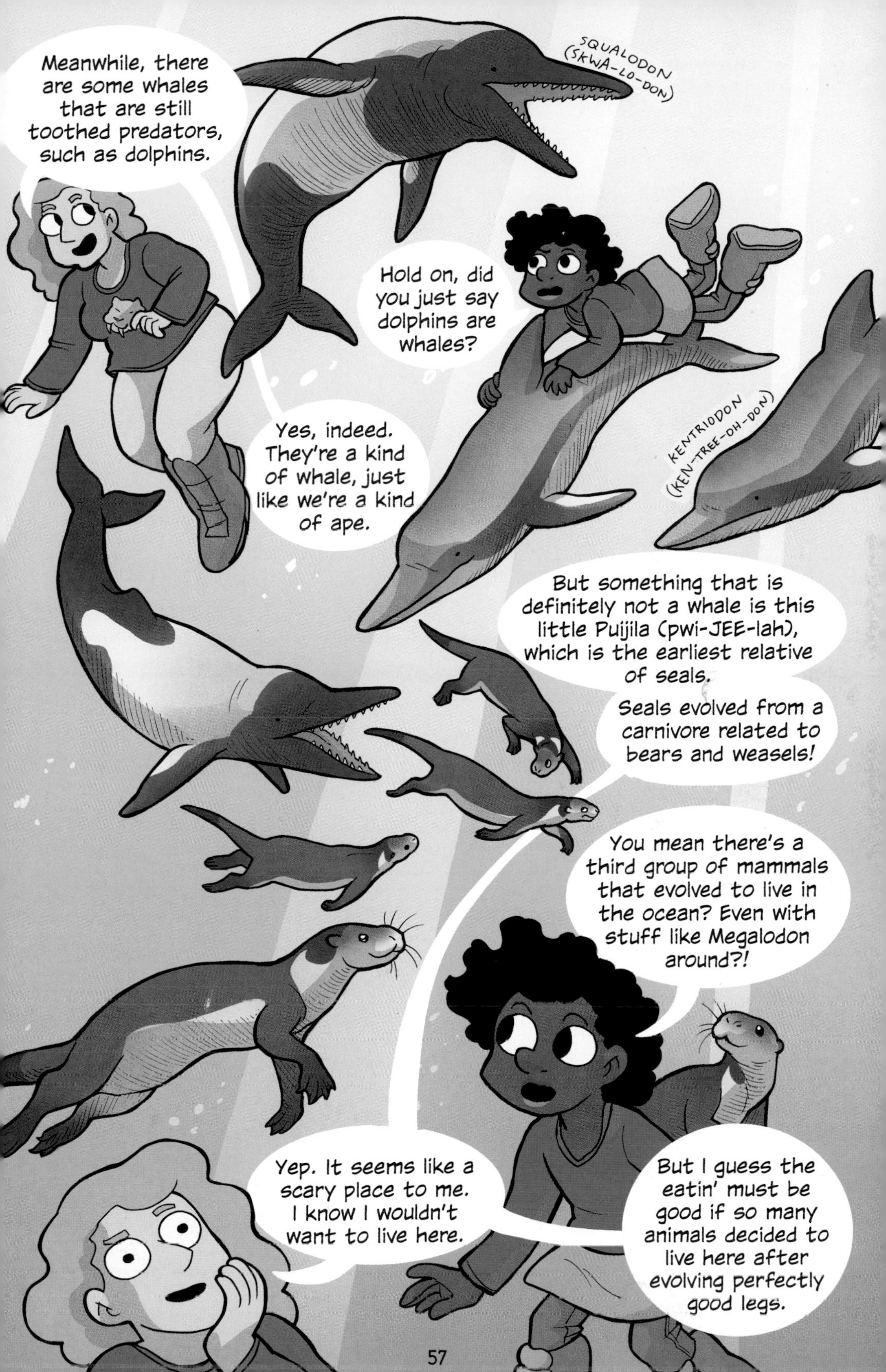
Meanwhile, there are some whales that are still toothed predators, such as dolphins.
SQUALODON (SKWA-LO-DON)
Hold on, did you just say dolphins are whales?
Yes, indeed. They're a kind of whale, just like we're a kind of ape.
KENTRIODON (KEN-TREE-OH-DON)
But something that is definitely not a whale is this little Puijila (pwi-JEE-lah), which is the earliest relative of seals.
Seals evolved from a carnivore related to bears and weasels!
You mean there's a third group of mammals that evolved to live in the ocean? Even with stuff like Megalodon around?!
Yep. It seems like a scary place to me. I know I wouldn't want to live here.
But I guess the eatin' must be good if so many animals decided to live here after evolving perfectly good legs.

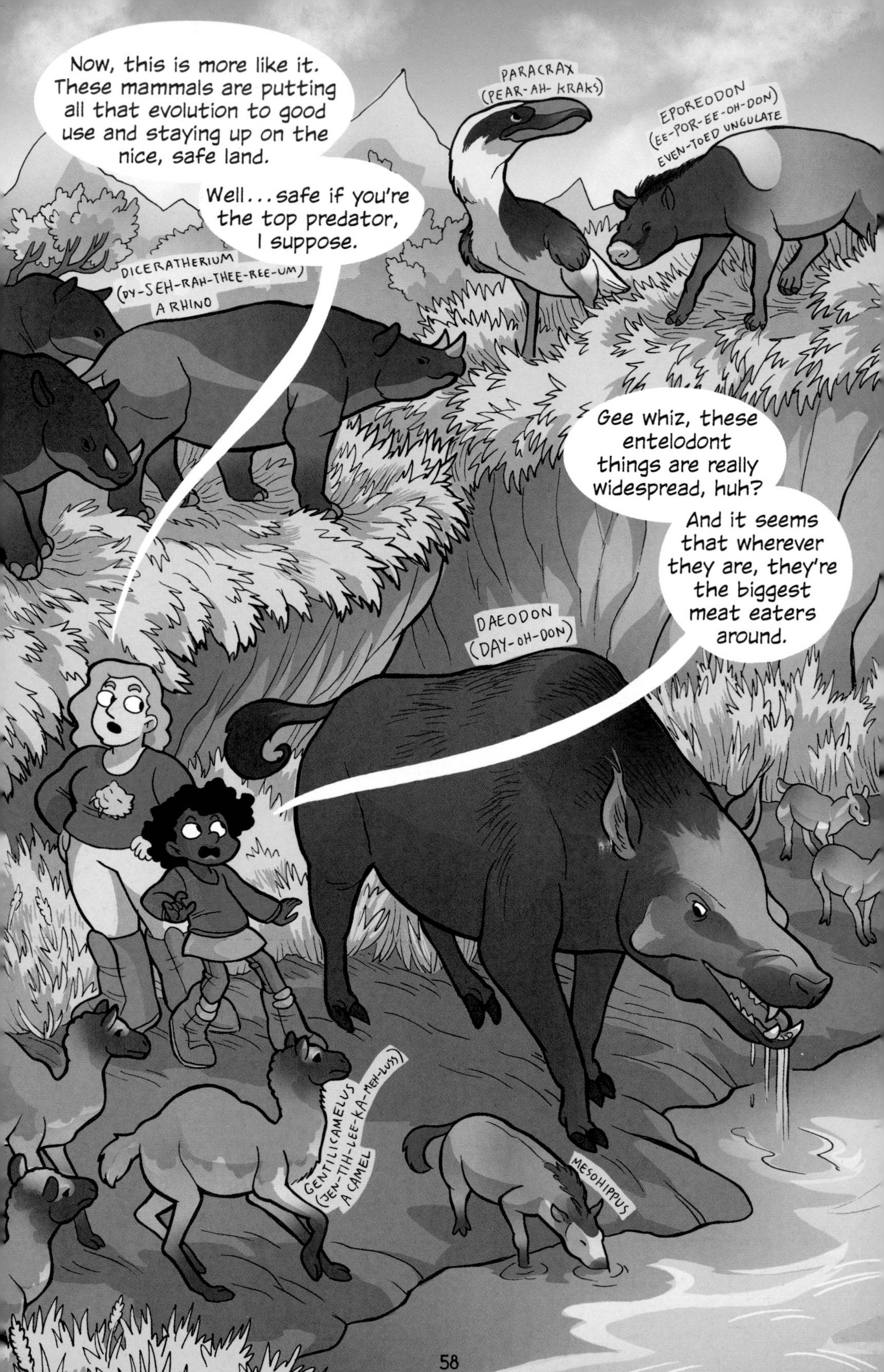
Now, this is more like it. These mammals are putting all that evolution to good use and staying up on the nice, safe land.
Well... safe if you're the top predator, I suppose.
PARACRAX (PEAR-AH-KRAKS)
EPOREODON (EE-POR-EE-OH-DON) EVEN-TOED UNGULATE
DICERATHERIUM (DY-SEH-RAH-THEE-REE-UM) A RHINO
Gee whiz, these entelodont things are really widespread, huh?
And it seems that wherever they are, they're the biggest meat eaters around.
DAEODON (DAY-OH-DON)
GENTILICAMELUS (JEN-TIH-LEE-KA-MEH-LUSS) A CAMEL
MESOHIPPUS

Of course, that doesn't make them the biggest things in general.
Some of the herbivores in this region have reached a pretty considerable size, such as the semi-aquatic rhino, Metamynodon (MEH-tah-MY-no-don).
EKGMOWECHASHAUSA (EK-GMO-WEH-CHA-SHA-OO-SA) A PRIMATE
Though most mammals in North America are still small, like the tree-dwelling rodents and little grass-eating ungulates.
ISCHYROMYS (IH-SHEE-RO-MISS) A RODENT
STENOMYLUS (STEH-NO-MY-LUSS) A CAMEL
Which makes them the perfect size for a non-mammalian predator that stalks these plains...
POGONODON (PO-GO-NO-DON)
FALSE SABER-TOOTHED CAT
LEPTOMERYX (LEP-TO-MEH-RIKS) EVEN-TOED UNGULATES
ALLIGATOR
BATHORNIS (BAH-THOR-NISS)
MERYCOCHOEIRUS (MEH-REE-SO-KO-EY-RUSS) EVEN-TOED UNGULATES

Oh no, another huge bird! These things were all over the place, huh?
Yeah, isn't that exciting? All these huge predatory birds are a lovely reminder that the dinosaurs never died out, and they can still kick our mammalian butts.
BATHORNIS
NIMRAVUS (NIM-RAH-VUSS) FALSE SABER-TOOTHED CAT
PARACRAX
ARCHAEOCYON (AR-KAY-OH-SY-ON) BONE-CRUSHING DOG
PALAEOCASTOR (PAY-LEE-OH-KASS-TOR)
A RODENT
OTAROCYON (OH-TAR-OH-SY-ON) BONE-CRUSHING DOG
It's not the only huge bird around, either, as you can see by this Pelagornis sandersi (peh-lah-GOR-niss san-DUR-see)...
...a bird with possibly the largest wingspan ever at 21 feet across.
Yeesh, and it's one of those creepy toothed birds.
There are way too many large and intimidating birds in the Oligocene. I've had about enough of them.
Well, bad news...

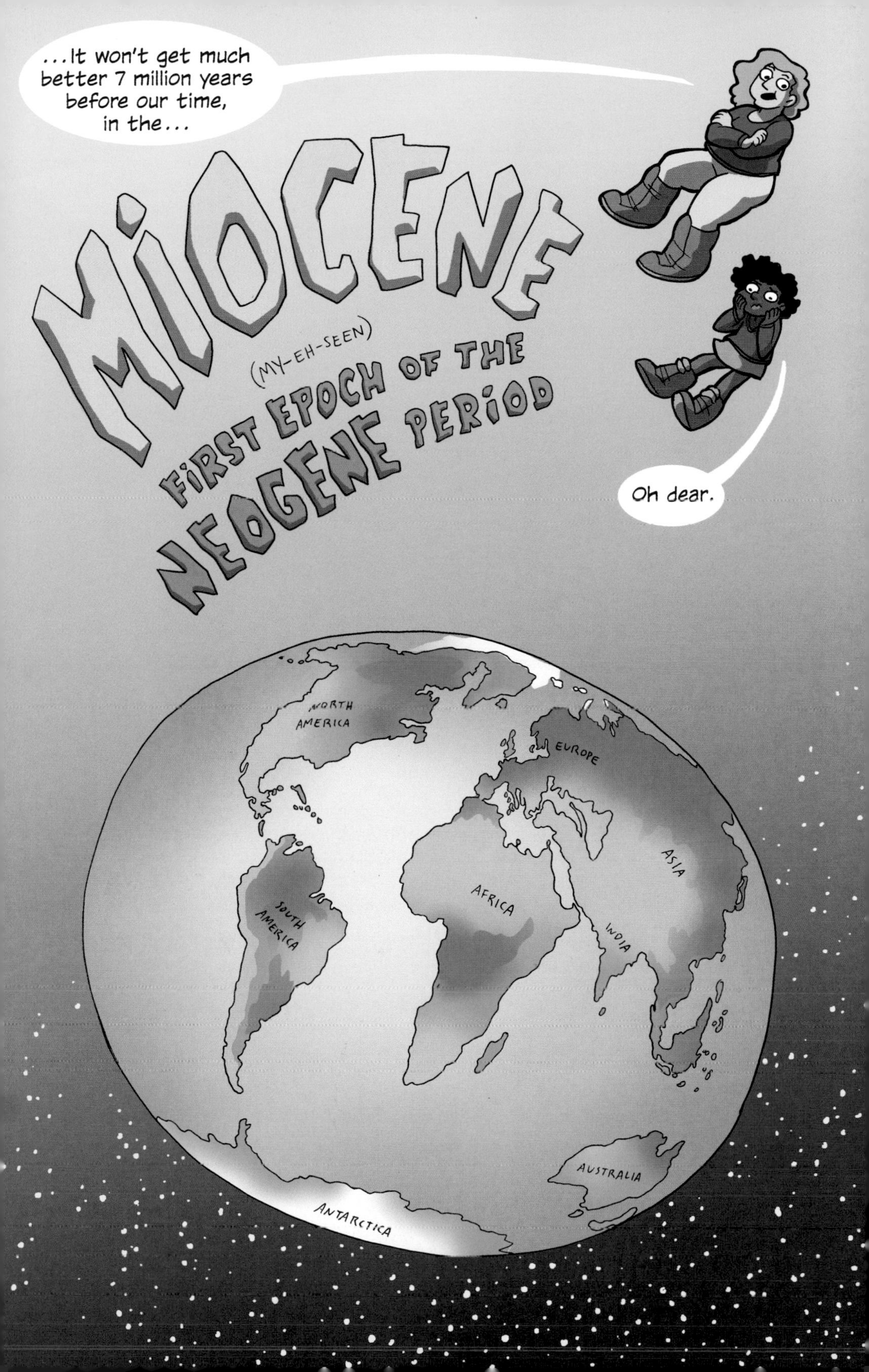
...It won't get much better 7 million years before our time, in the...
MIOCENE
(MY-EH-SEEN)
FIRST EPOCH OF THE NEOGENE PERIOD
Oh dear.
NORTH AMERICA
EUROPE
ASIA
AFRICA
SOUTH AMERICA
INDIA
AUSTRALIA
ANTARCTICA

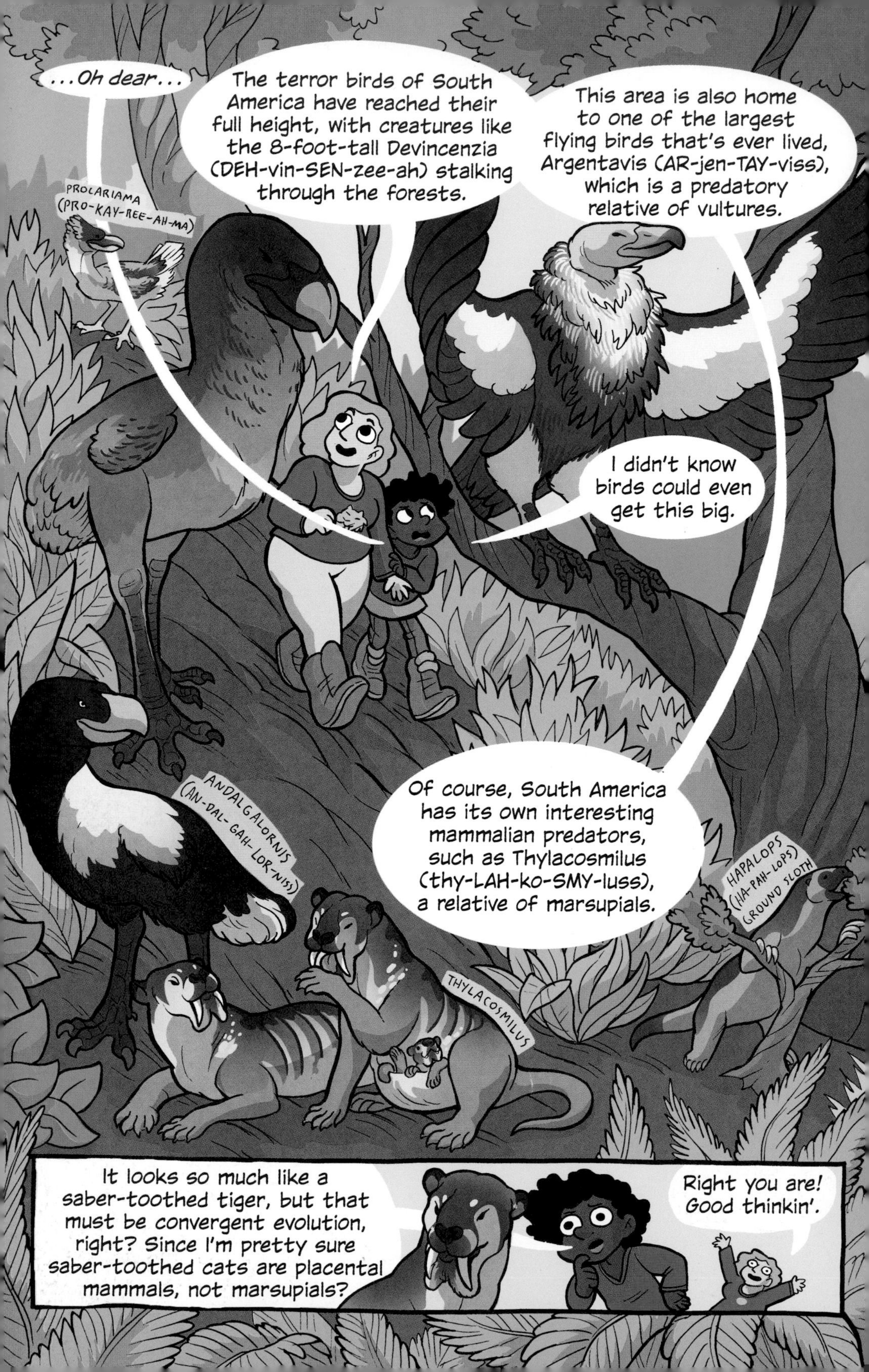

...Oh dear...
The terror birds of South America have reached their full height, with creatures like the 8-foot-tall Devincenzia (DEH-vin-SEN-zee-ah) stalking through the forests.
This area is also home to one of the largest flying birds that's ever lived, Argentavis (AR-jen-TAY-viss), which is a predatory relative of vultures.
PROCARIAMA (PRO-KAY-REE-AH-MA)
I didn't know birds could even get this big.
ANDALGALORNIS (AN-DAL-GAH-LOR-NISS)
Of course, South America has its own interesting mammalian predators, such as Thylacosmilus (thy-LAH-ko-SMY-luss), a relative of marsupials.
HAPALOPS (HA-PAH-LOPS) GROUND SLOTH
THYLACOSMILUS
It looks so much like a saber-toothed tiger, but that must be convergent evolution, right? Since I'm pretty sure saber-toothed cats are placental mammals, not marsupials?
Right you are! Good thinkin'.

SOUTH AMERICAN UNGULATES
DIPLASIOTHERIUM (DIH-PLAY-ZEE-OH-THEE-REE-UM)
TOXODON (TOKS-OH-DON)
Most placental mammals in this region are herbivores.
DIADIAPHORUS (DEE-AH-DY-AH-FOR-USS) SOUTH AMERICAN UNGULATE
Which isn't to say there aren't placental predators. This little relative of raccoons came all the way down from North America!
ADINOTHERIUM (AH-DI-NO-THEE-REE-UM) SOUTH AMERICAN UNGULATE
There are some neat native predators, as well, though they look a little odd compared to the northerners.
CYONASUA (SY-O-NA-SOO-AH) RACCOON RELATIVE
MACROEUPHRACTUS (MAK-RO-YOO-FRAK-TUSS)
Um... Is that an armadillo?
Yep, but a huge one that eats meat.
South America is a strange place.
You said it. And you haven't even seen what's swimming around nearby...

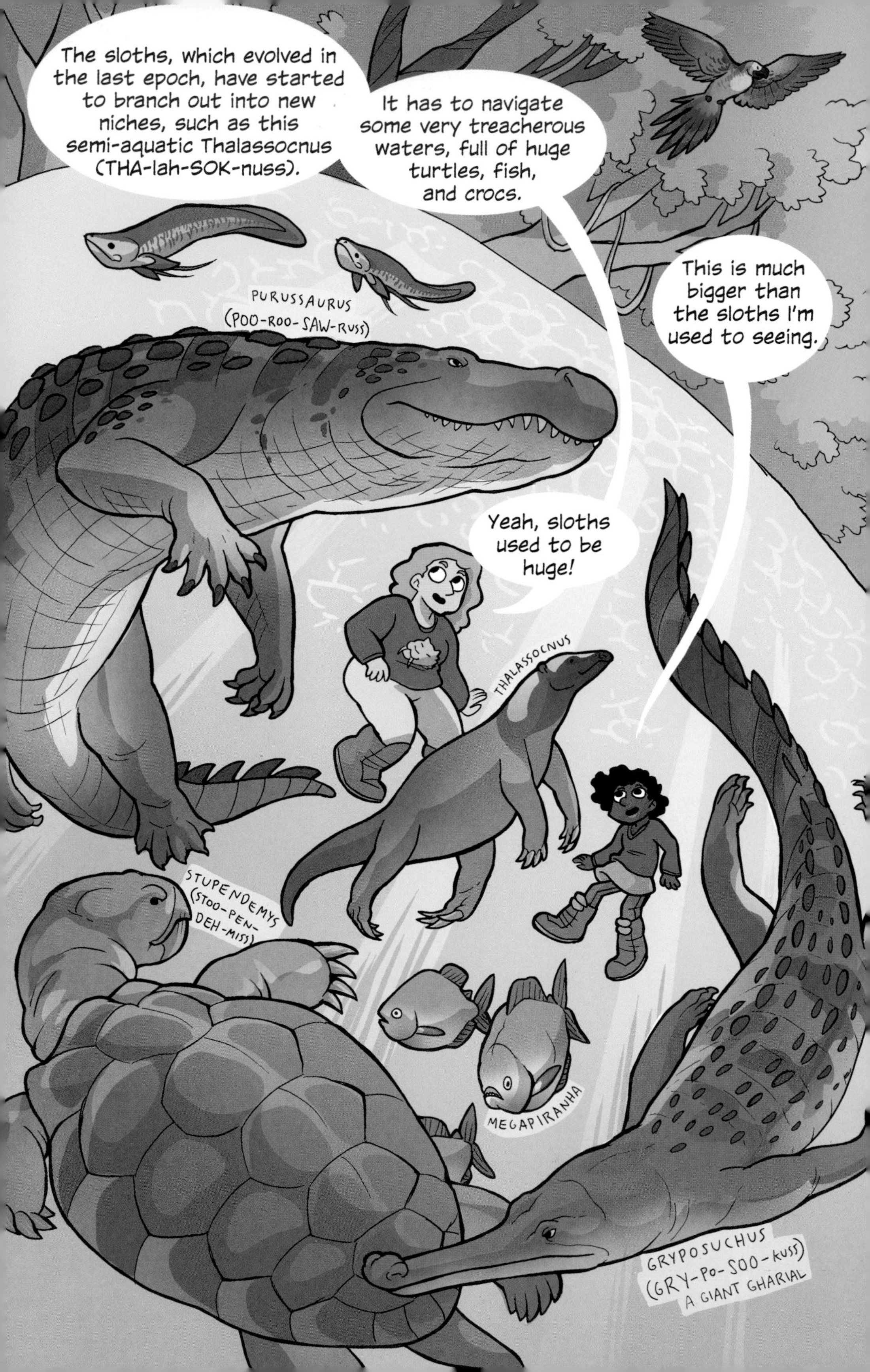

The sloths, which evolved in the last epoch, have started to branch out into new niches, such as this semi-aquatic Thalassocnus (THA-lah-SOK-nuss).
It has to navigate some very treacherous waters, full of huge turtles, fish, and crocs.
This is much bigger than the sloths I'm used to seeing.
Yeah, sloths used to be huge!
PURUSSAURUS (POO-ROO-SAW-RUSS)
THALASSOCNUS
STUPENDEMYS (STOO-PEN-DEH-MISS)
MEGAPIRANHA
GRYPOSUCHUS (GRY-PO-SOO-KUSS) A GIANT GHARIAL

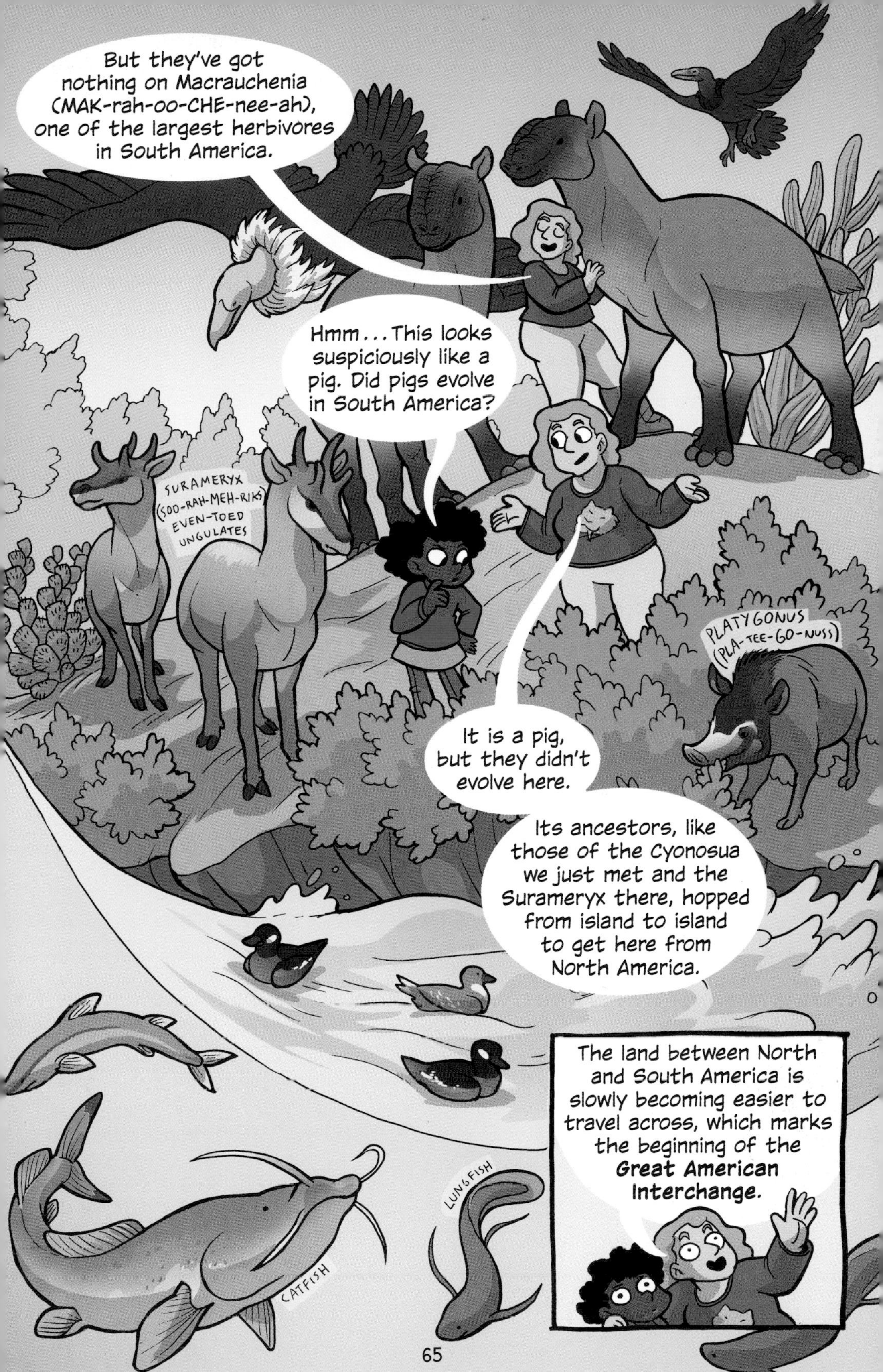
But they've got nothing on Macrauchenia (MAK-rah-oo-CHE-nee-ah), one of the largest herbivores in South America.
Hmm... This looks suspiciously like a pig. Did pigs evolve in South America?
SURAMERYX (SOO-RAH-MEH-RIKS) EVEN-TOED UNGULATES
It is a pig, but they didn't evolve here.
PLATYGONUS (PLA-TEE-GO-NUSS)
Its ancestors, like those of the Cyonosua we just met and the Surameryx there, hopped from island to island to get here from North America.
The land between North and South America is slowly becoming easier to travel across, which marks the beginning of the **Great American Interchange.**
LUNGFISH
CATFISH

And the interchange goes both ways. South American creatures have also found their way up into North America.
These look like that aquatic sloth. Did they come from South America?
THINOBADISTES (THY-NO-BAH-DISS-TEEZ)
Yep, you got it. These are giant ground sloths, and they've started to make a lovely home for themselves alongside the usual North American fauna.
MEGALONYX (MEH-GA-LO-NIKS)
This one isn't so familiar... Is it a sloth, too?
This one is a chalicothere (kah-LIH-ko-theer), and it's an odd-toed ungulate that has no living relatives.
Oh! So that means it's related to horses and rhinos.
It looks so different from them, like a horse is trying to be a gorilla.
HIPPARION
ANISODON (AH-NEE-SO-DON)
CANIS LEPOPHAGUS (KAY-NISS LEH-PO-FAY-GUSS)
CLOSE RELATIVE OF WOLVES
An apt description! It's especially weird seeing them next to actual horses, like Hipparion (chih-PARE-ee-on).
CERATOGAULUS (SEH-RAH-TO-GAW-LUSS) A RODENT

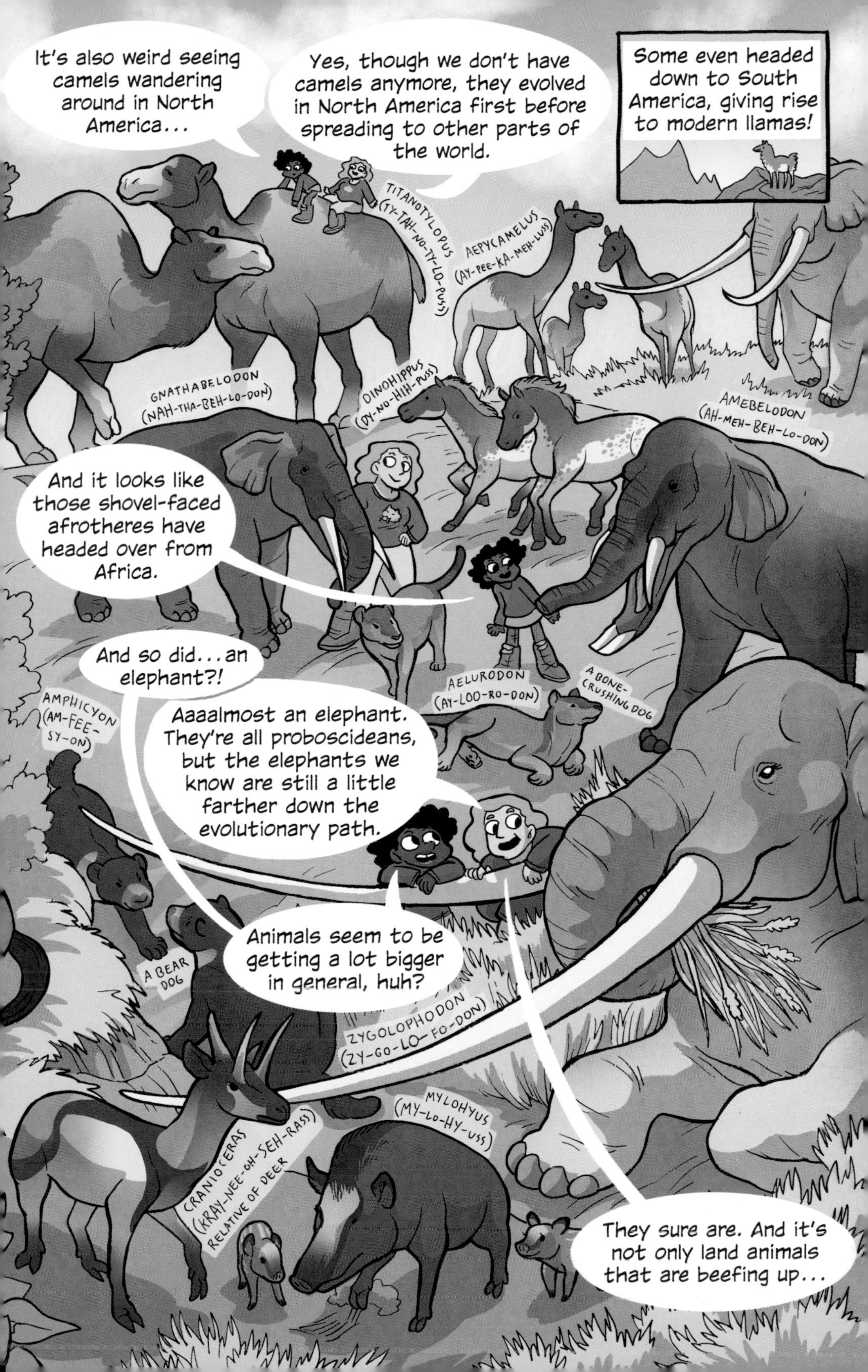
It's also weird seeing camels wandering around in North America...
Yes, though we don't have camels anymore, they evolved in North America first before spreading to other parts of the world.
Some even headed down to South America, giving rise to modern llamas!
TITANOTYLOPUS (TY-TAH-NO-TY-LO-PUSS)
AEPYCAMELUS (AY-PEE-KA-MEH-LUSS)
GNATHABELODON (NAH-THA-BEH-LO-DON)
DINOHIPPUS (DY-NO-HIH-PUSS)
AMEBELODON (AH-MEH-BEH-LO-DON)
And it looks like those shovel-faced afrotheres have headed over from Africa.
And so did...an elephant?!
AMPHICYON (AM-FEE-SY-ON)
AELURODON (AY-LOO-RO-DON)
A BONE-CRUSHING DOG
Aaaalmost an elephant. They're all proboscideans, but the elephants we know are still a little farther down the evolutionary path.
Animals seem to be getting a lot bigger in general, huh?
A BEAR DOG
ZYGOLOPHODON (ZY-GO-LO-FO-DON)
MYLOHYUS (MY-LO-HY-USS)
CRANIOCERAS (KRAY-NEE-OH-SEH-RASS) RELATIVE OF DEER
They sure are. And it's not only land animals that are beefing up...

...The creatures of the sea have gotten quite big, as you can see by this Livyatan (LIV-yah-tan), a formidable sperm whale.
That whale has some serious teeth!
GREAT WHITE SHARK
MEGALODON

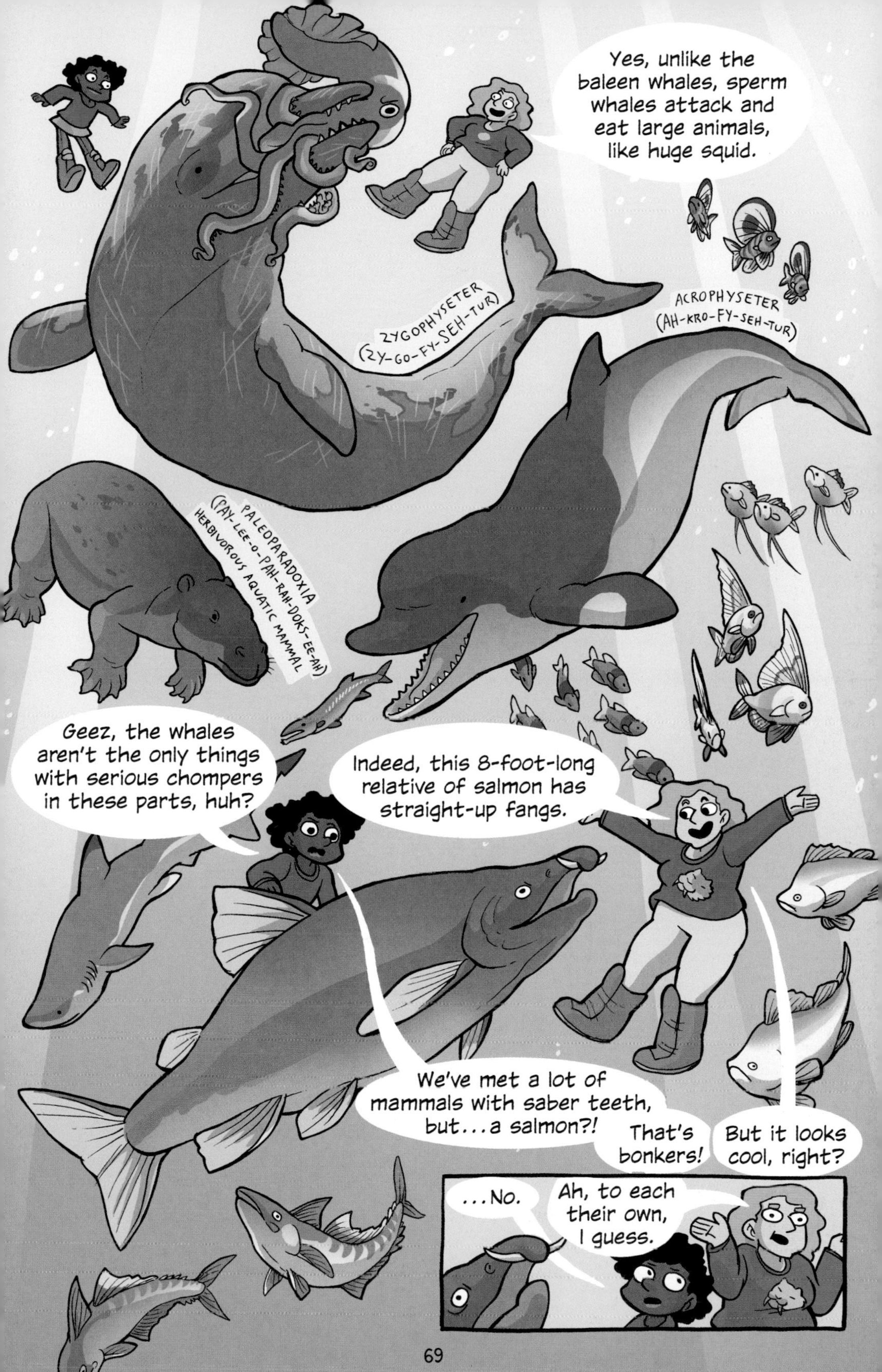
Yes, unlike the baleen whales, sperm whales attack and eat large animals, like huge squid.
ZYGOPHYSETER (ZY-GO-FY-SEH-TUR)
ACROPHYSETER (AH-KRO-FY-SEH-TUR)
PALEOPARADOXIA (PAY-LEE-O-PAH-RAH-DOKS-EE-AH) HERBIVOROUS AQUATIC MAMMAL
Geez, the whales aren't the only things with serious chompers in these parts, huh?
Indeed, this 8-foot-long relative of salmon has straight-up fangs.
We've met a lot of mammals with saber teeth, but...a salmon?!
That's bonkers!
But it looks cool, right?
...No.
Ah, to each their own, I guess.

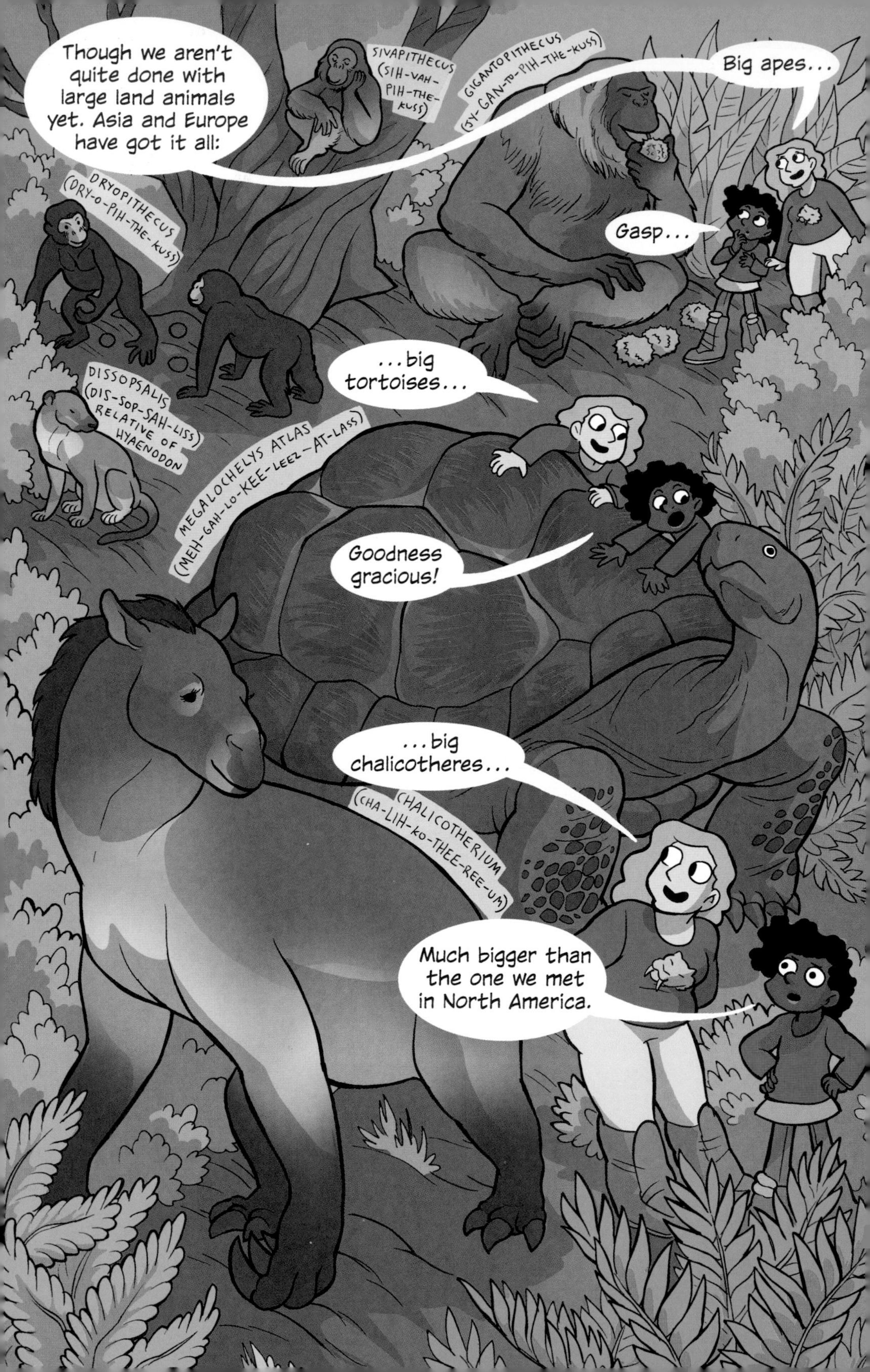
Though we aren't quite done with large land animals yet. Asia and Europe have got it all:
SIVAPITHECUS (SIH-VAH-PIH-THE-KUSS)
GIGANTOPITHECUS (JY-GAN-TO-PIH-THE-KUSS)
Big apes...
DRYOPITHECUS (DRY-O-PIH-THE-KUSS)
Gasp...
DISSOPSALIS (DIS-SOP-SAH-LISS) RELATIVE OF HYAENODON
...big tortoises...
MEGALOCHELYS ATLAS (MEH-GAH-LO-KEE-LEEZ-AT-LASS)
Goodness gracious!
...big chalicotheres...
CHALICOTHERIUM (CHA-LIH-KO-THEE-REE-UM)
Much bigger than the one we met in North America.

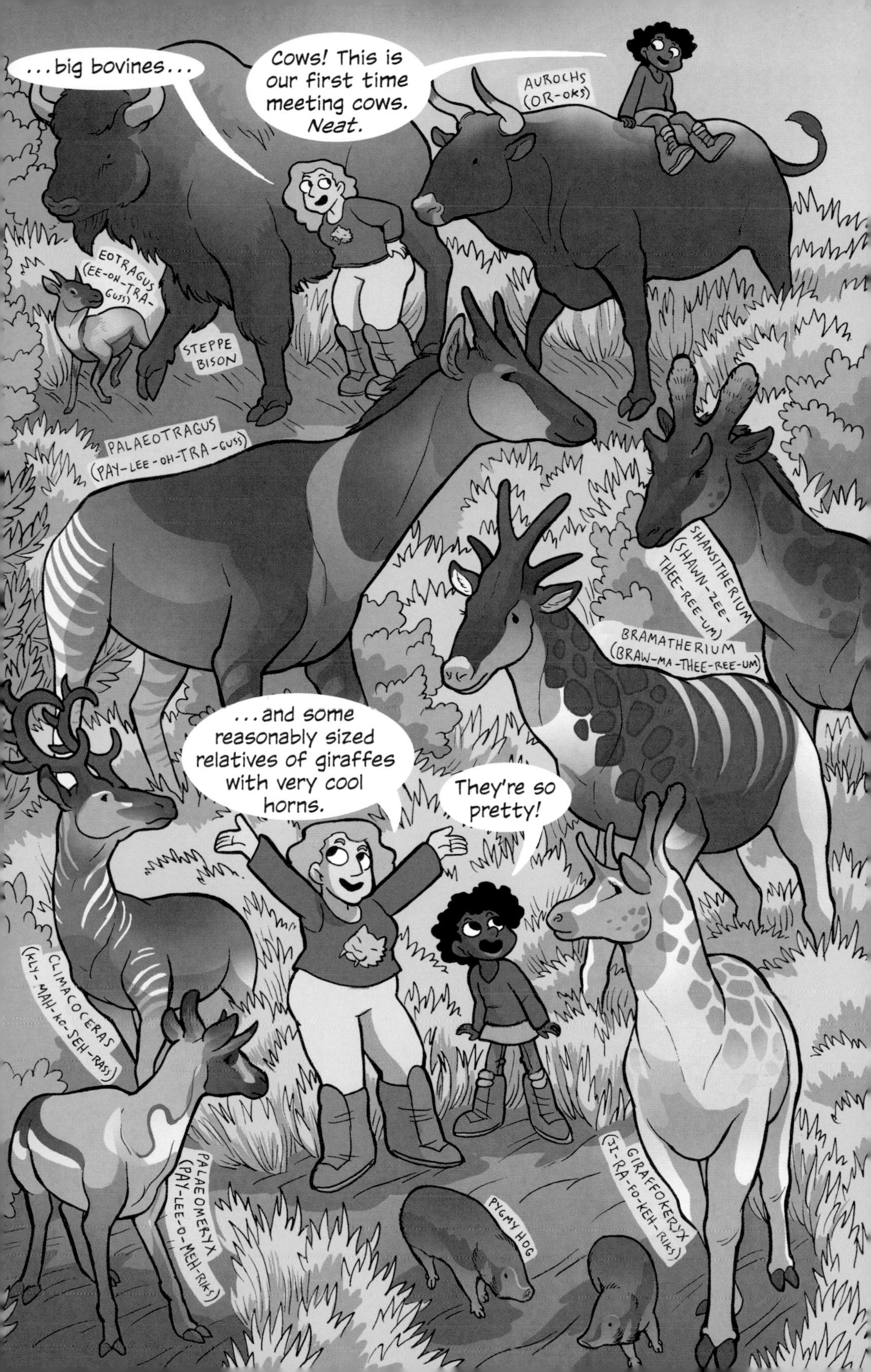
...big bovines...
Cows! This is our first time meeting cows. Neat.
AUROCHS (OR-OKS)
EOTRAGUS (EE-OH-TRA-GUSS)
STEPPE BISON
PALAEOTRAGUS (PAY-LEE-OH-TRA-GUSS)
SHANSITHERIUM (SHAWN-ZEE-THEE-REE-UM)
BRAMATHERIUM (BRAW-MA-THEE-REE-UM)
...and some reasonably sized relatives of giraffes with very cool horns.
They're so pretty!
CLIMACOCERAS (KLY-MAH-KO-SEH-RASS)
PALAEOMERYX (PAY-LEE-O-MEH-RIKS)
PYGMY HOG
GIRAFFOKERYX (JI-RA-FO-KEH-RIKS)

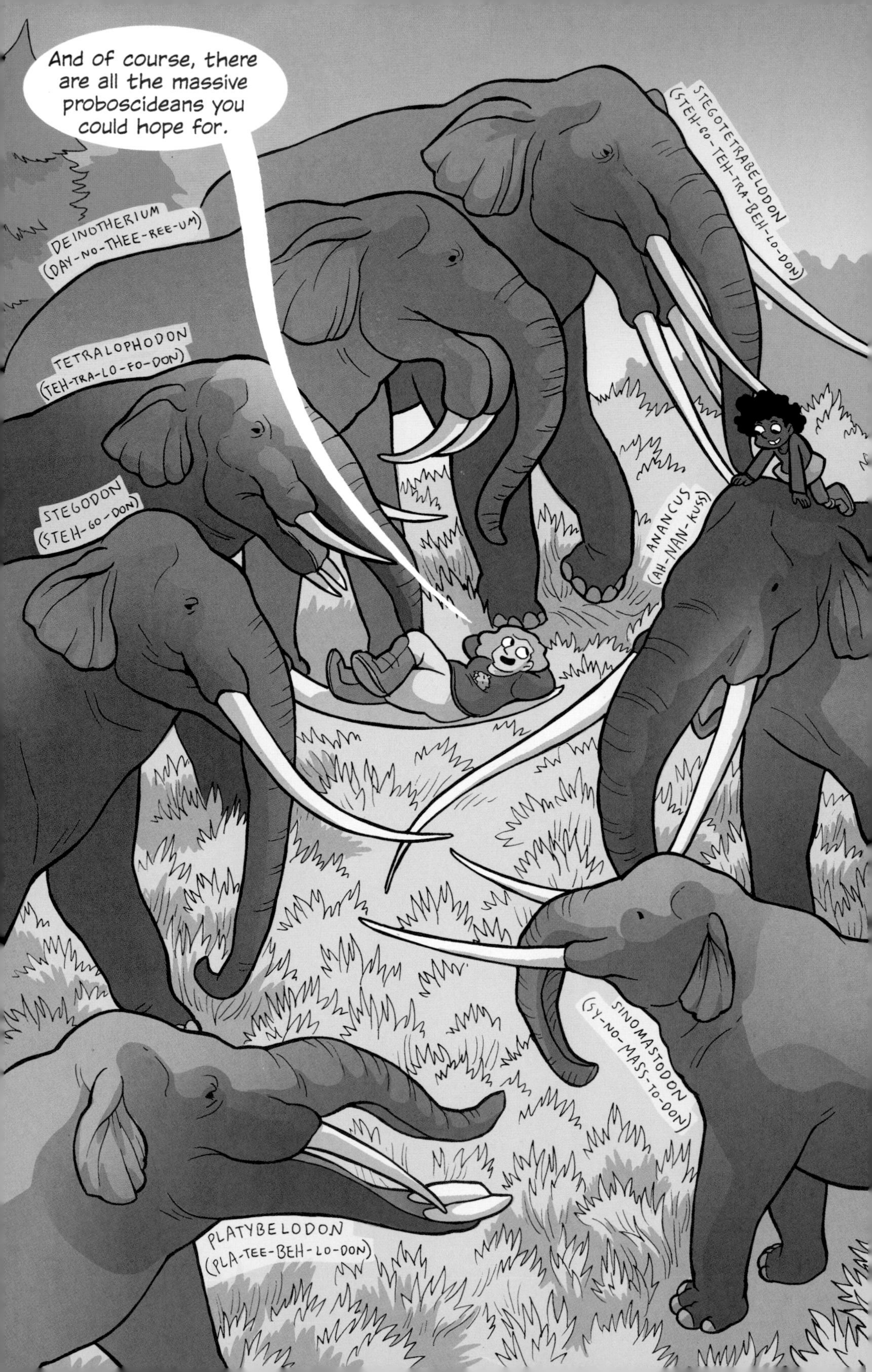
And of course, there are all the massive proboscideans you could hope for.
STEGOTETRABELODON (STEH-GO-TEH-TRA-BEH-LO-DON)
DEINOTHERIUM (DAY-NO-THEE-REE-UM)
TETRALOPHODON (TEH-TRA-LO-FO-DON)
STEGODON (STEH-GO-DON)
ANANCUS (AH-NAN-KUSS)
SINOMASTODON (SY-NO-MASS-TO-DON)
PLATYBELODON (PLA-TEE-BEH-LO-DON)

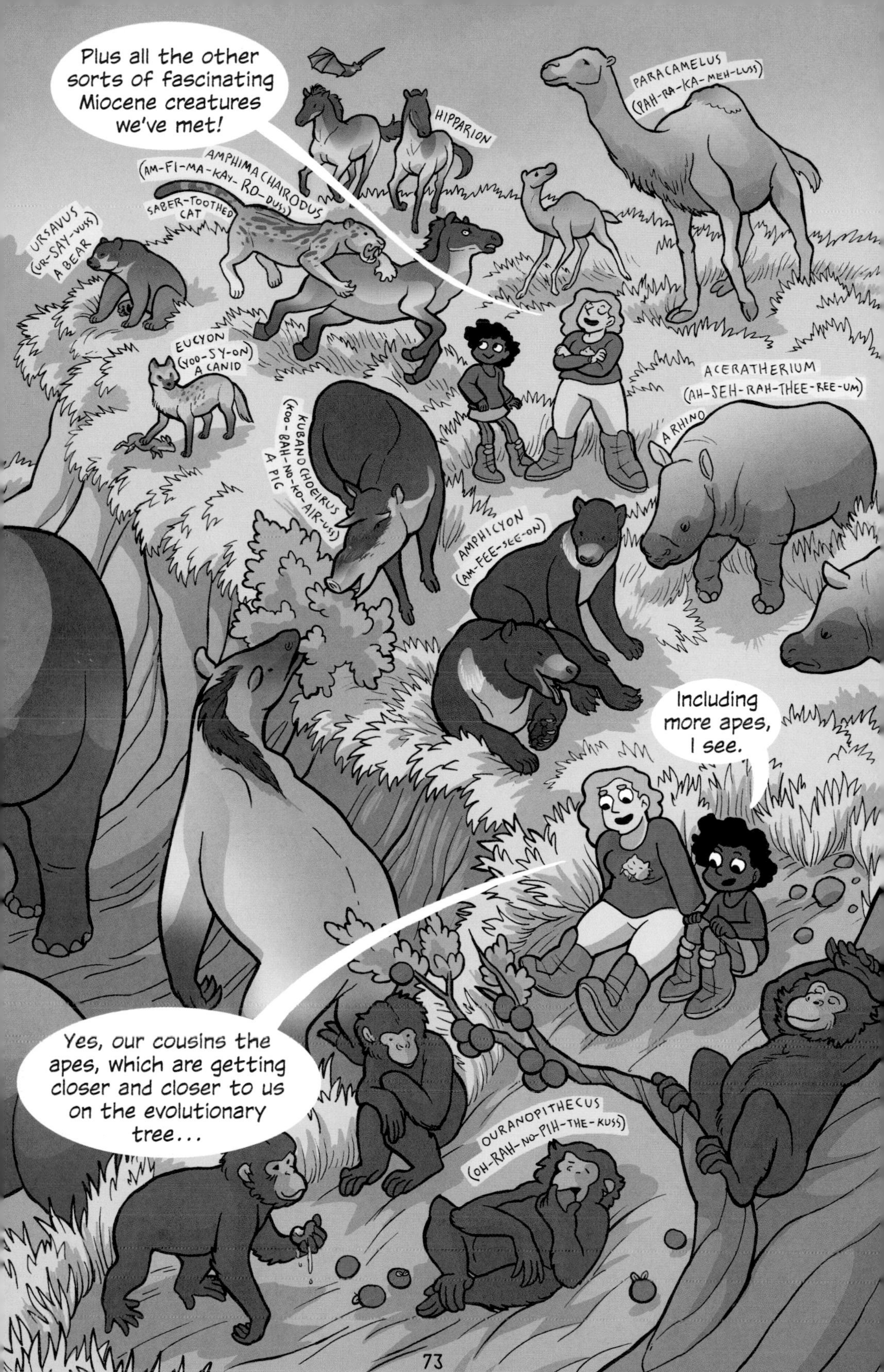
Plus all the other sorts of fascinating Miocene creatures we've met!
HIPPARION
PARACAMELUS (PAH-RA-KA-MEH-LUSS)
AMPHIMACHAIRODUS (AM-FI-MA-KAY-RO-DUSS)
SABER-TOOTHED CAT
URSAVUS (UR-SAY-VUSS) A BEAR
EUCYON (YOO-SY-ON) A CANID
KUBANOCHOEIRUS (KOO-BAH-NO-KO-AIR-USS) A PIG
ACERATHERIUM (AH-SEH-RAH-THEE-REE-UM)
A RHINO
AMPHICYON (AM-FEE-SEE-ON)
Including more apes, I see.
Yes, our cousins the apes, which are getting closer and closer to us on the evolutionary tree...
OURANOPITHECUS (OH-RAH-NO-PIH-THE-KUSS)

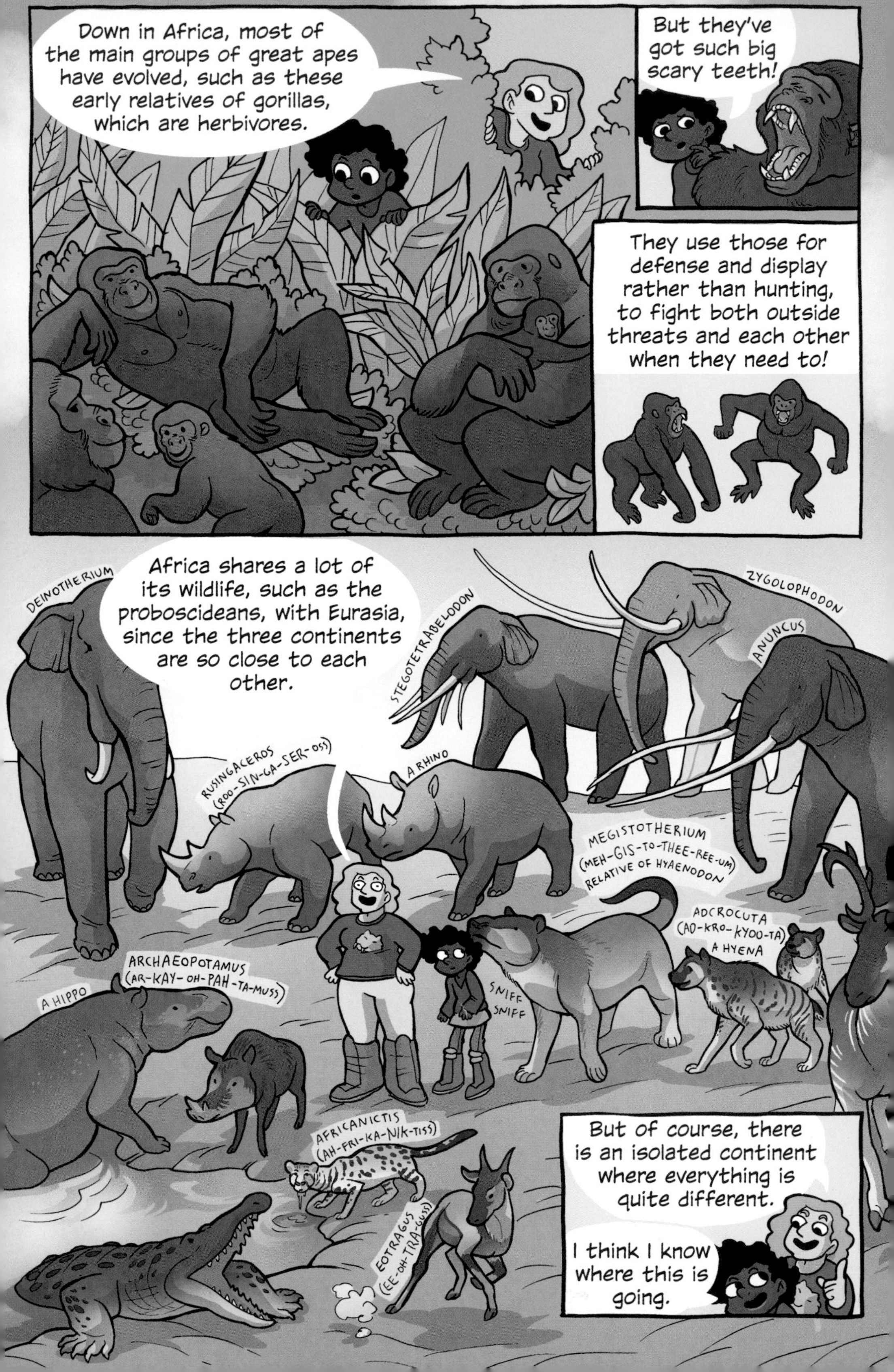

Down in Africa, most of the main groups of great apes have evolved, such as these early relatives of gorillas, which are herbivores.
But they've got such big scary teeth!
They use those for defense and display rather than hunting, to fight both outside threats and each other when they need to!
Africa shares a lot of its wildlife, such as the proboscideans, with Eurasia, since the three continents are so close to each other.
DEINOTHERIUM
STEGOTETRABELODON
ZYGOLOPHODON
ANUNCUS
RUSINGACEROS (ROO-SIN-GA-SER-OSS)
A RHINO
MEGISTOTHERIUM (MEH-GIS-TO-THEE-REE-UM) RELATIVE OF HYAENODON
ADCROCUTA (AD-KRO-KYOO-TA) A HYENA
SNIFF SNIFF
ARCHAEOPOTAMUS (AR-KAY-OH-PAH-TA-MUSS)
A HIPPO
AFRICANICTIS (AH-FRI-KA-NIK-TISS)
EOTRAGUS (EE-OH-TRA-GUSS)
But of course, there is an isolated continent where everything is quite different.
I think I know where this is going.

Australia! I knew it.
Does that mean this huge bird is another one of those vicious meat eaters?
Yes, Australia, where mammals are still pretty low on the food chain.
Actually, this Dromornis (dro-MOR-niss) is an herbivore, so it's not what the local mammals have to worry about...
...which is the dreaded Quinkana, still alive and well.
MEIOLANIA (MY-OH-LAH-NEE-AH)
QUINKANA
KOLOPSIS (KO-LOP-SIS)
GANGUROO (GAN-GUH-ROO)
PALORCHESTES (PAH-LOR-KESS TEEZ)
ZAGLOSSUS (ZA-GLAW-SUS) AN ECHIDNA
OBDURODON

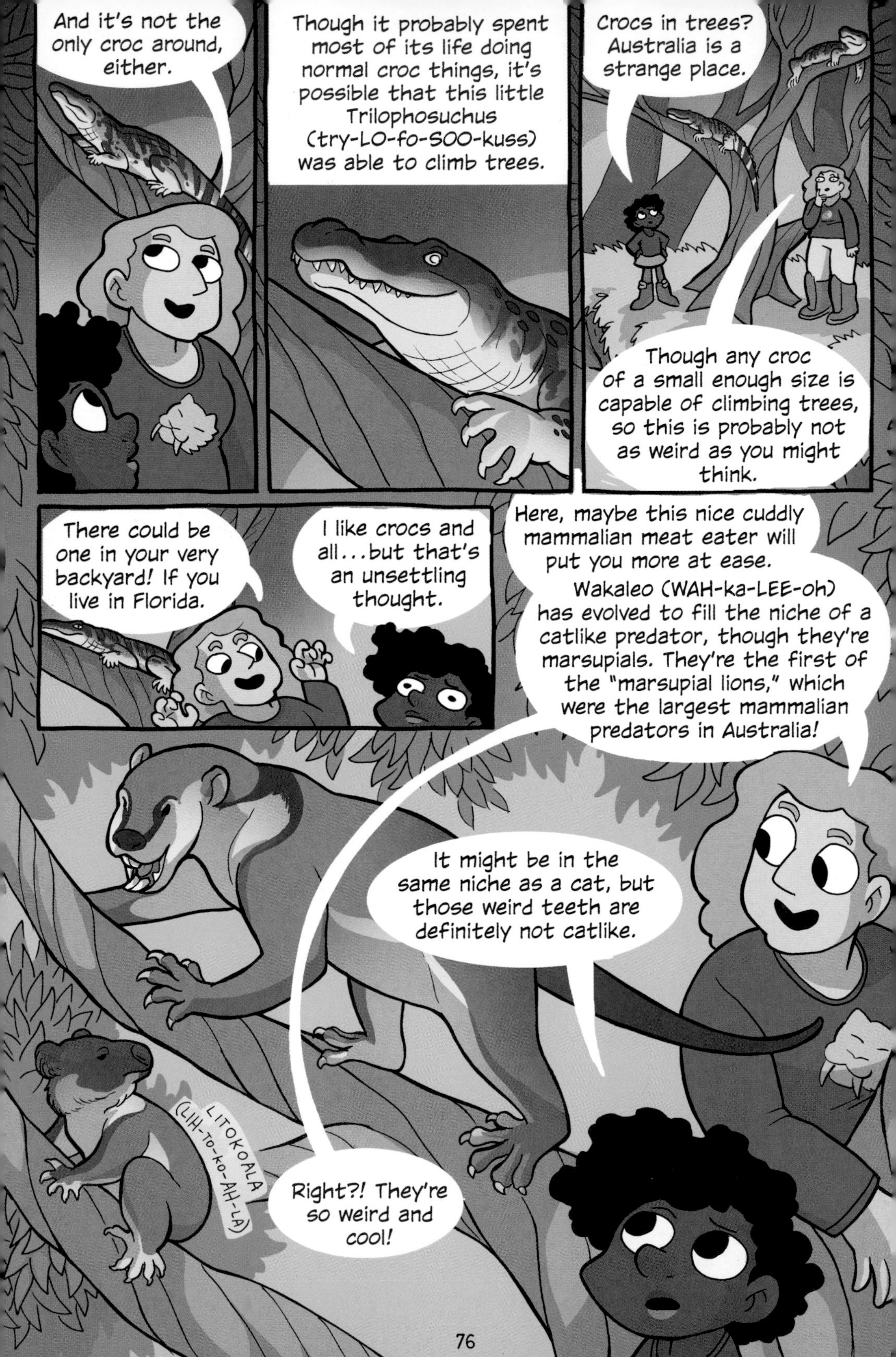
And it's not the only croc around, either.
Though it probably spent most of its life doing normal croc things, it's possible that this little Trilophosuchus (try-LO-fo-SOO-kuss) was able to climb trees.
Crocs in trees? Australia is a strange place.
Though any croc of a small enough size is capable of climbing trees, so this is probably not as weird as you might think.
There could be one in your very backyard! If you live in Florida.
I like crocs and all...but that's an unsettling thought.
Here, maybe this nice cuddly mammalian meat eater will put you more at ease.
Wakaleo (WAH-ka-LEE-oh) has evolved to fill the niche of a catlike predator, though they're marsupials. They're the first of the "marsupial lions," which were the largest mammalian predators in Australia!
It might be in the same niche as a cat, but those weird teeth are definitely not catlike.
LITOKOALA (LIH-to-ko-AH-LA)
Right?! They're so weird and cool!

It's been amazing watching the world slowly change into the one we live in.
It's quite magical, isn't it? And things are about to take a pretty dramatic turn as we head to about 3 million years ago, 2.7 to be precise, and enter the...
PLIOCENE
(PLY-EH-SEEN)
FINAL EPOCH OF THE NOGENE PERIOD
It's the very start of the Ice Age!
Oh no, it's gonna be so cold. I came back in time with you to escape the snow. I'll freeze down there.
Don't worry, it's only just started, so it's not that cold yet.
Plus, there are many parts of the world that stay quite warm and free of snow, especially along the equator.

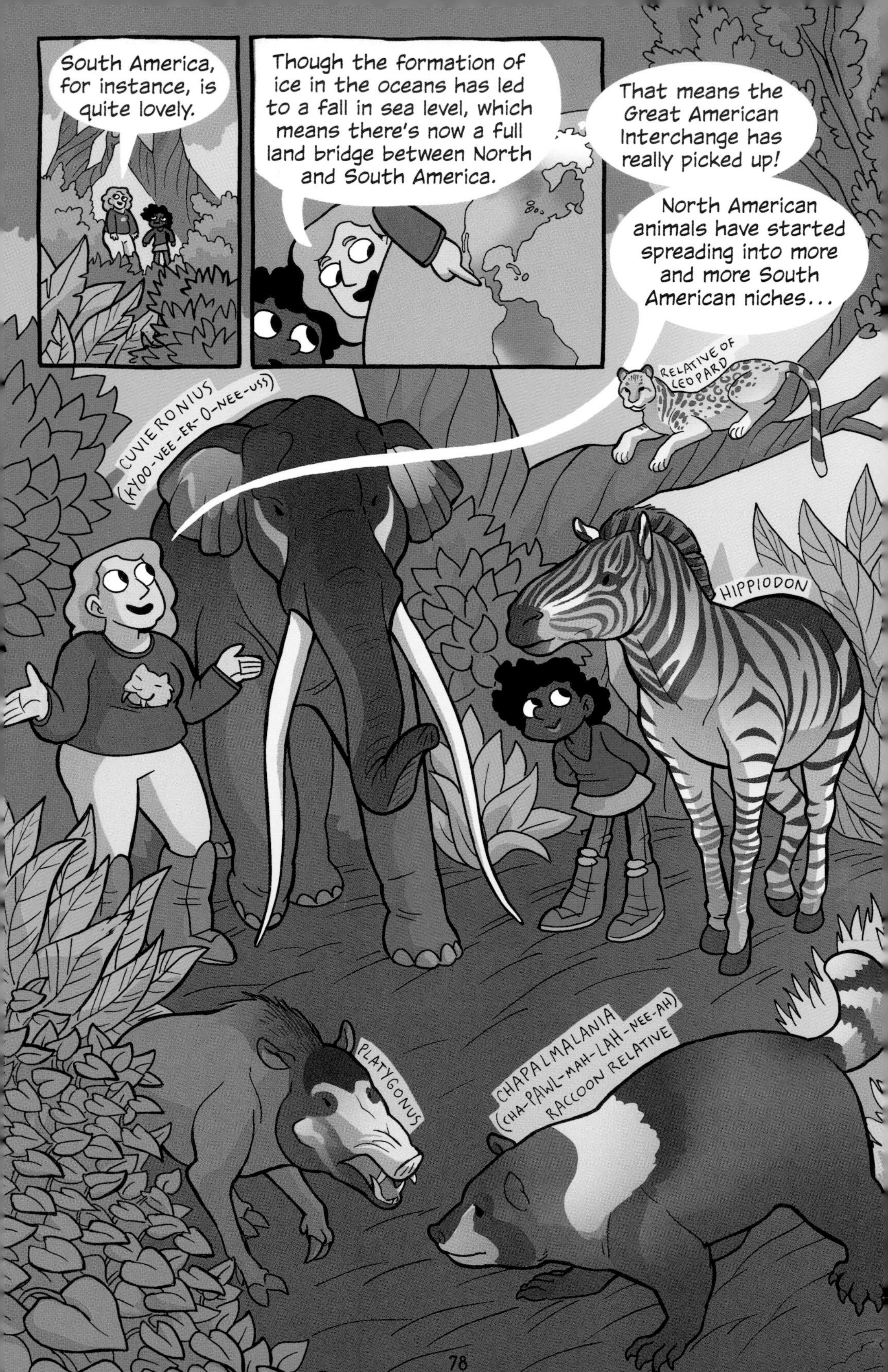

South America, for instance, is quite lovely.
Though the formation of ice in the oceans has led to a fall in sea level, which means there's now a full land bridge between North and South America.
That means the Great American Interchange has really picked up!
North American animals have started spreading into more and more South American niches...
RELATIVE OF LEOPARD
CUVIERONIUS (KYOO-VEE-ER-O-NEE-USS)
HIPPIODON
PLATYGONUS
CHAPALMALANIA (CHA-PAWL-MAH-LAH-NEE-AH) RACCOON RELATIVE

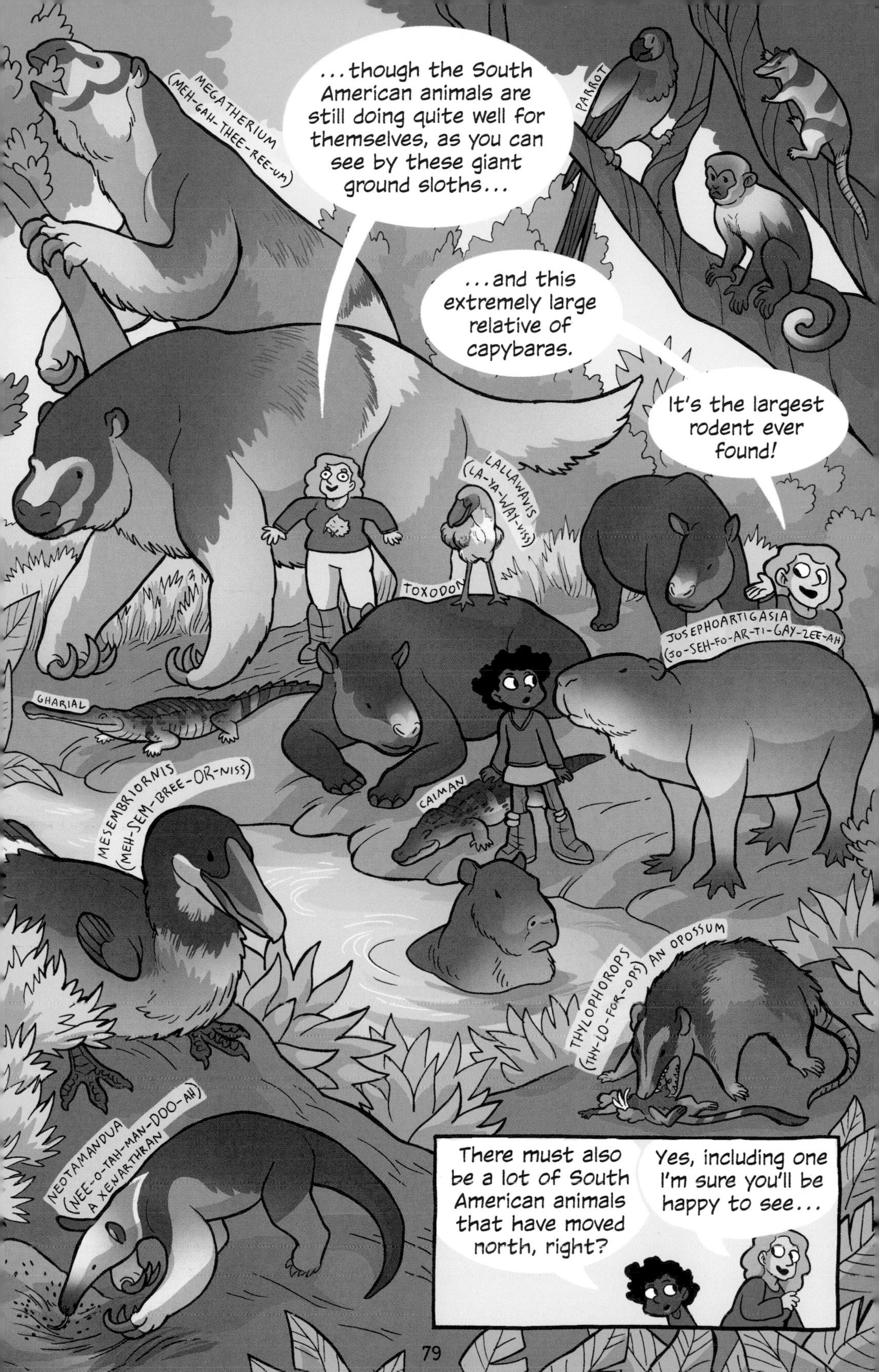

...though the South American animals are still doing quite well for themselves, as you can see by these giant ground sloths...
...and this extremely large relative of capybaras.
It's the largest rodent ever found!
MEGATHERIUM (MEH-GAH-THEE-REE-UM)
PARROT
LALLAWAVIS (LA-YA-WAY-VISS)
TOXODON
JOSEPHOARTIGASIA (JO-SEH-FO-AR-TI-GAY-ZEE-AH)
GHARIAL
CAIMAN
MESEMBRIORNIS (MEH-SEM-BREE-OR-NISS)
THYLOPHOROPS (THY-LO-FOR-OPS) AN OPOSSUM
NEOTAMANDUA (NEE-O-TAH-MAN-DOO-AH) A XENARTHRAN
There must also be a lot of South American animals that have moved north, right?
Yes, including one I'm sure you'll be happy to see...

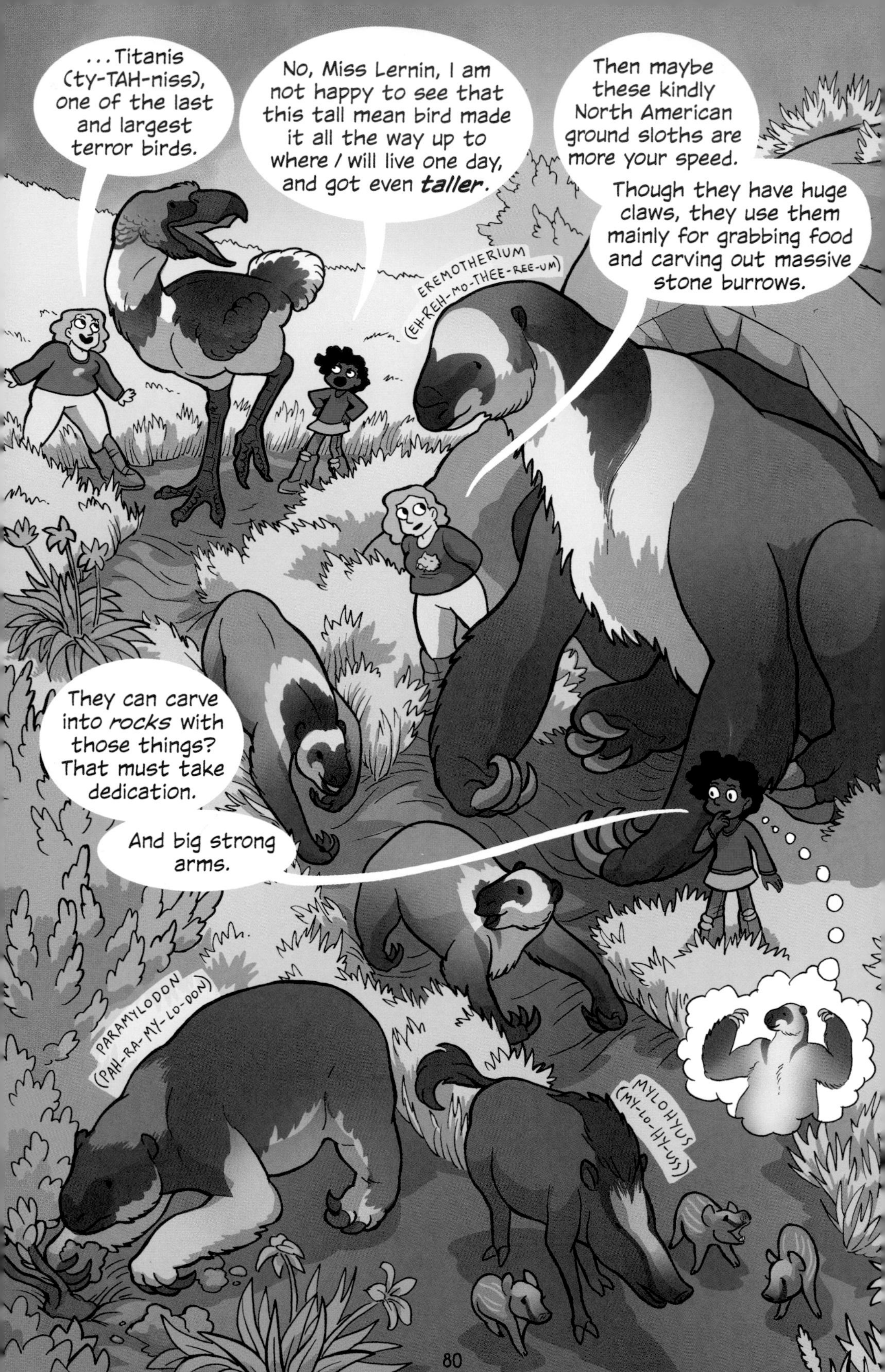
...Titanis (ty-TAH-niss), one of the last and largest terror birds.
No, Miss Lernin, I am not happy to see that this tall mean bird made it all the way up to where I will live one day, and got even *taller*.
Then maybe these kindly North American ground sloths are more your speed.
Though they have huge claws, they use them mainly for grabbing food and carving out massive stone burrows.
EREMOTHERIUM (EH-REH-MO-THEE-REE-UM)
They can carve into *rocks* with those things? That must take dedication.
And big strong arms.
PARAMYLODON (PAH-RA-MY-LO-DON)
MYLOHYUS (MY-LO-HY-USS)

Too bad living in North America means they're now at the mercy of creatures like the giant false saber-toothed cat Barbourfelis (BAR-bor-FEH-liss).
Why do so many of the saber-toothed animals we've met have big weird chins?
Good question! Their weird elongated chin bones support long, fleshy, saliva-covered lips, which are probably helpful in keeping their teeth clean.
GOT GUNK ON YOUR FANGIES?
SCRAPE SOME OF THAT GUNK OFF WITH YOUR BIG WET LIPS!
MEGANTEREON
Then why wouldn't *all* saber-toothed animals have big chins and long lips?
We aren't really sure. Actual saber-toothed cats, such as Megantereon (MEH-gan-TEE-ree-on) here, usually have smaller chins despite their larger teeth...
DINOFELIS (DY-NO-FEH-LISS)
And in our time, there are a fair number of saber-toothed deer that have neither a big chin nor large lips!
It's a mystery why some saber-toothed animals have the chin and lip situation while others don't.
There are so many mysteries that still need solving...

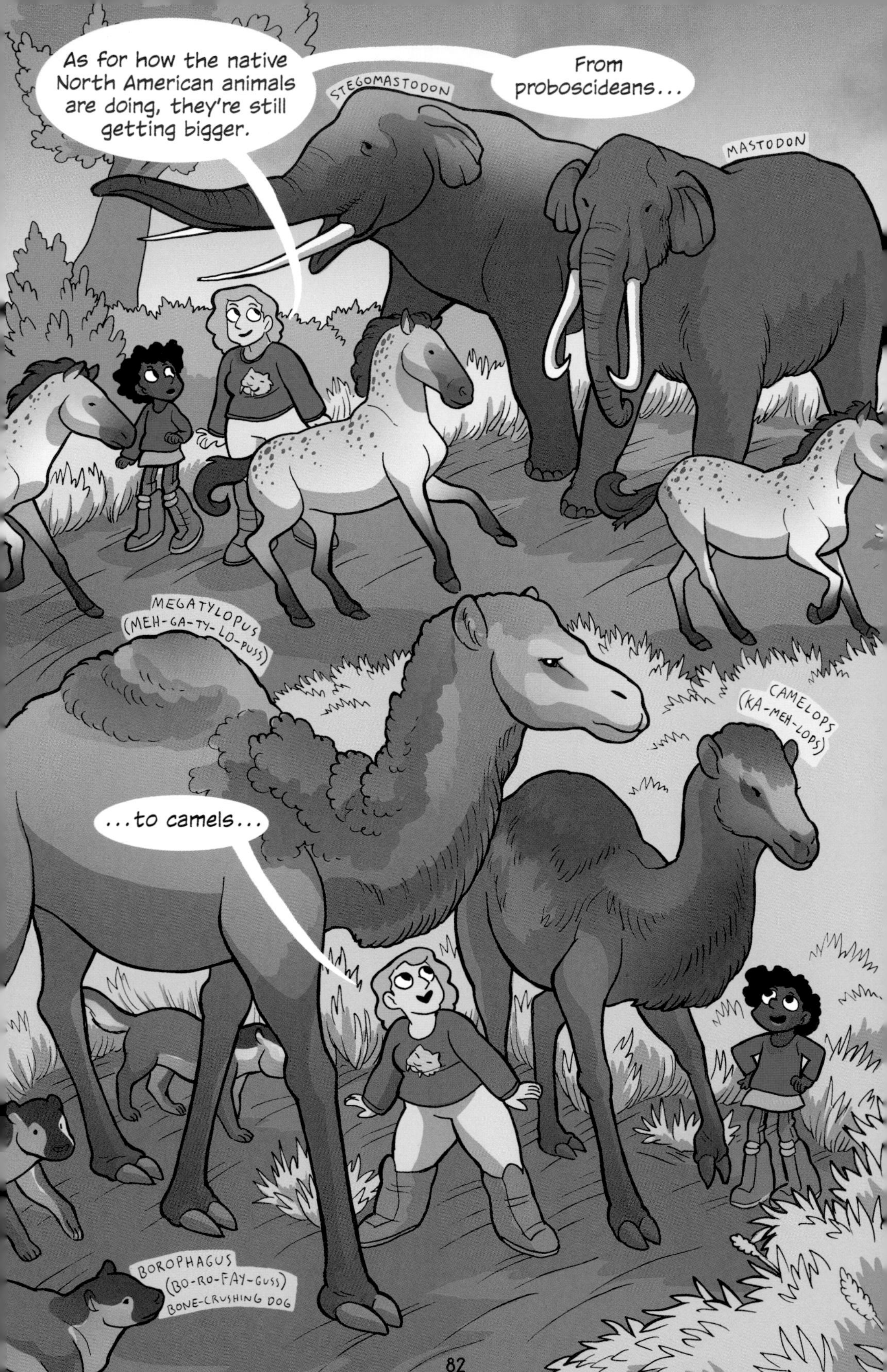
As for how the native North American animals are doing, they're still getting bigger.
From proboscideans...
STEGOMASTODON
MASTODON
MEGATYLOPUS (MEH-GA-TY-LO-PUSS)
CAMELOPS (KA-MEH-LOPS)
...to camels...
BOROPHAGUS (BO-RO-FAY-GUSS) BONE-CRUSHING DOG

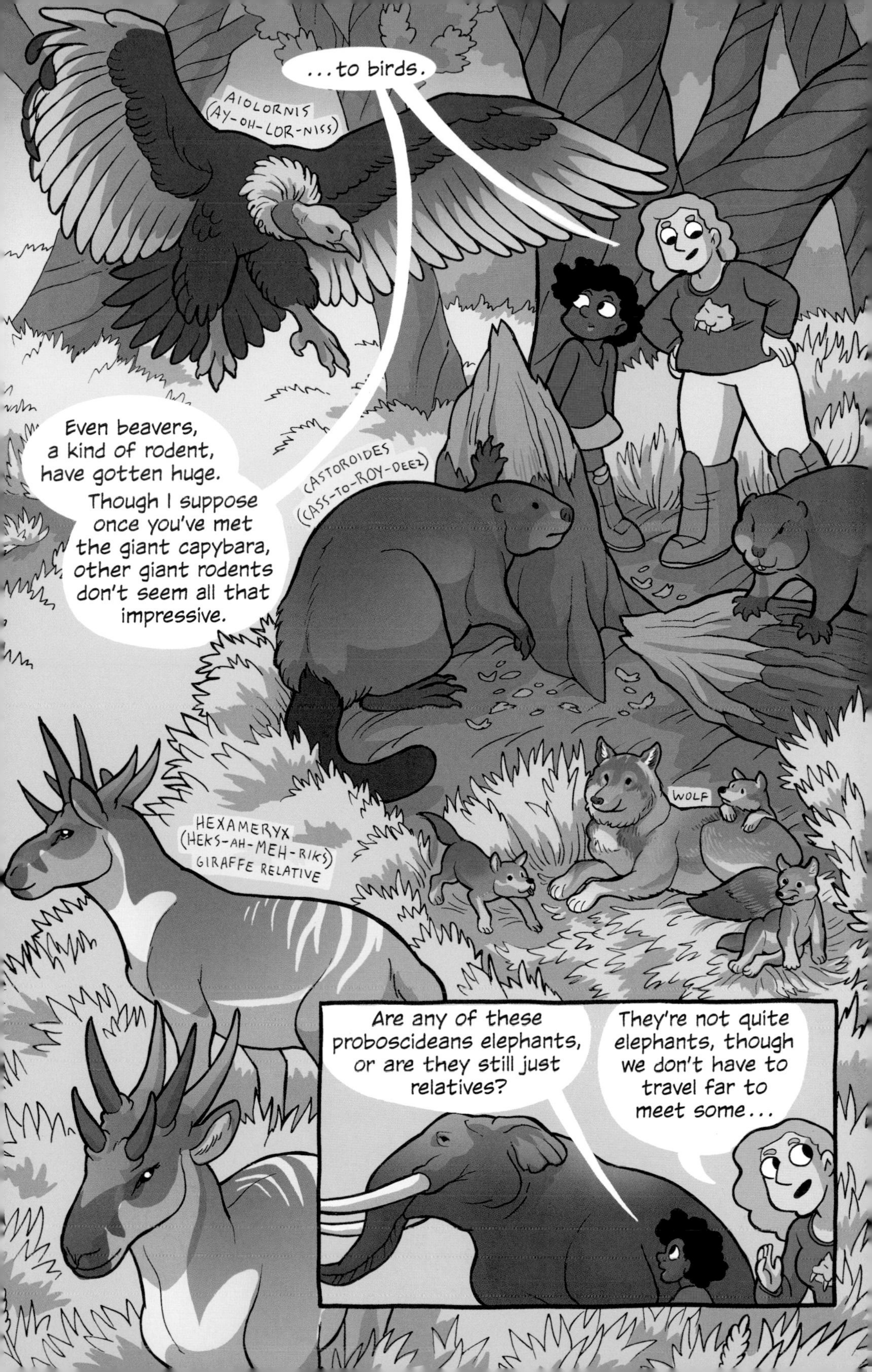
...to birds.
AIOLORNIS (AY-OH-LOR-NISS)
Even beavers, a kind of rodent, have gotten huge.
Though I suppose once you've met the giant capybara, other giant rodents don't seem all that impressive.
CASTOROIDES (CASS-TO-ROY-DEEZ)
HEXAMERYX (HEKS-AH-MEH-RIKS) GIRAFFE RELATIVE
WOLF
Are any of these proboscideans elephants, or are they still just relatives?
They're not quite elephants, though we don't have to travel far to meet some...

We just have to cross the land bridge into Asia...
RUSSIA, ASIAN CONTINENT
ALASKA, NORTH AMERICA
SOUTHERN MAMMOTH
...where Asian elephants, one of the two groups of elephants we have in our time, have arrived on the scene.
ASIAN ELEPHANT
EUCLADOCEROS (YOO-KLA-DO-SEH-ROSS) A DEER
Besides elephants, most of the Eurasian mammals are quite similar to those we just visited in North America...
SHEEP
...with the notable exception of the giant rhino Elasmotherium (ee-LAZ-mo-THEE-ree-um), also called the Siberian unicorn.
That horn is bigger than I am!
DINOFELIS
RELATIVE OF BIG CATS
CELEBOCHOEIRUS (SEH-LEH-BO-KU-AIR-US)
This rhino lived on into human times, and legends were written about it long before it was ever documented by paleontologists.
It's a real-life mythical creature!
As for the second group of elephants that live in our time, they're currently wandering the plains of...

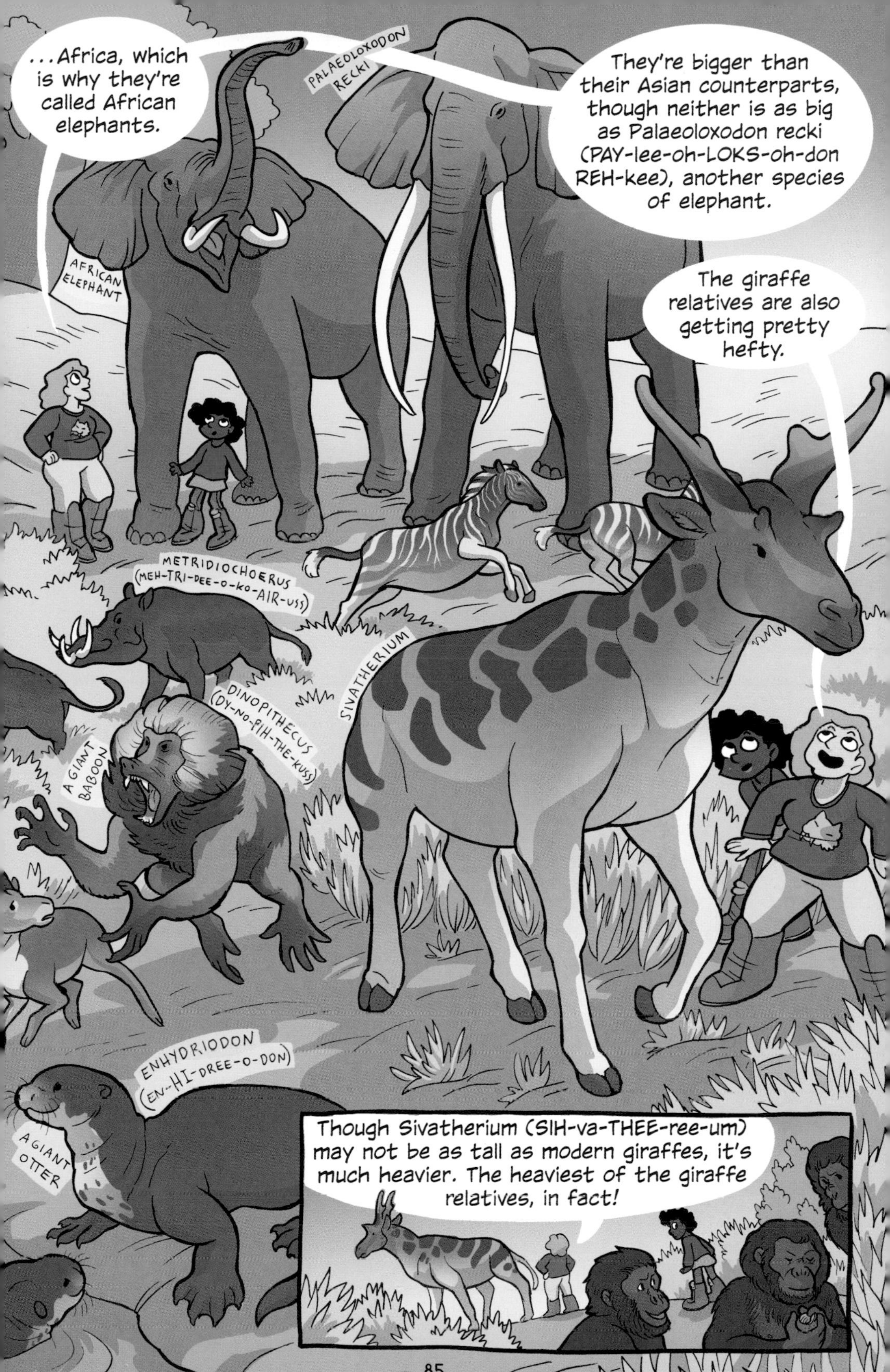
...Africa, which is why they're called African elephants.
PALAEOLOXODON RECKI
They're bigger than their Asian counterparts, though neither is as big as Palaeoloxodon recki (PAY-lee-oh-LOKS-oh-don REH-kee), another species of elephant.
AFRICAN ELEPHANT
The giraffe relatives are also getting pretty hefty.
METRIDIOCHOERUS (MEH-TRI-DEE-O-KO-AIR-USS)
SIVATHERIUM
DINOPITHECUS (DY-NO-PIH-THE-KUSS)
A GIANT BABOON
ENHYDRIODON (EN-HI-DREE-O-DON)
A GIANT OTTER
Though Sivatherium (SIH-va-THEE-ree-um) may not be as tall as modern giraffes, it's much heavier. The heaviest of the giraffe relatives, in fact!

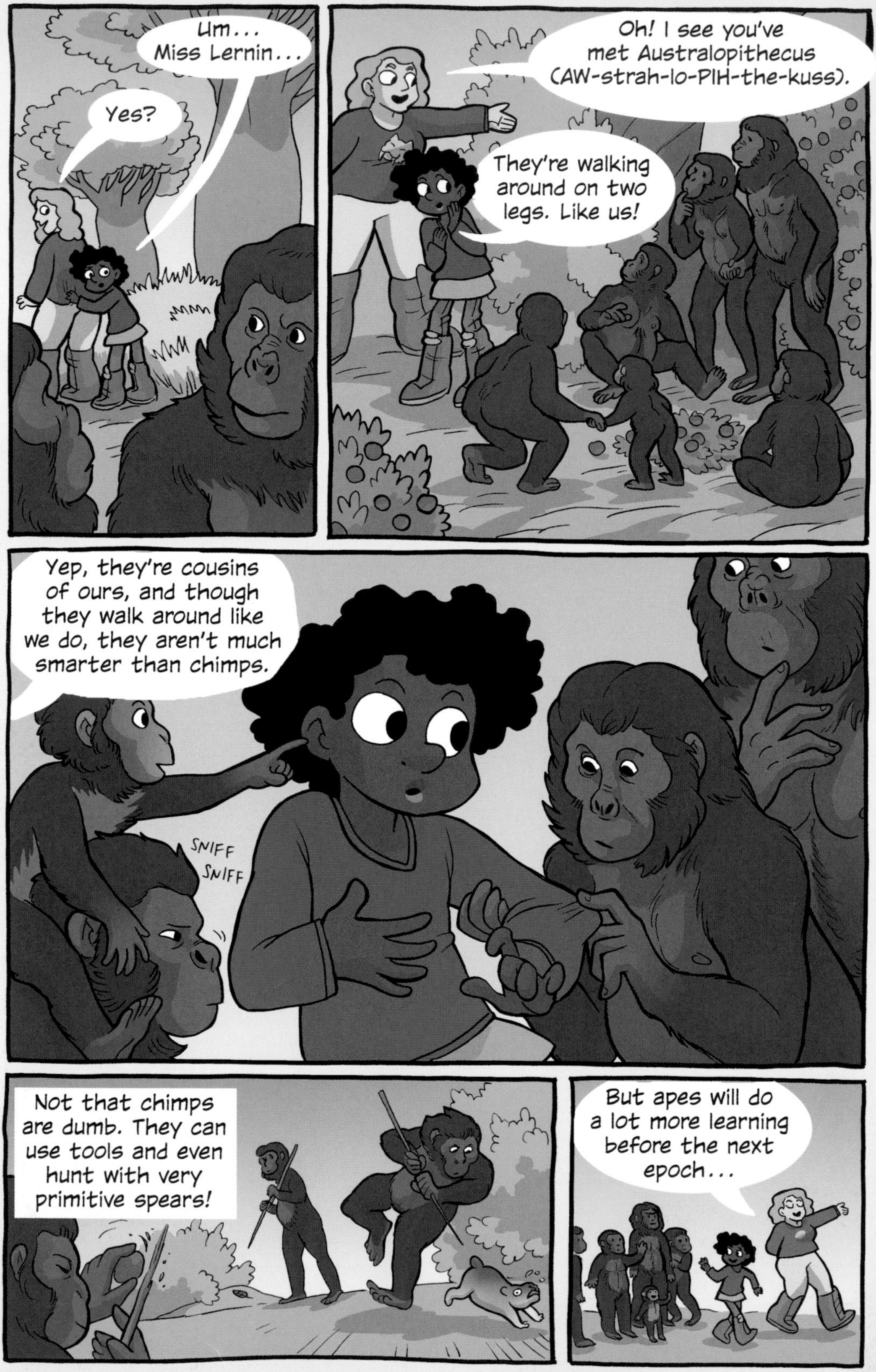
Um... Miss Lernin...
Yes?
Oh! I see you've met Australopithecus (AW-strah-lo-PIH-the-kuss).
They're walking around on two legs. Like us!
Yep, they're cousins of ours, and though they walk around like we do, they aren't much smarter than chimps.
SNIFF SNIFF
Not that chimps are dumb. They can use tools and even hunt with very primitive spears!
But apes will do a lot more learning before the next epoch...

Welcome to the...
PLEISTOCENE
(PLY-STEH-SEEN)
FIRST EPOCH OF THE QUATERNARY PERIOD
(KWA-TUR-NARE-EE)
The Pleistocene was only a couple hundred thousand years ago, which is extremely recent if you consider how long animals have been growing and changing.
That means this epoch is very similar to modern day.
Though it is chillier, since the Ice Age is at its coldest.
So how about we visit a nice warm place first?
Yes, please!

Like Australia, for instance.
Oh boy, I can't wait to see what weird stuff there is now.
And you won't be disappointed. There are large, adorable mammalian herbivores now, like Diprotodon (dy-PRO-to-don)...
EURYZYGOMA (YOO-REE-ZY-GO-MA)
...and large mammalian carnivores, too, like the marsupial lion Thylacoleo (thy-LAH-ko-LEE-oh).
PALORCHESTES
Again with the weird teeth! These marsupial lions are so odd.
Australia is also home to some very odd sights, like this giant kangaroo that doesn't hop. Instead it walks around like a weird buff person.
PROCOPTODON (PRO-KOP-TO-DON)
But the oddest and perhaps most frightening creatures around are the reptiles.

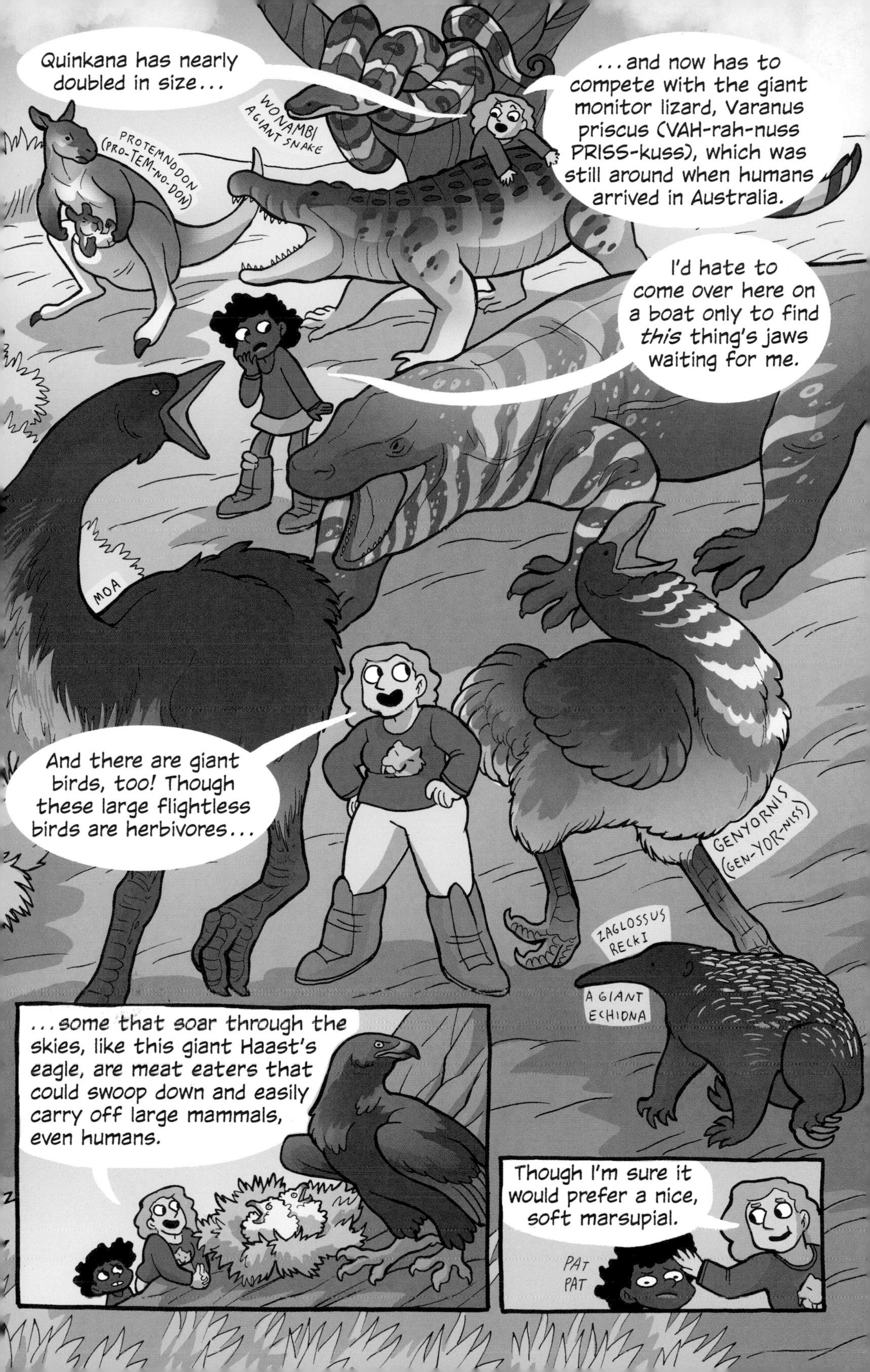
Quinkana has nearly doubled in size...
WONAMBI
A GIANT SNAKE
PROTEMNODON
(PRO-TEM-NO-DON)
...and now has to compete with the giant monitor lizard, Varanus priscus (VAH-rah-nuss PRISS-kuss), which was still around when humans arrived in Australia.
I'd hate to come over here on a boat only to find *this* thing's jaws waiting for me.
MOA
And there are giant birds, too! Though these large flightless birds are herbivores...
GENYORNIS
(GEN-YOR-NISS)
ZAGLOSSUS
RECKI
A GIANT
ECHIDNA
...some that soar through the skies, like this giant Haast's eagle, are meat eaters that could swoop down and easily carry off large mammals, even humans.
Though I'm sure it would prefer a nice, soft marsupial.
PAT
PAT

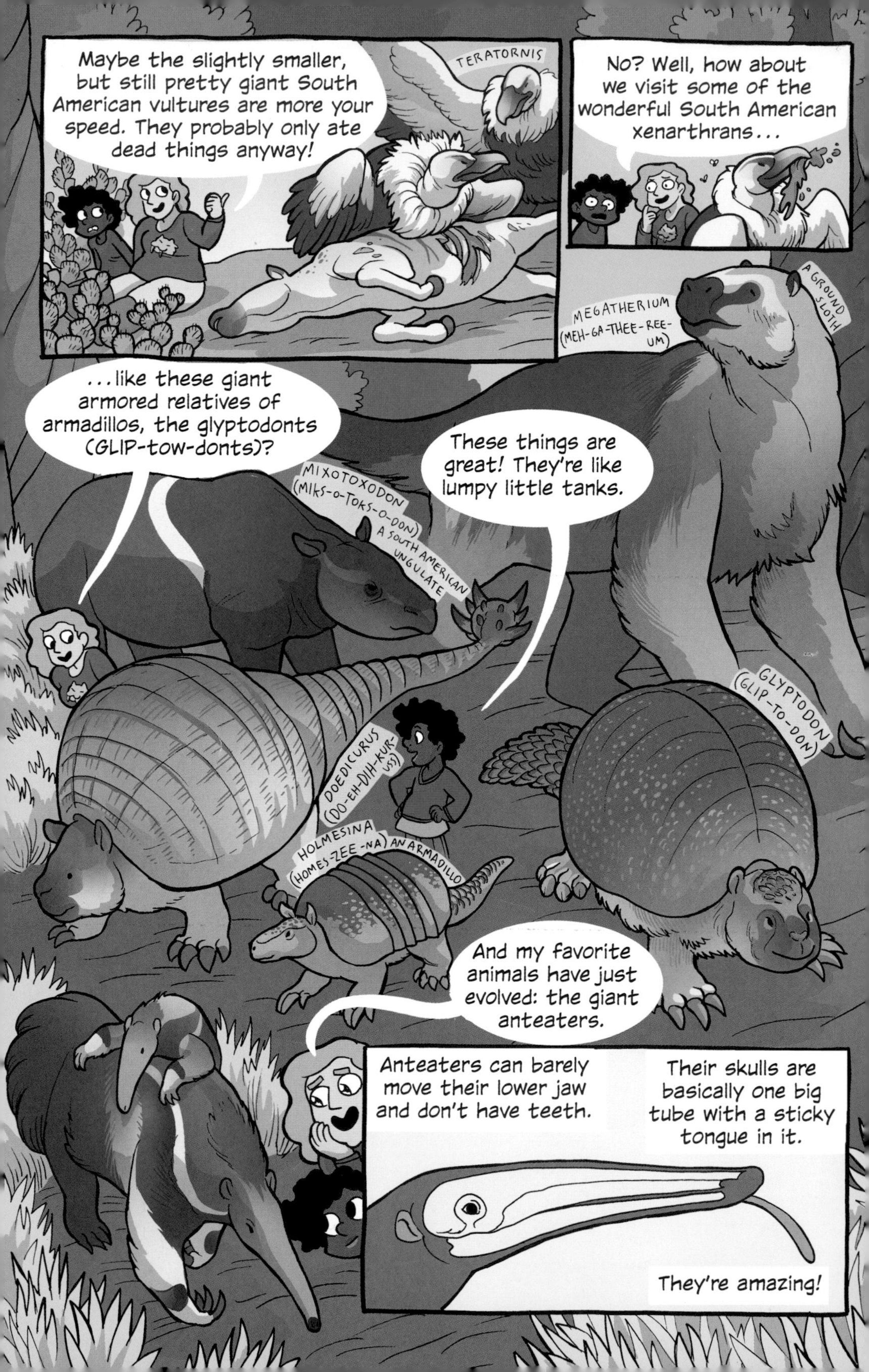
Maybe the slightly smaller, but still pretty giant South American vultures are more your speed. They probably only ate dead things anyway!
TERATORNIS
No? Well, how about we visit some of the wonderful South American xenarthrans...
MEGATHERIUM (MEH-GA-THEE-REE-UM)
A GROUND SLOTH
...like these giant armored relatives of armadillos, the glyptodonts (GLIP-tow-donts)?
These things are great! They're like lumpy little tanks.
MIXOTOXODON (MIKS-O-TOKS-O-DON)
A SOUTH AMERICAN UNGULATE
GLYPTODON (GLIP-TO-DON)
DOEDICURUS (DO-EH-DIH-KUR-US)
HOLMESINA (HOMES-ZEE-NA) AN ARMADILLO
And my favorite animals have just evolved: the giant anteaters.
Anteaters can barely move their lower jaw and don't have teeth.
Their skulls are basically one big tube with a sticky tongue in it.
They're amazing!

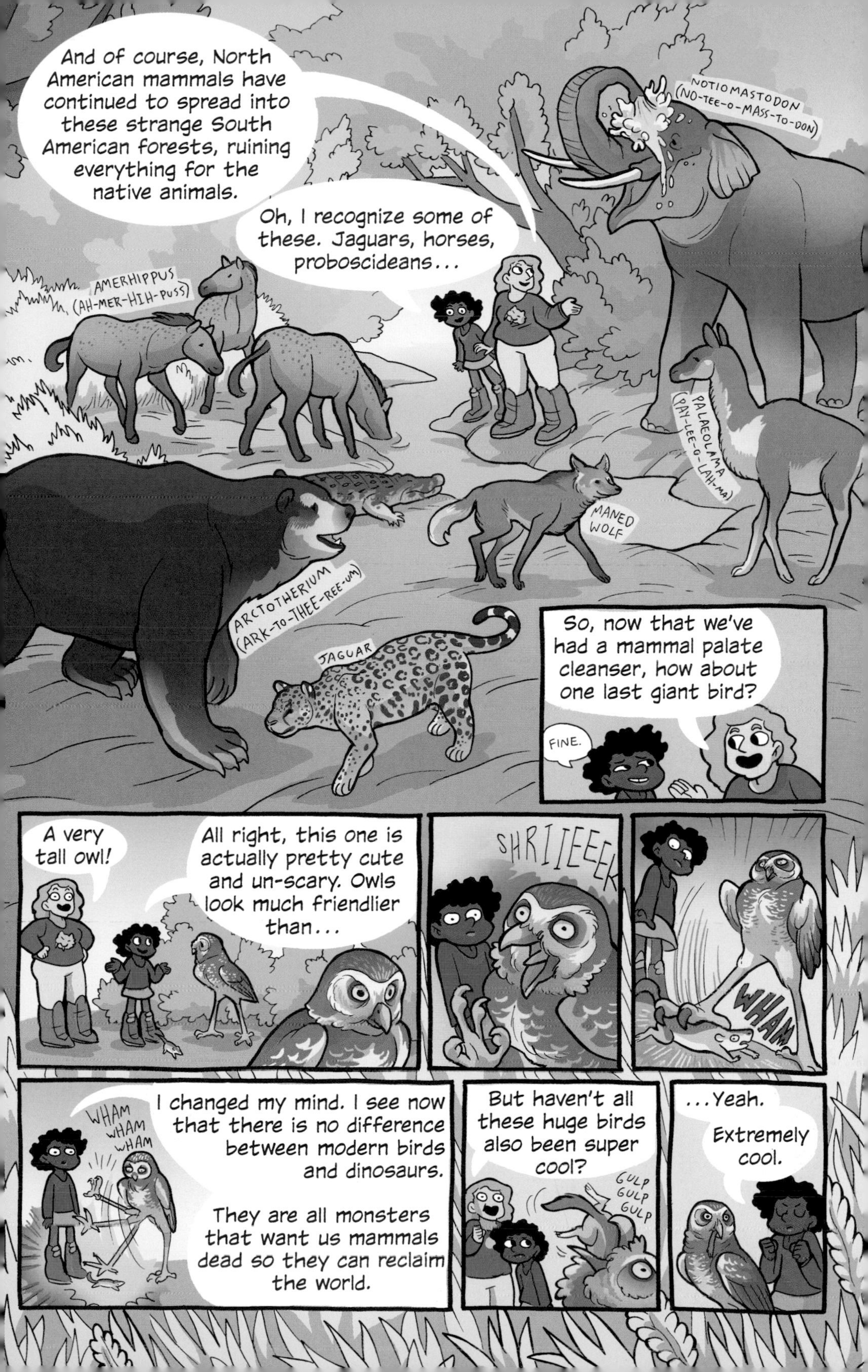

And of course, North American mammals have continued to spread into these strange South American forests, ruining everything for the native animals.
Oh, I recognize some of these. Jaguars, horses, proboscideans...
NOTIOMASTODON (NO-TEE-O-MASS-TO-DON)
AMERHIPPUS (AH-MER-HIH-PUSS)
PALAEOLAMA (PAY-LEE-O-LAH-MA)
MANED WOLF
ARCTOTHERIUM (ARK-TO-THEE-REE-UM)
JAGUAR
So, now that we've had a mammal palate cleanser, how about one last giant bird?
FINE.
A very tall owl!
All right, this one is actually pretty cute and un-scary. Owls look much friendlier than...
SHRIIEEEK
WHAM
WHAM WHAM WHAM
I changed my mind. I see now that there is no difference between modern birds and dinosaurs.
They are all monsters that want us mammals dead so they can reclaim the world.
But haven't all these huge birds also been super cool?
GULP GULP GULP
...Yeah.
Extremely cool.

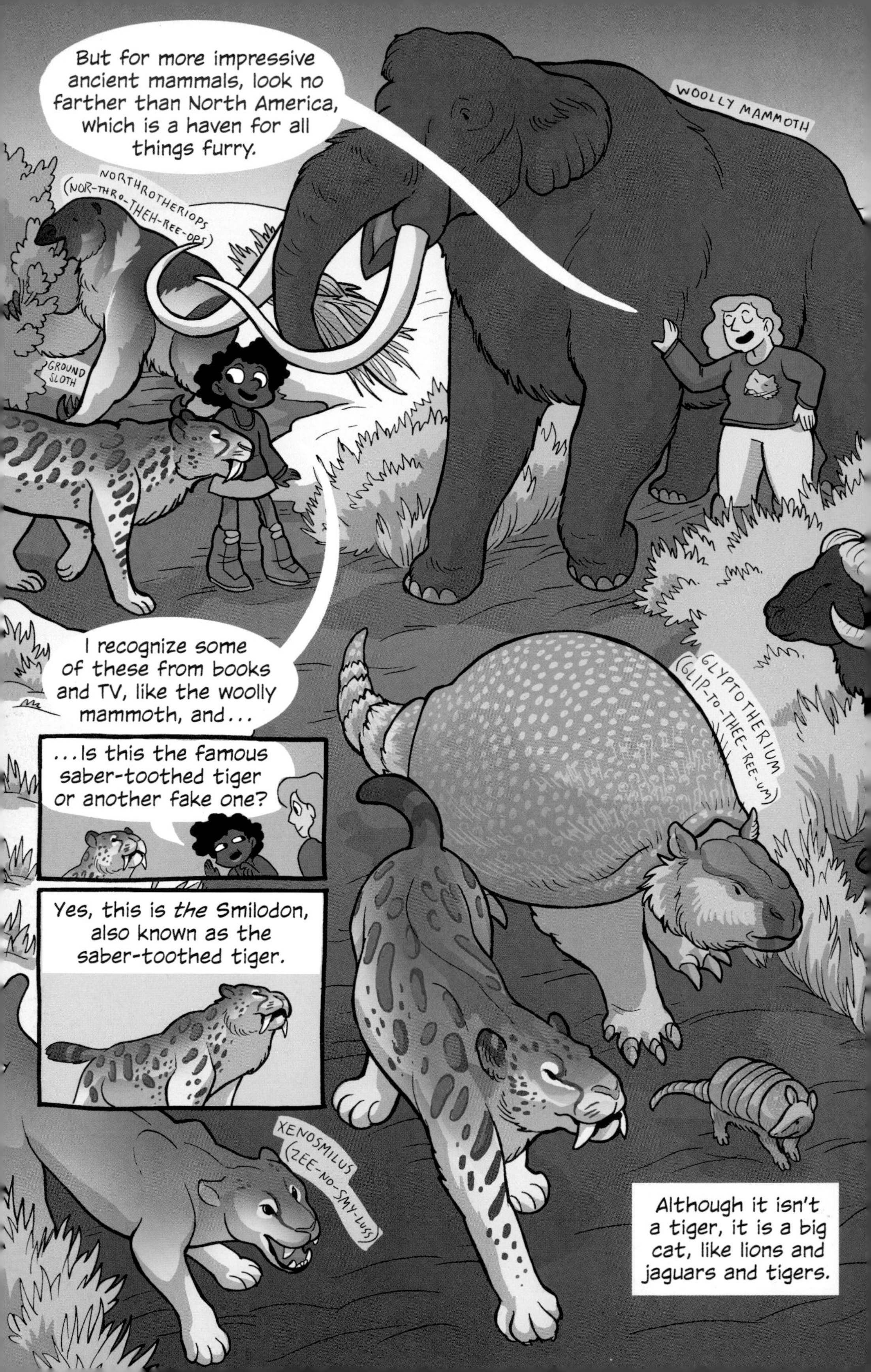

But for more impressive ancient mammals, look no farther than North America, which is a haven for all things furry.
WOOLLY MAMMOTH
NORTHROTHERIOPS (NOR-THRO-THEH-REE-OPS)
GROUND SLOTH
I recognize some of these from books and TV, like the woolly mammoth, and...
GLYPTOTHERIUM (GLIP-TO-THEE-REE-UM)
...Is this the famous saber-toothed tiger or another fake one?
Yes, this is *the* Smilodon, also known as the saber-toothed tiger.
XENOSMILUS (ZEE-NO-SMY-LUSS)
Although it isn't a tiger, it is a big cat, like lions and jaguars and tigers.

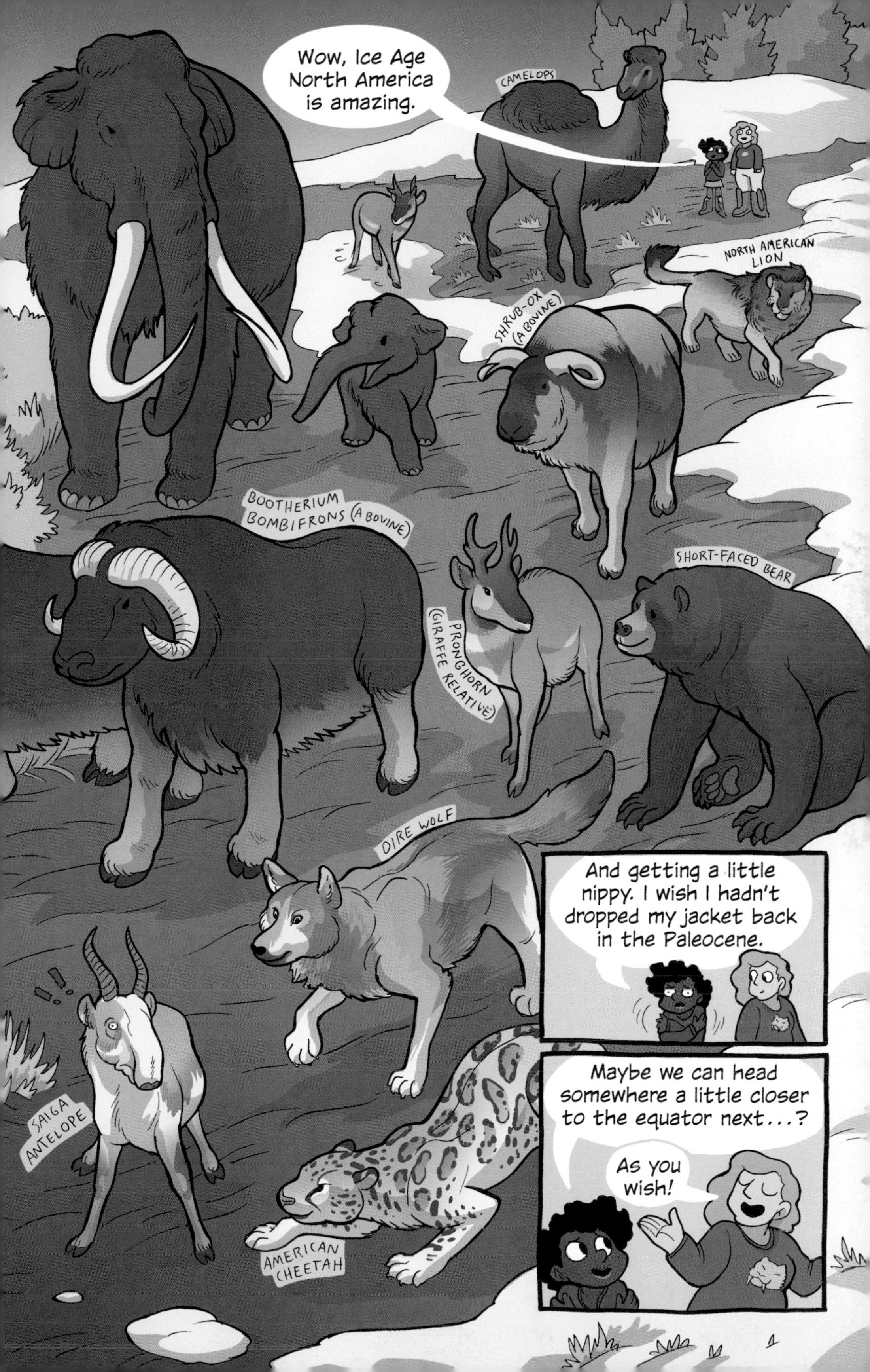
Wow, Ice Age North America is amazing.
CAMELOPS
NORTH AMERICAN LION
SHRUB-OX (A BOVINE)
BOOTHERIUM BOMBIFRONS (A BOVINE)
PRONGHORN (GIRAFFE RELATIVE)
SHORT-FACED BEAR
DIRE WOLF
And getting a little nippy. I wish I hadn't dropped my jacket back in the Paleocene.
SAIGA ANTELOPE
AMERICAN CHEETAH
Maybe we can head somewhere a little closer to the equator next...?
As you wish!

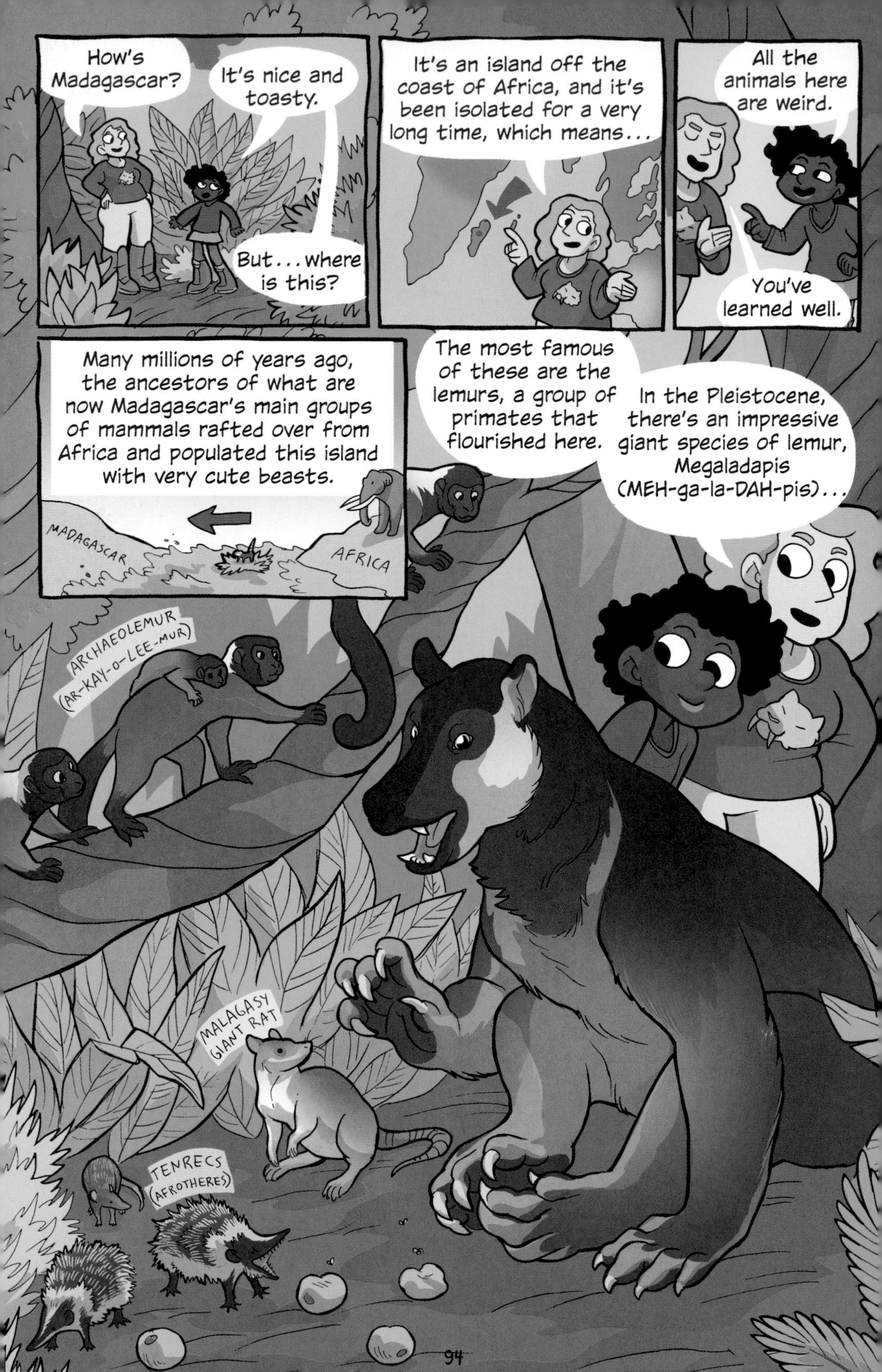
How's Madagascar?
It's nice and toasty.
But...where is this?
It's an island off the coast of Africa, and it's been isolated for a very long time, which means...
All the animals here are weird.
You've learned well.
Many millions of years ago, the ancestors of what are now Madagascar's main groups of mammals rafted over from Africa and populated this island with very cute beasts.
MADAGASCAR
AFRICA
The most famous of these are the lemurs, a group of primates that flourished here.
In the Pleistocene, there's an impressive giant species of lemur, Megaladapis (MEH-ga-la-DAH-pis)...
ARCHAEOLEMUR (AR-KAY-o-LEE-MUR)
MALAGASY GIANT RAT
TENRECS (AFROTHERES)

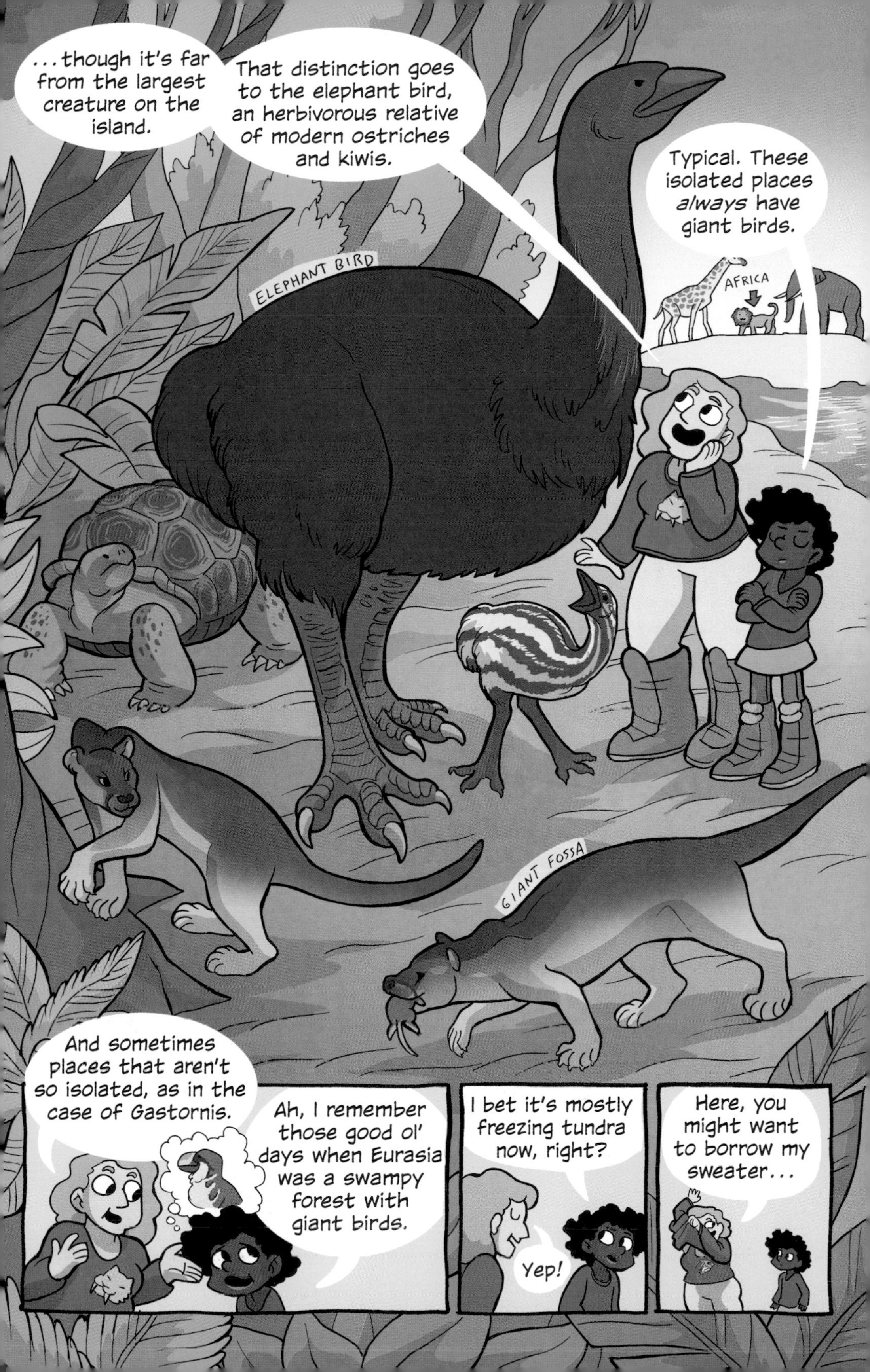
...though it's far from the largest creature on the island.
That distinction goes to the elephant bird, an herbivorous relative of modern ostriches and kiwis.
Typical. These isolated places *always* have giant birds.
ELEPHANT BIRD
AFRICA
GIANT FOSSA
And sometimes places that aren't so isolated, as in the case of Gastornis.
Ah, I remember those good ol' days when Eurasia was a swampy forest with giant birds.
I bet it's mostly freezing tundra now, right?
Yep!
Here, you might want to borrow my sweater...

...as we traverse the icy plains of Eurasia.
A-aren't you...c-cold?
STEPPE MAMMOTH
STRAIGHT-TUSKED ELEPHANT
WOOLLY RHINO
Not when I have the majesty of Eurasian wildlife to warm me!
ELASMOTHERIUM
CAVE LION
CAVE HYENA

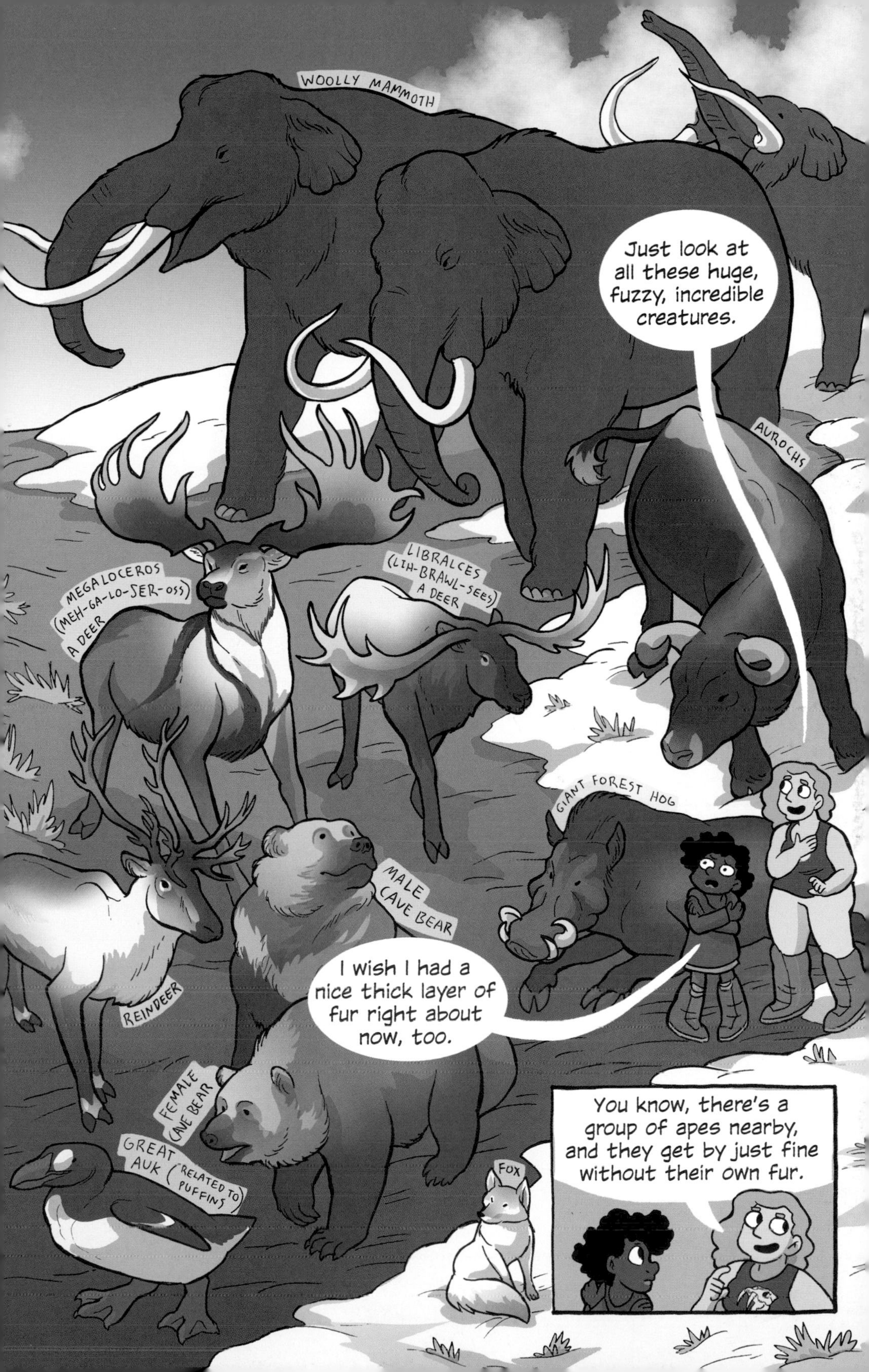

WOOLLY MAMMOTH
Just look at all these huge, fuzzy, incredible creatures.
AUROCHS
MEGALOCEROS (MEH-GA-LO-SER-OSS) A DEER
LIBRALCES (LIH-BRAWL-SEES) A DEER
GIANT FOREST HOG
MALE CAVE BEAR
REINDEER
I wish I had a nice thick layer of fur right about now, too.
FEMALE CAVE BEAR
GREAT AUK (RELATED TO PUFFINS)
FOX
You know, there's a group of apes nearby, and they get by just fine without their own fur.

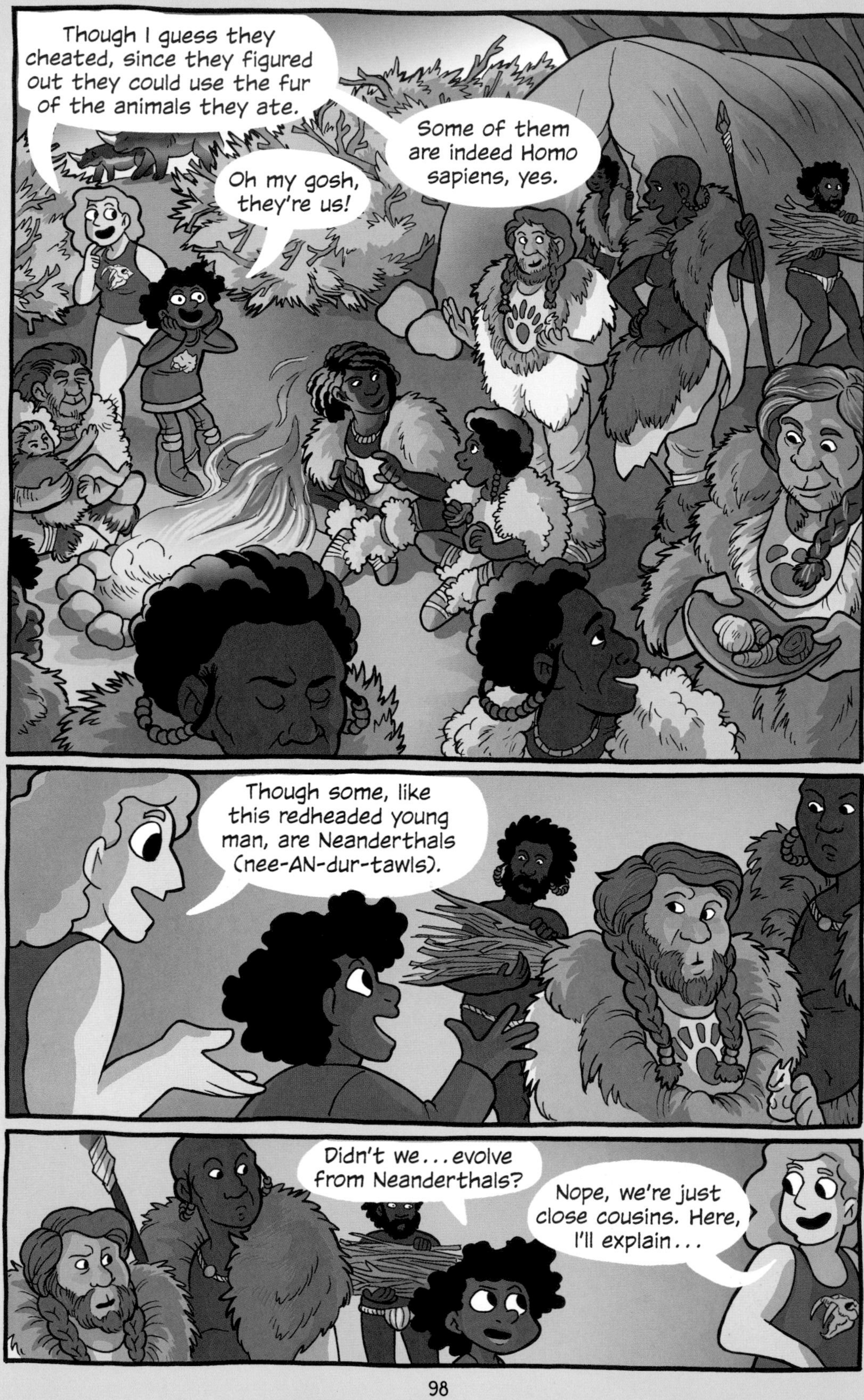
Though I guess they cheated, since they figured out they could use the fur of the animals they ate.
Oh my gosh, they're us!
Some of them are indeed Homo sapiens, yes.
Though some, like this redheaded young man, are Neanderthals (nee-AN-dur-tawls).
Didn't we... evolve from Neanderthals?
Nope, we're just close cousins. Here, I'll explain...

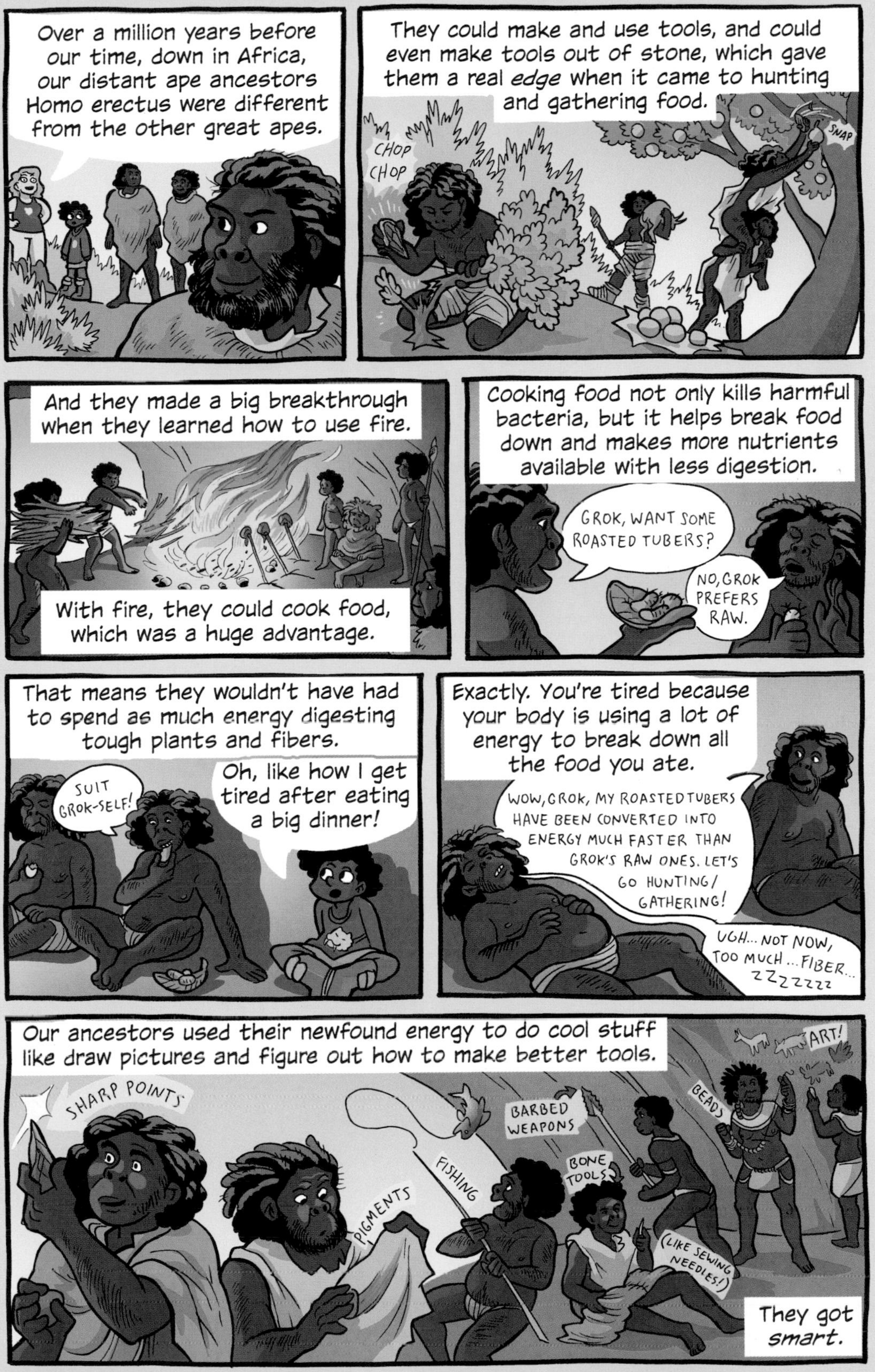
Over a million years before our time, down in Africa, our distant ape ancestors Homo erectus were different from the other great apes.
They could make and use tools, and could even make tools out of stone, which gave them a real *edge* when it came to hunting and gathering food.
CHOP CHOP
SNAP
And they made a big breakthrough when they learned how to use fire.
With fire, they could cook food, which was a huge advantage.
Cooking food not only kills harmful bacteria, but it helps break food down and makes more nutrients available with less digestion.
GROK, WANT SOME ROASTED TUBERS?
NO, GROK PREFERS RAW.
That means they wouldn't have had to spend as much energy digesting tough plants and fibers.
SUIT GROK-SELF!
Oh, like how I get tired after eating a big dinner!
Exactly. You're tired because your body is using a lot of energy to break down all the food you ate.
WOW, GROK, MY ROASTED TUBERS HAVE BEEN CONVERTED INTO ENERGY MUCH FASTER THAN GROK'S RAW ONES. LET'S GO HUNTING/GATHERING!
UGH... NOT NOW, TOO MUCH... FIBER... ZZZZZZZ
Our ancestors used their newfound energy to do cool stuff like draw pictures and figure out how to make better tools.
SHARP POINTS
PIGMENTS
FISHING
BARBED WEAPONS
BONE TOOLS
(LIKE SEWING NEEDLES!)
BEADS
ART!
They got *smart*.

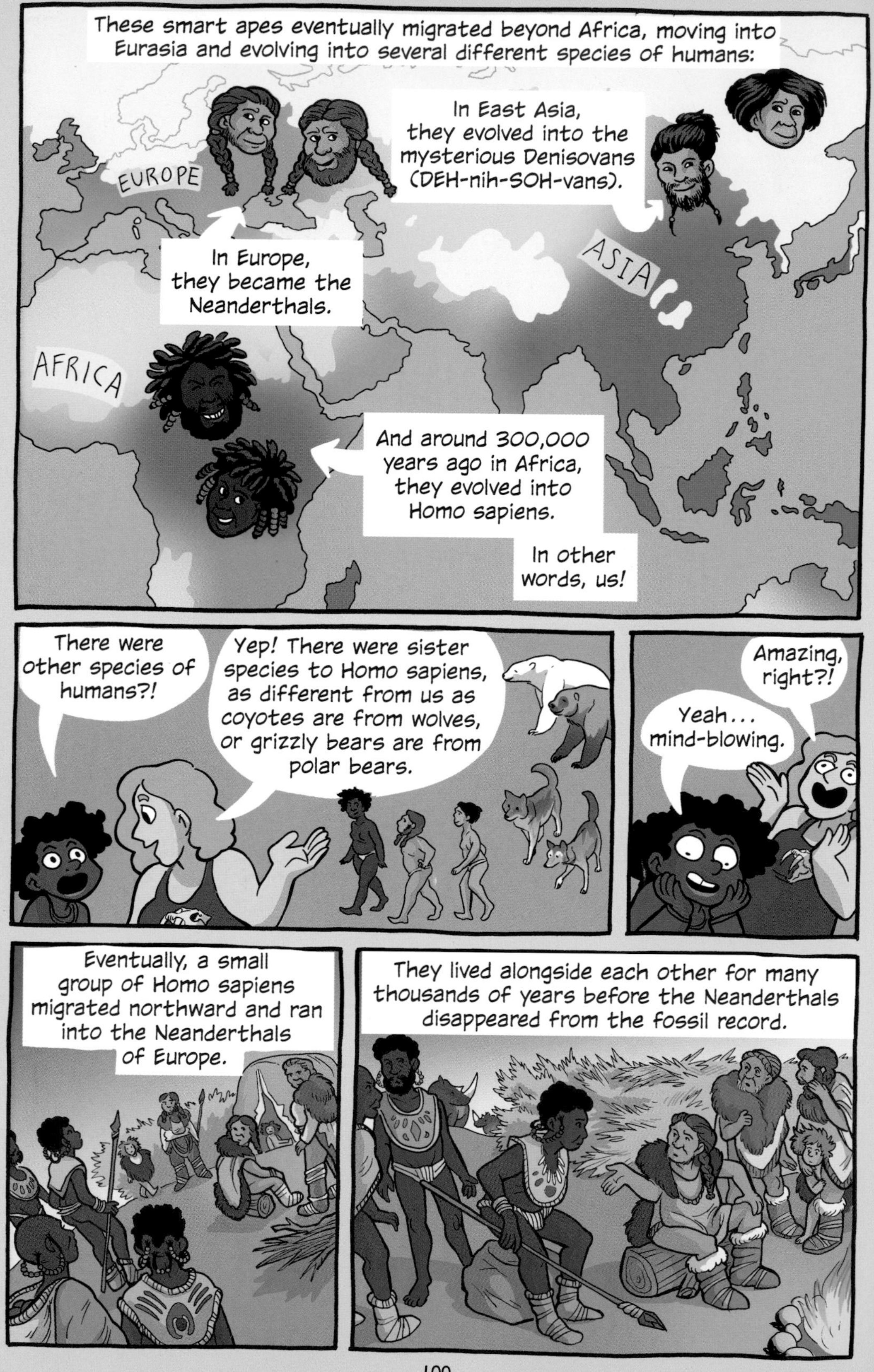
These smart apes eventually migrated beyond Africa, moving into Eurasia and evolving into several different species of humans:
EUROPE
In Europe, they became the Neanderthals.
In East Asia, they evolved into the mysterious Denisovans (DEH-nih-SOH-vans).
ASIA
AFRICA
And around 300,000 years ago in Africa, they evolved into Homo sapiens.
In other words, us!
There were other species of humans?!
Yep! There were sister species to Homo sapiens, as different from us as coyotes are from wolves, or grizzly bears are from polar bears.
Amazing, right?!
Yeah... mind-blowing.
Eventually, a small group of Homo sapiens migrated northward and ran into the Neanderthals of Europe.
They lived alongside each other for many thousands of years before the Neanderthals disappeared from the fossil record.

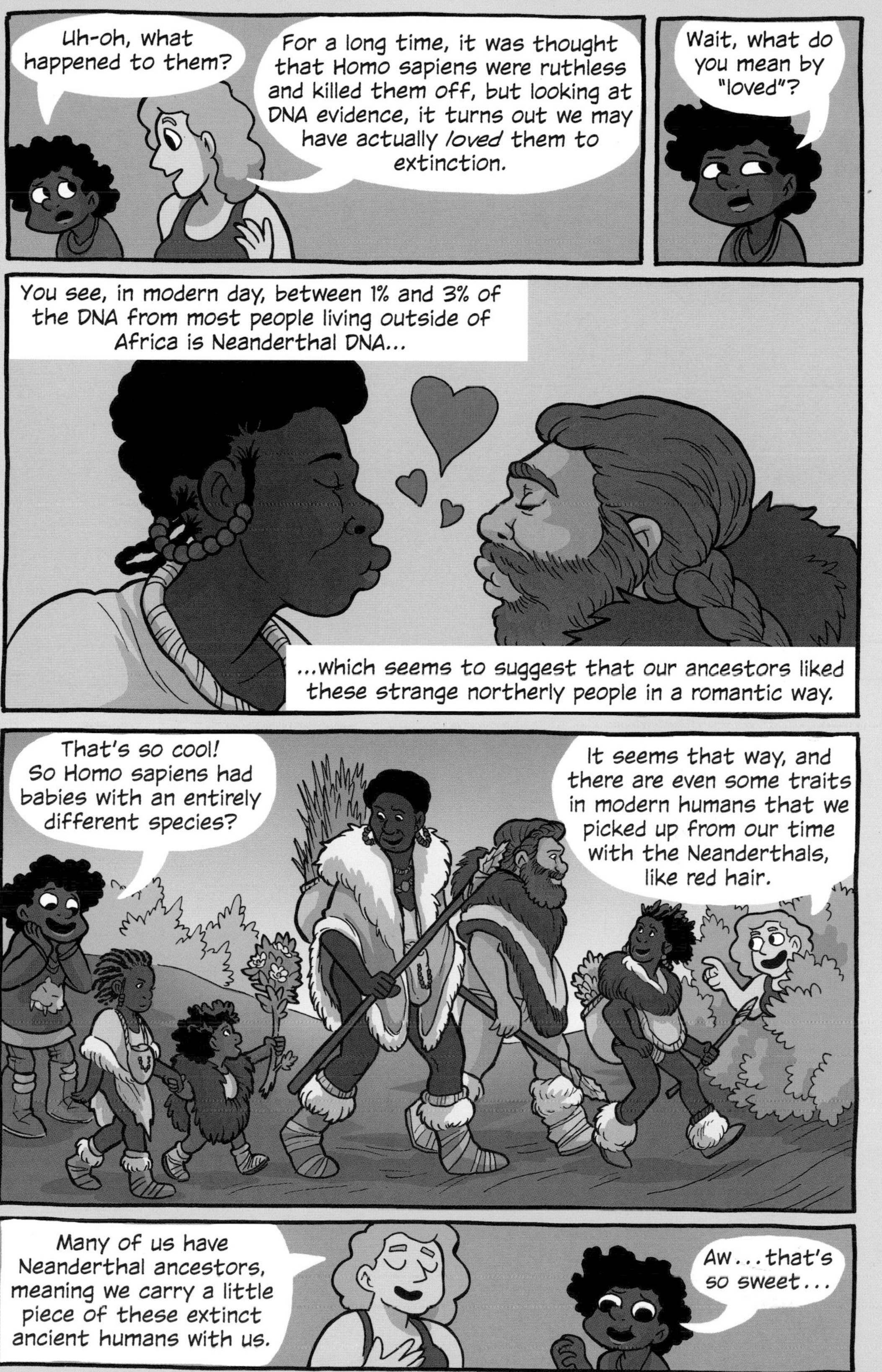
Uh-oh, what happened to them?
For a long time, it was thought that Homo sapiens were ruthless and killed them off, but looking at DNA evidence, it turns out we may have actually *loved* them to extinction.
Wait, what do you mean by "loved"?
You see, in modern day, between 1% and 3% of the DNA from most people living outside of Africa is Neanderthal DNA...
...which seems to suggest that our ancestors liked these strange northerly people in a romantic way.
That's so cool! So Homo sapiens had babies with an entirely different species?
It seems that way, and there are even some traits in modern humans that we picked up from our time with the Neanderthals, like red hair.
Many of us have Neanderthal ancestors, meaning we carry a little piece of these extinct ancient humans with us.
Aw... that's so sweet...

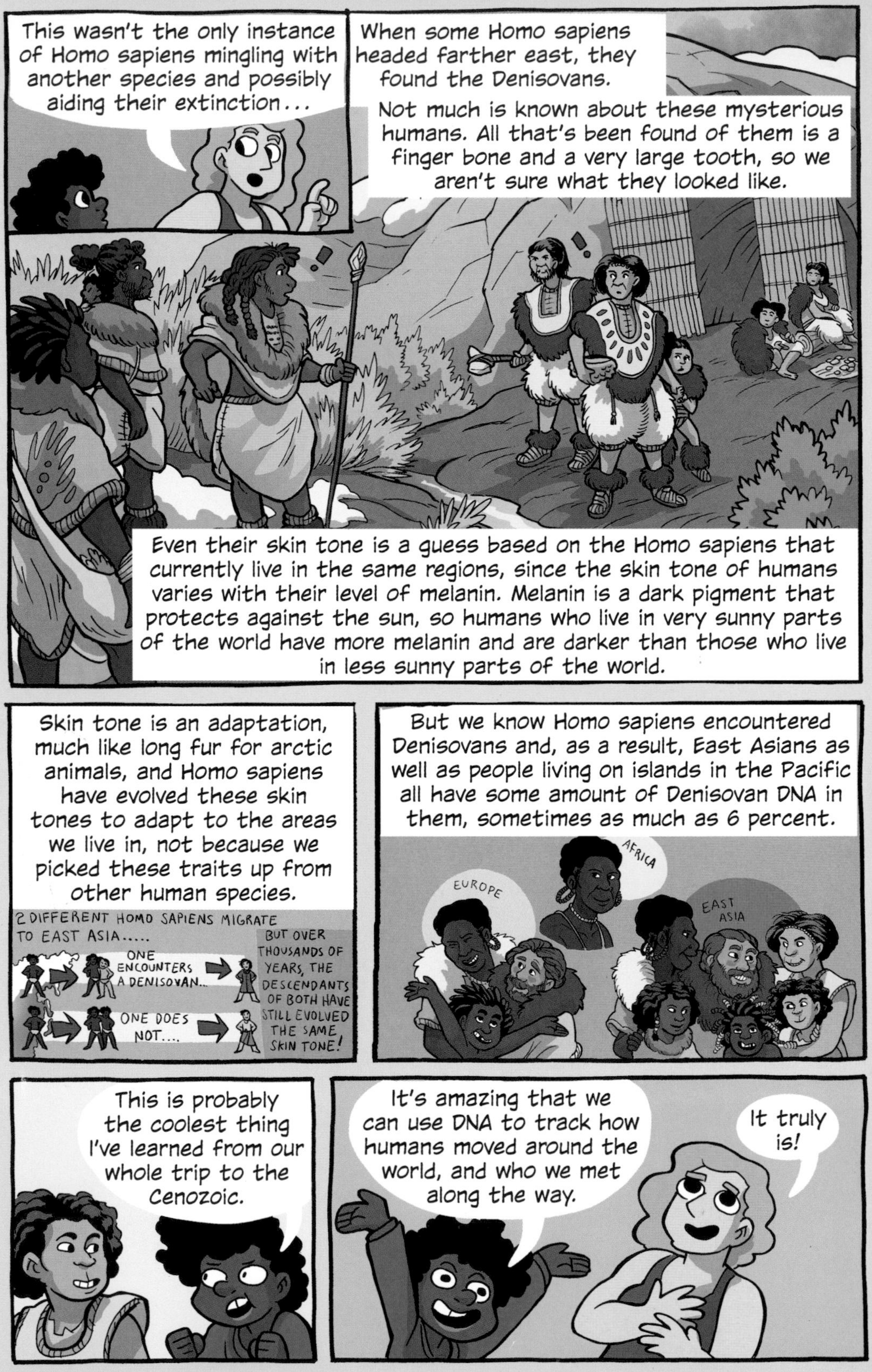
This wasn't the only instance of Homo sapiens mingling with another species and possibly aiding their extinction...
When some Homo sapiens headed farther east, they found the Denisovans.
Not much is known about these mysterious humans. All that's been found of them is a finger bone and a very large tooth, so we aren't sure what they looked like.
Even their skin tone is a guess based on the Homo sapiens that currently live in the same regions, since the skin tone of humans varies with their level of melanin. Melanin is a dark pigment that protects against the sun, so humans who live in very sunny parts of the world have more melanin and are darker than those who live in less sunny parts of the world.
Skin tone is an adaptation, much like long fur for arctic animals, and Homo sapiens have evolved these skin tones to adapt to the areas we live in, not because we picked these traits up from other human species.
2 DIFFERENT HOMO SAPIENS MIGRATE TO EAST ASIA.....
ONE ENCOUNTERS A DENISOVAN...
ONE DOES NOT....
BUT OVER THOUSANDS OF YEARS, THE DESCENDANTS OF BOTH HAVE STILL EVOLVED THE SAME SKIN TONE!
But we know Homo sapiens encountered Denisovans and, as a result, East Asians as well as people living on islands in the Pacific all have some amount of Denisovan DNA in them, sometimes as much as 6 percent.
AFRICA
EUROPE
EAST ASIA
This is probably the coolest thing I've learned from our whole trip to the Cenozoic.
It's amazing that we can use DNA to track how humans moved around the world, and who we met along the way.
It truly is!

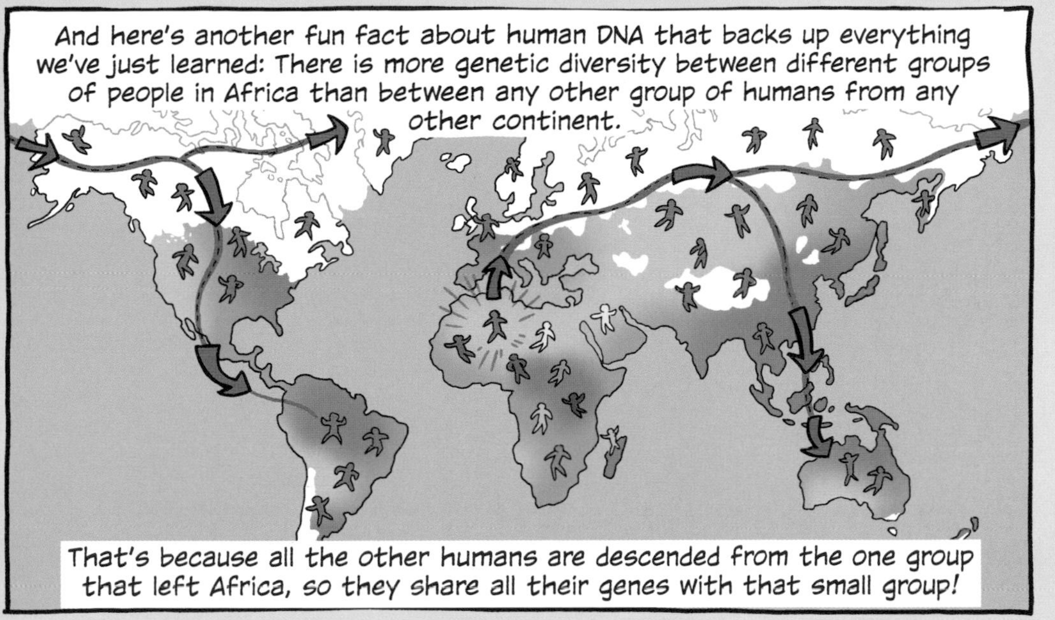
And here's another fun fact about human DNA that backs up everything we've just learned: There is more genetic diversity between different groups of people in Africa than between any other group of humans from any other continent.
That's because all the other humans are descended from the one group that left Africa, so they share all their genes with that small group!

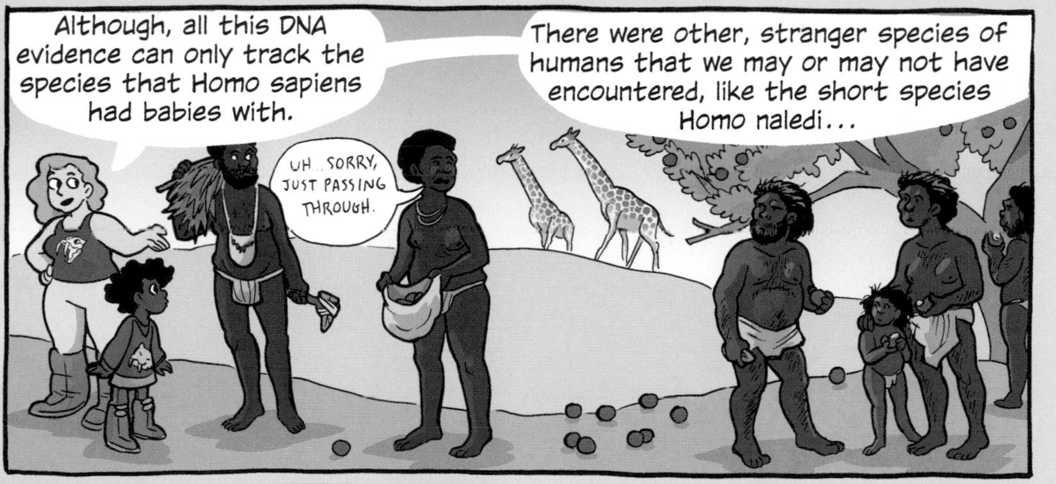
Although, all this DNA evidence can only track the species that Homo sapiens had babies with.
There were other, stranger species of humans that we may or may not have encountered, like the short species Homo naledi...
UH... SORRY, JUST PASSING THROUGH.

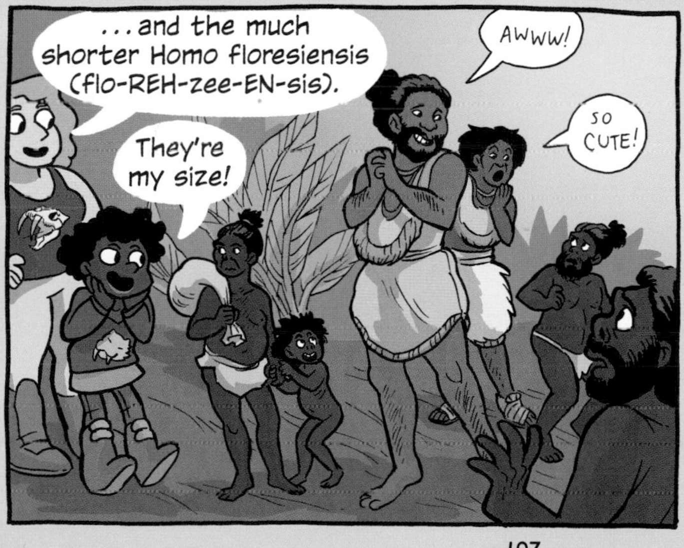
...and the much shorter Homo floresiensis (flo-REH-zee-EN-sis).
AWWW!
They're my size!
SO CUTE!

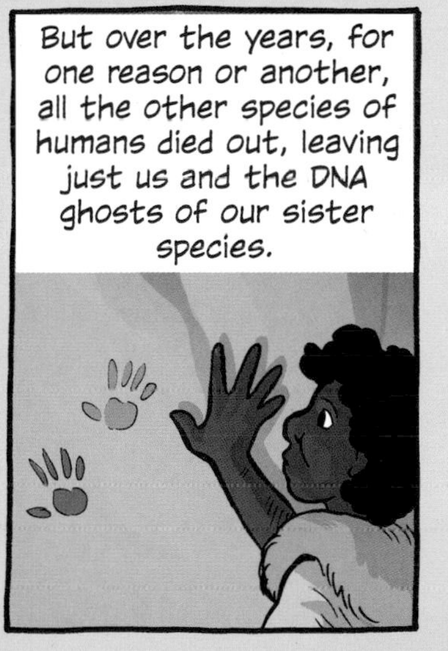
But over the years, for one reason or another, all the other species of humans died out, leaving just us and the DNA ghosts of our sister species.

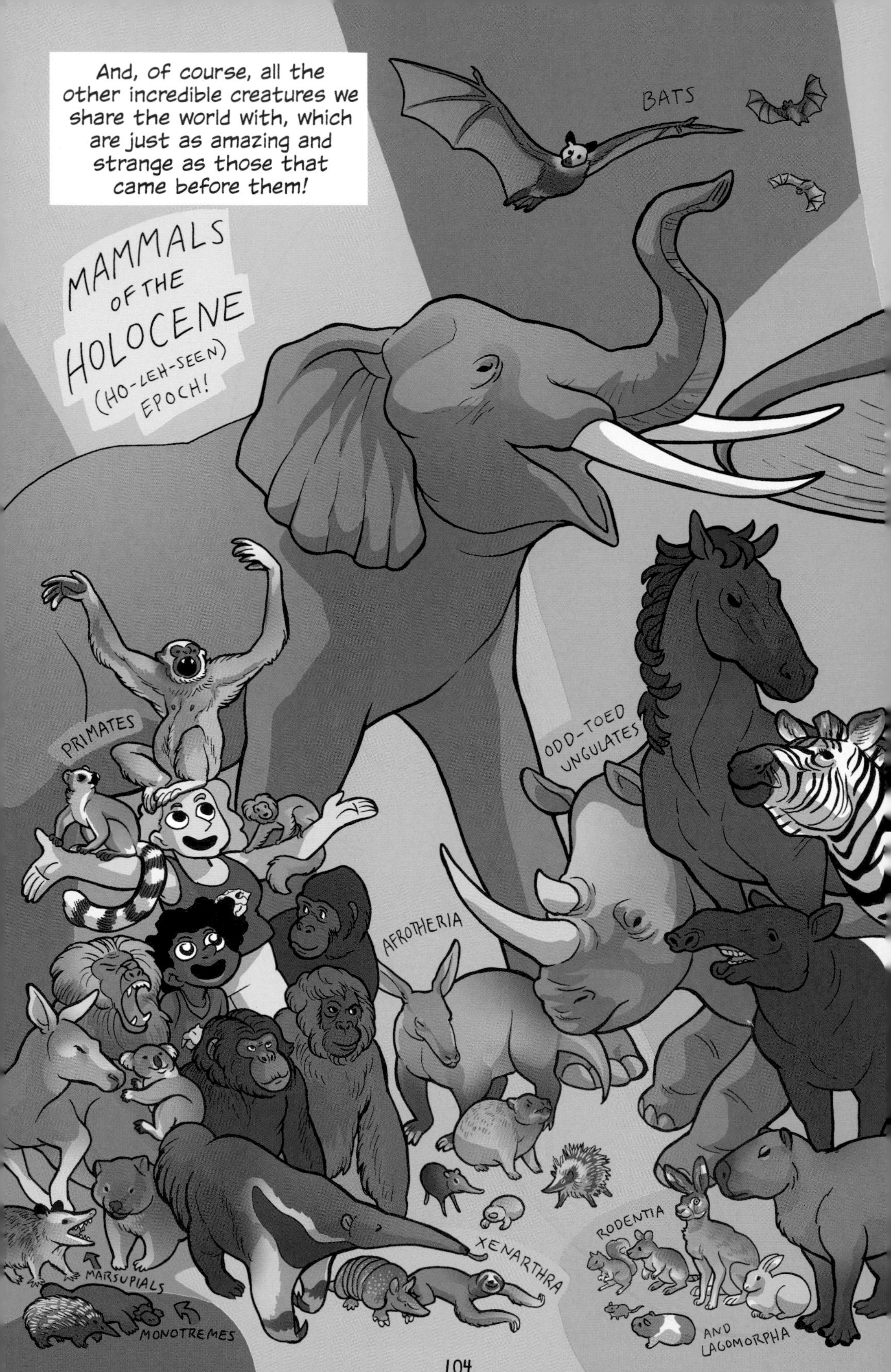
And, of course, all the other incredible creatures we share the world with, which are just as amazing and strange as those that came before them!
MAMMALS OF THE HOLOCENE (HO-LEH-SEEN) EPOCH!
BATS
PRIMATES
ODD-TOED UNGULATES
AFROTHERIA
XENARTHRA
MARSUPIALS
MONOTREMES
RODENTIA
AND LAGOMORPHA

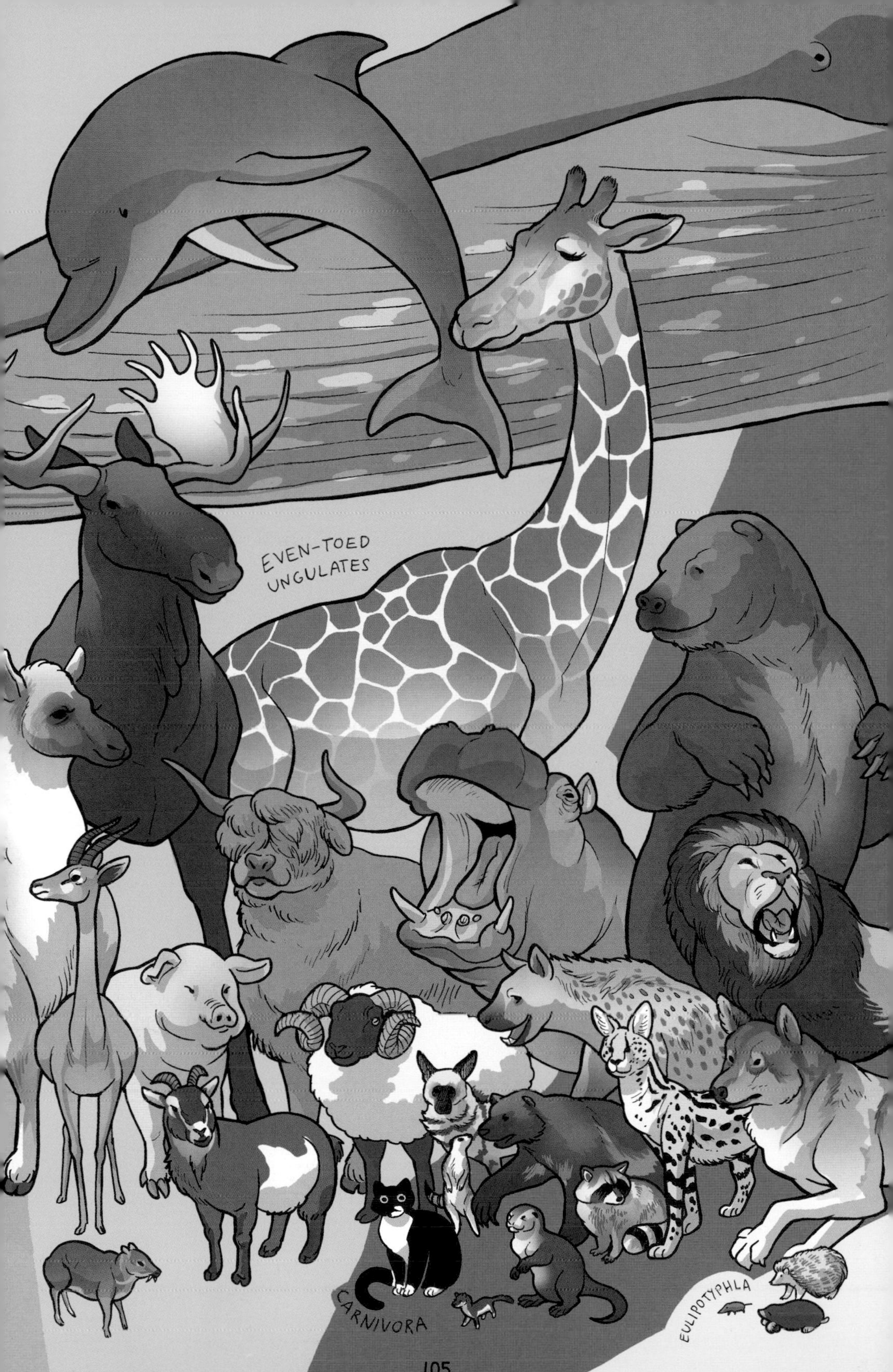
EVEN-TOED UNGULATES
CARNIVORA
EULIPOTYPHLA

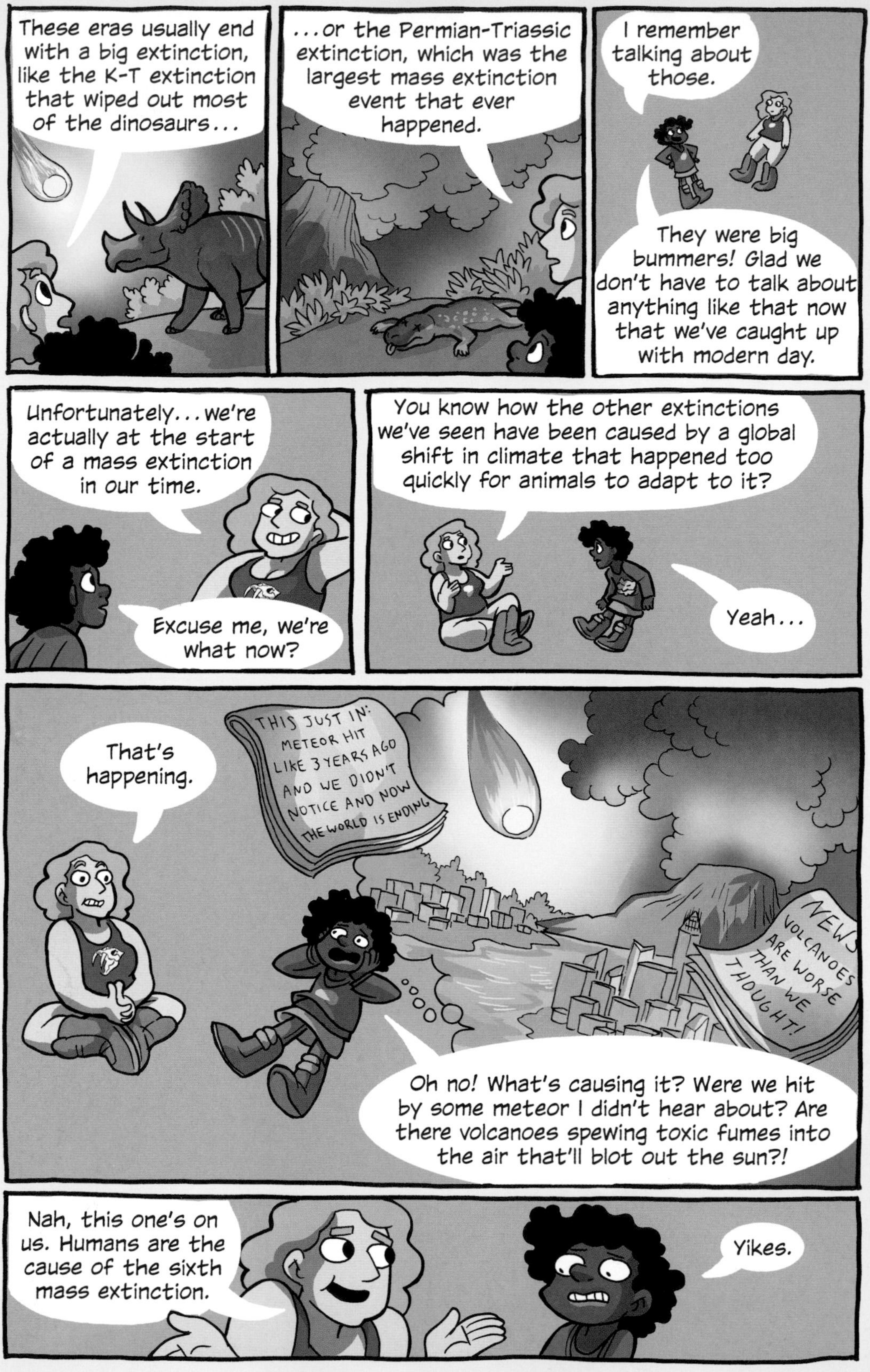
These eras usually end with a big extinction, like the K-T extinction that wiped out most of the dinosaurs...
...or the Permian-Triassic extinction, which was the largest mass extinction event that ever happened.
I remember talking about those.
They were big bummers! Glad we don't have to talk about anything like that now that we've caught up with modern day.
Unfortunately...we're actually at the start of a mass extinction in our time.
Excuse me, we're what now?
You know how the other extinctions we've seen have been caused by a global shift in climate that happened too quickly for animals to adapt to it?
Yeah...
That's happening.
THIS JUST IN: METEOR HIT LIKE 3 YEARS AGO AND WE DIDN'T NOTICE AND NOW THE WORLD IS ENDING
NEWS
VOLCANOES ARE WORSE THAN WE THOUGHT!
Oh no! What's causing it? Were we hit by some meteor I didn't hear about? Are there volcanoes spewing toxic fumes into the air that'll blot out the sun?!
Nah, this one's on us. Humans are the cause of the sixth mass extinction.
Yikes.

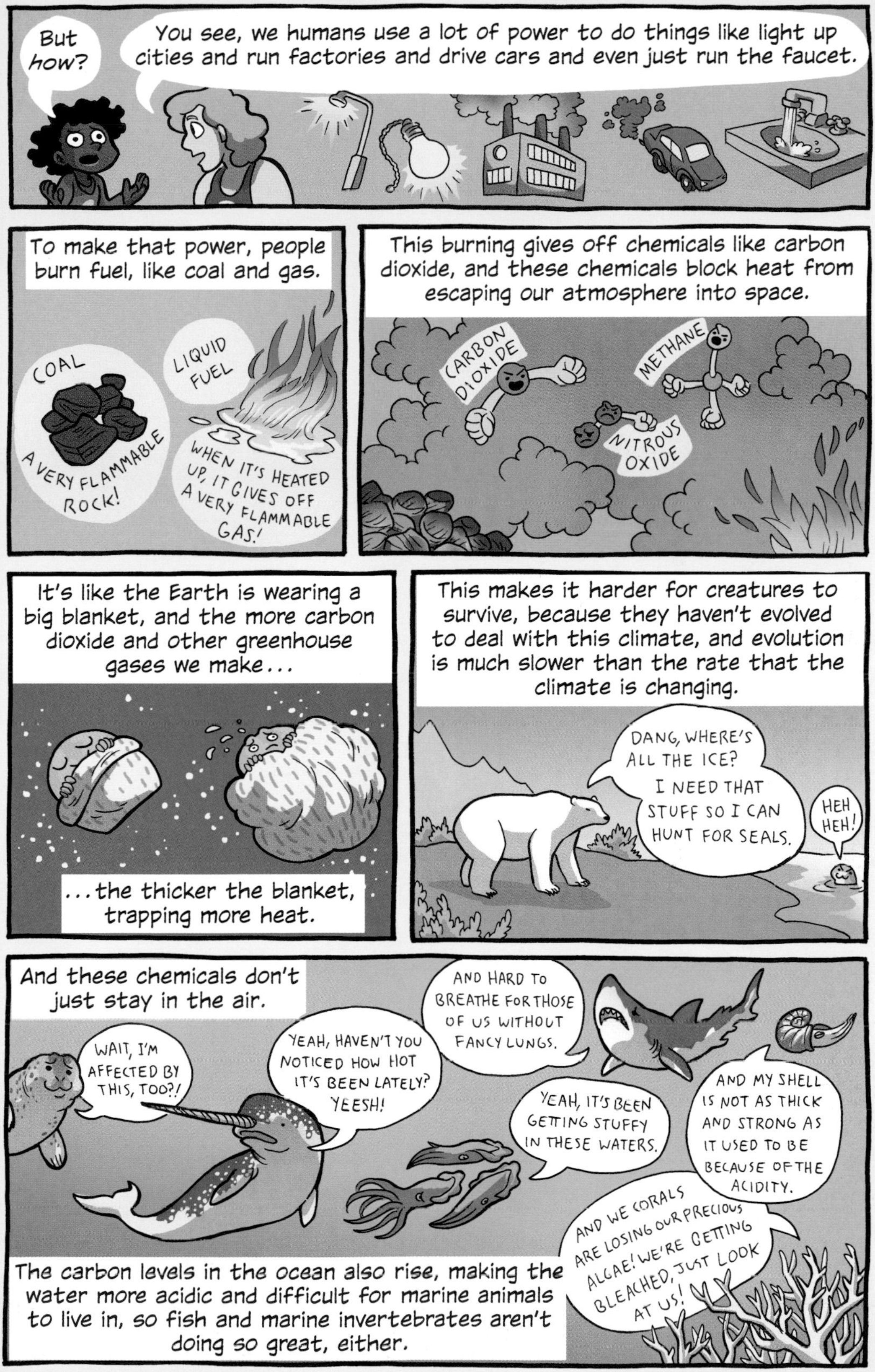

But how?
You see, we humans use a lot of power to do things like light up cities and run factories and drive cars and even just run the faucet.
To make that power, people burn fuel, like coal and gas.
COAL
A VERY FLAMMABLE ROCK!
LIQUID FUEL
WHEN IT'S HEATED UP, IT GIVES OFF A VERY FLAMMABLE GAS!
This burning gives off chemicals like carbon dioxide, and these chemicals block heat from escaping our atmosphere into space.
CARBON DIOXIDE
METHANE
NITROUS OXIDE
It's like the Earth is wearing a big blanket, and the more carbon dioxide and other greenhouse gases we make...
...the thicker the blanket, trapping more heat.
This makes it harder for creatures to survive, because they haven't evolved to deal with this climate, and evolution is much slower than the rate that the climate is changing.
DANG, WHERE'S ALL THE ICE?
I NEED THAT STUFF SO I CAN HUNT FOR SEALS.
HEH HEH!
And these chemicals don't just stay in the air.
WAIT, I'M AFFECTED BY THIS, TOO?!
YEAH, HAVEN'T YOU NOTICED HOW HOT IT'S BEEN LATELY? YEESH!
AND HARD TO BREATHE FOR THOSE OF US WITHOUT FANCY LUNGS.
YEAH, IT'S BEEN GETTING STUFFY IN THESE WATERS.
AND MY SHELL IS NOT AS THICK AND STRONG AS IT USED TO BE BECAUSE OF THE ACIDITY.
AND WE CORALS ARE LOSING OUR PRECIOUS ALGAE! WE'RE GETTING BLEACHED, JUST LOOK AT US!
The carbon levels in the ocean also rise, making the water more acidic and difficult for marine animals to live in, so fish and marine invertebrates aren't doing so great, either.

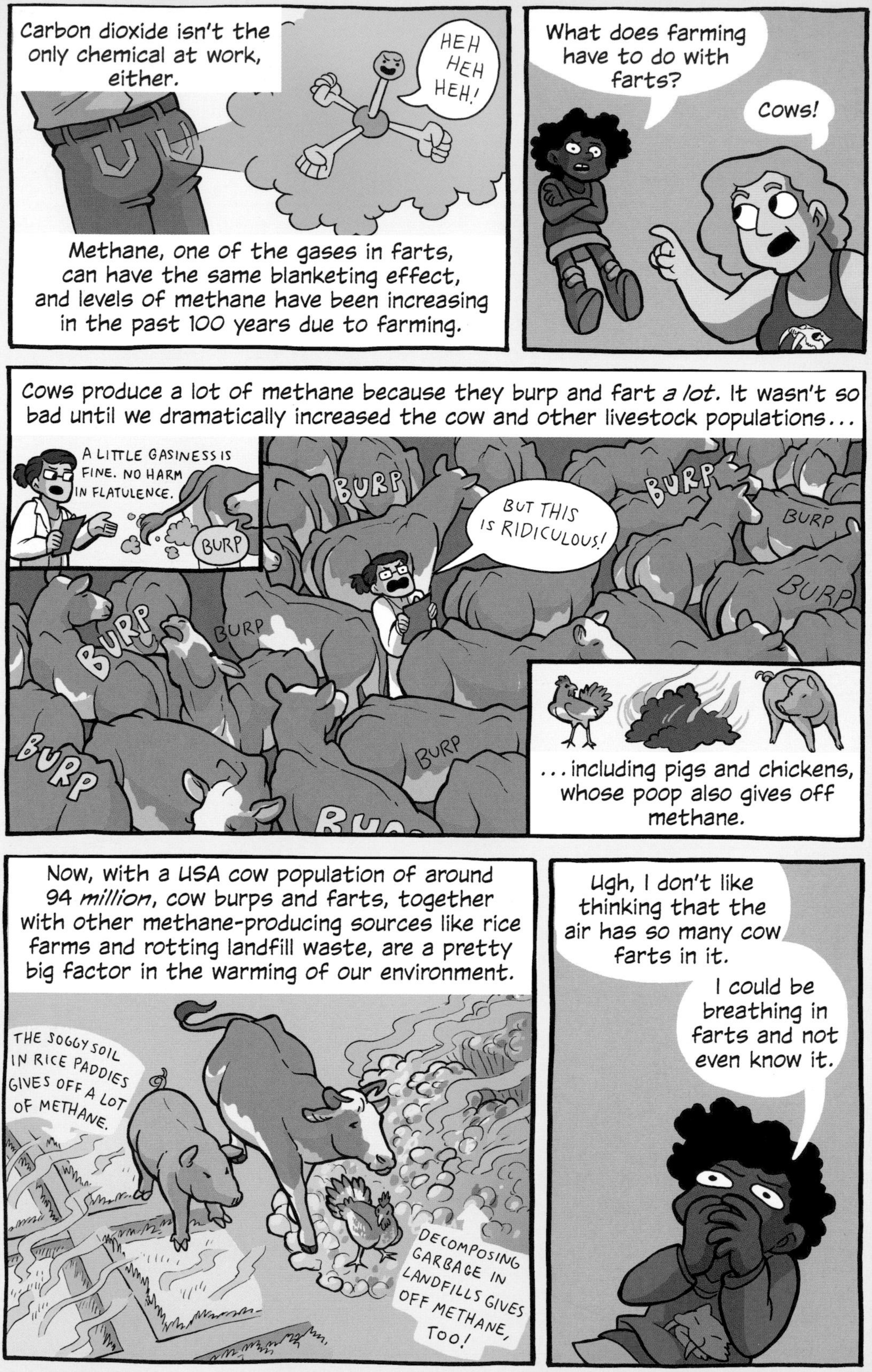
Carbon dioxide isn't the only chemical at work, either.
HEH HEH HEH!
Methane, one of the gases in farts, can have the same blanketing effect, and levels of methane have been increasing in the past 100 years due to farming.
What does farming have to do with farts?
Cows!
Cows produce a lot of methane because they burp and fart *a lot*. It wasn't so bad until we dramatically increased the cow and other livestock populations...
A LITTLE GASINESS IS FINE. NO HARM IN FLATULENCE.
BURP
BURP
BUT THIS IS RIDICULOUS!
BURP
BURP
BURP
BURP
BURP
BURP
BURP
BURP
...including pigs and chickens, whose poop also gives off methane.
Now, with a USA cow population of around 94 *million*, cow burps and farts, together with other methane-producing sources like rice farms and rotting landfill waste, are a pretty big factor in the warming of our environment.
THE SOGGY SOIL IN RICE PADDIES GIVES OFF A LOT OF METHANE.
DECOMPOSING GARBAGE IN LANDFILLS GIVES OFF METHANE, TOO!
Ugh, I don't like thinking that the air has so many cow farts in it.
I could be breathing in farts and not even know it.

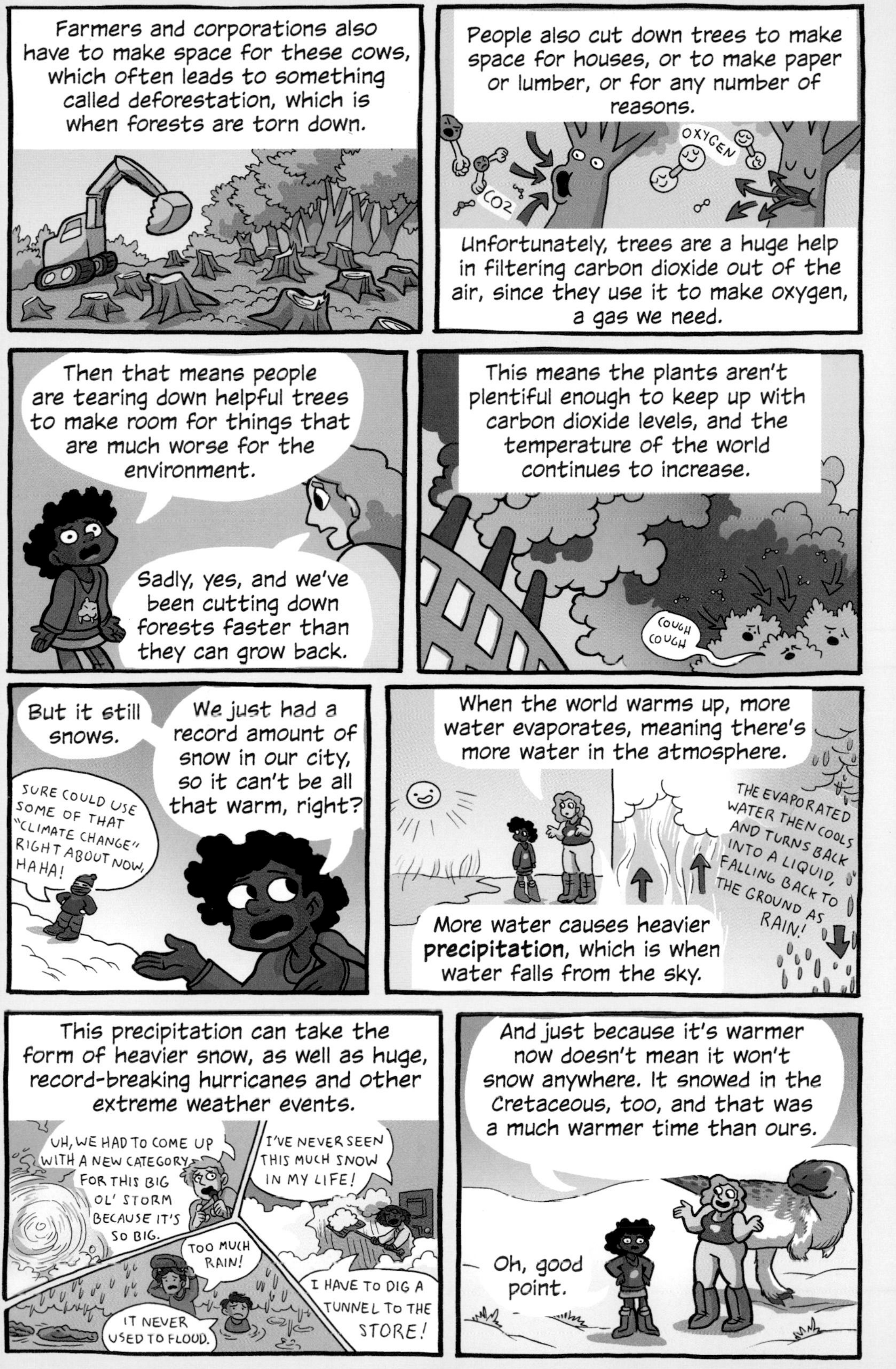

Farmers and corporations also have to make space for these cows, which often leads to something called deforestation, which is when forests are torn down.
People also cut down trees to make space for houses, or to make paper or lumber, or for any number of reasons.
OXYGEN
CO_2
Unfortunately, trees are a huge help in filtering carbon dioxide out of the air, since they use it to make oxygen, a gas we need.
Then that means people are tearing down helpful trees to make room for things that are much worse for the environment.
Sadly, yes, and we've been cutting down forests faster than they can grow back.
This means the plants aren't plentiful enough to keep up with carbon dioxide levels, and the temperature of the world continues to increase.
COUGH COUGH
But it still snows.
We just had a record amount of snow in our city, so it can't be all that warm, right?
SURE COULD USE SOME OF THAT "CLIMATE CHANGE" RIGHT ABOUT NOW, HA HA!
When the world warms up, more water evaporates, meaning there's more water in the atmosphere.
THE EVAPORATED WATER THEN COOLS AND TURNS BACK INTO A LIQUID, FALLING BACK TO THE GROUND AS RAIN!
More water causes heavier **precipitation**, which is when water falls from the sky.
This precipitation can take the form of heavier snow, as well as huge, record-breaking hurricanes and other extreme weather events.
UH, WE HAD TO COME UP WITH A NEW CATEGORY FOR THIS BIG OL' STORM BECAUSE IT'S SO BIG.
I'VE NEVER SEEN THIS MUCH SNOW IN MY LIFE!
TOO MUCH RAIN!
IT NEVER USED TO FLOOD.
I HAVE TO DIG A TUNNEL TO THE STORE!
And just because it's warmer now doesn't mean it won't snow anywhere. It snowed in the Cretaceous, too, and that was a much warmer time than ours.
Oh, good point.

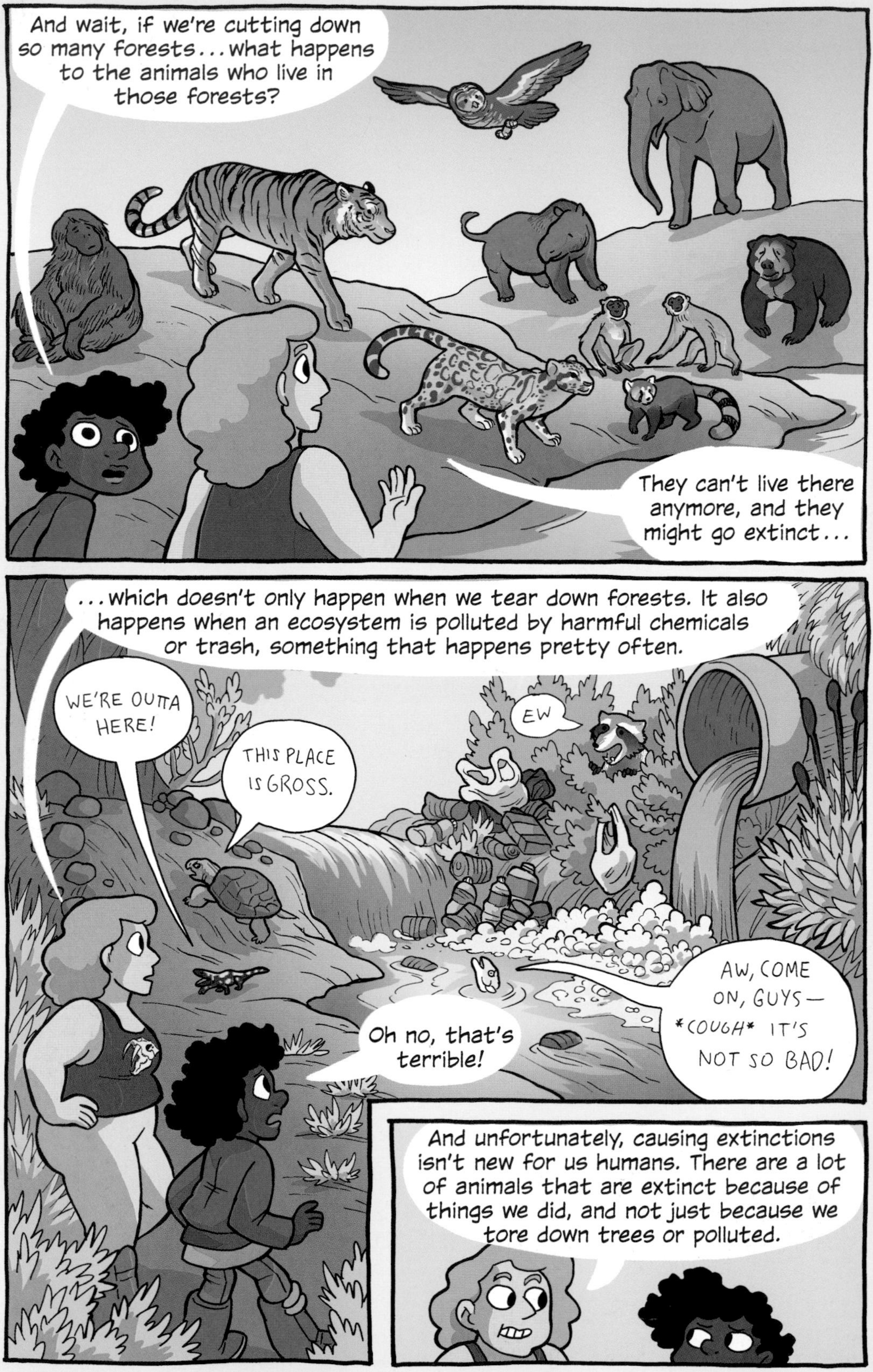
And wait, if we're cutting down so many forests...what happens to the animals who live in those forests?
They can't live there anymore, and they might go extinct...
...which doesn't only happen when we tear down forests. It also happens when an ecosystem is polluted by harmful chemicals or trash, something that happens pretty often.
WE'RE OUTTA HERE!
THIS PLACE IS GROSS.
EW
Oh no, that's terrible!
AW, COME ON, GUYS— *COUGH* IT'S NOT SO BAD!
And unfortunately, causing extinctions isn't new for us humans. There are a lot of animals that are extinct because of things we did, and not just because we tore down trees or polluted.

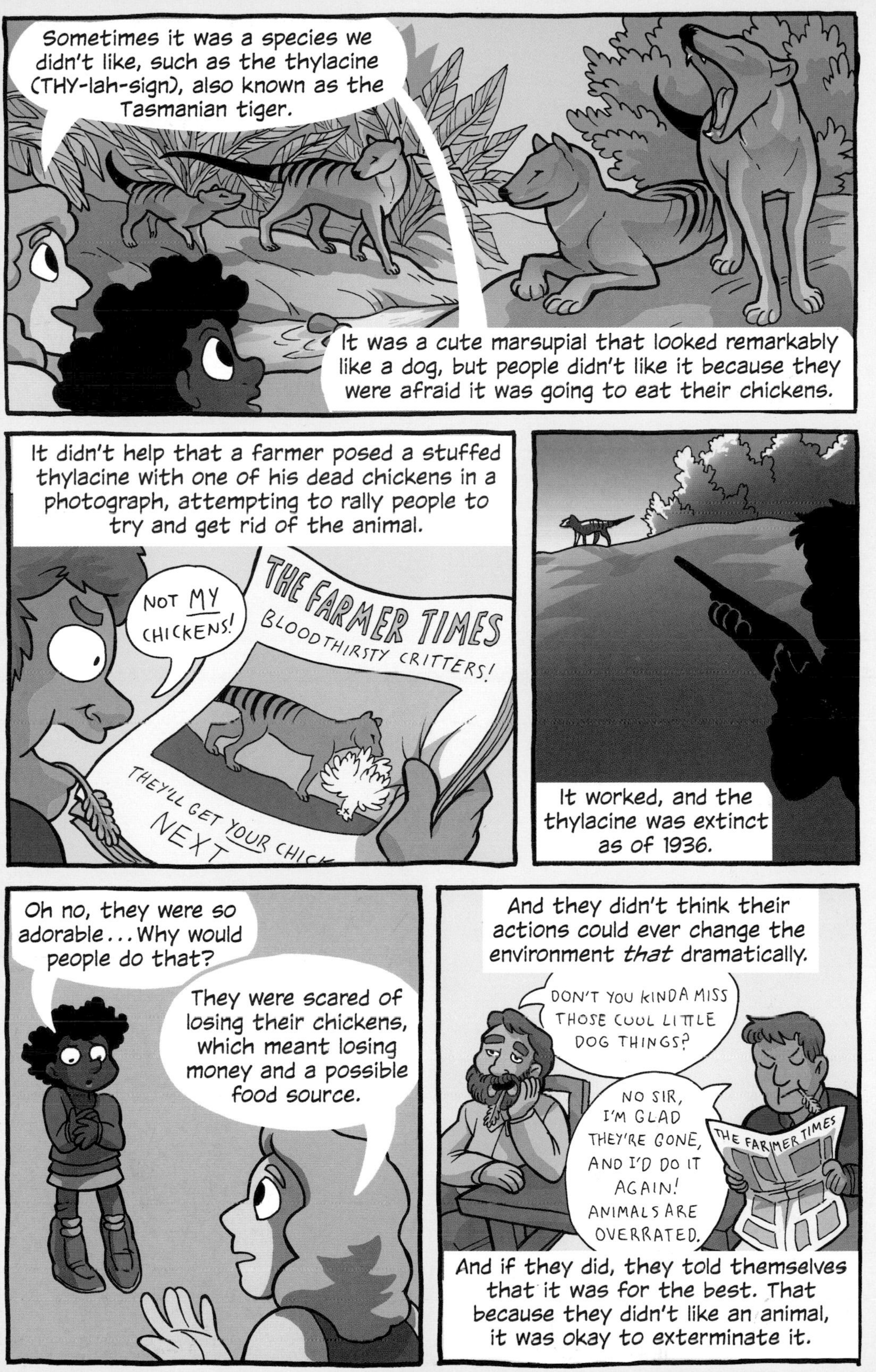

Sometimes it was a species we didn't like, such as the thylacine (THY-lah-sign), also known as the Tasmanian tiger.
It was a cute marsupial that looked remarkably like a dog, but people didn't like it because they were afraid it was going to eat their chickens.
It didn't help that a farmer posed a stuffed thylacine with one of his dead chickens in a photograph, attempting to rally people to try and get rid of the animal.
NOT MY CHICKENS!
THE FARMER TIMES
BLOODTHIRSTY CRITTERS!
THEY'LL GET YOUR CHICK
NEXT
It worked, and the thylacine was extinct as of 1936.
Oh no, they were so adorable...Why would people do that?
They were scared of losing their chickens, which meant losing money and a possible food source.
And they didn't think their actions could ever change the environment *that* dramatically.
DON'T YOU KINDA MISS THOSE COOL LITTLE DOG THINGS?
NO SIR, I'M GLAD THEY'RE GONE, AND I'D DO IT AGAIN! ANIMALS ARE OVERRATED.
THE FARMER TIMES
And if they did, they told themselves that it was for the best. That because they didn't like an animal, it was okay to exterminate it.

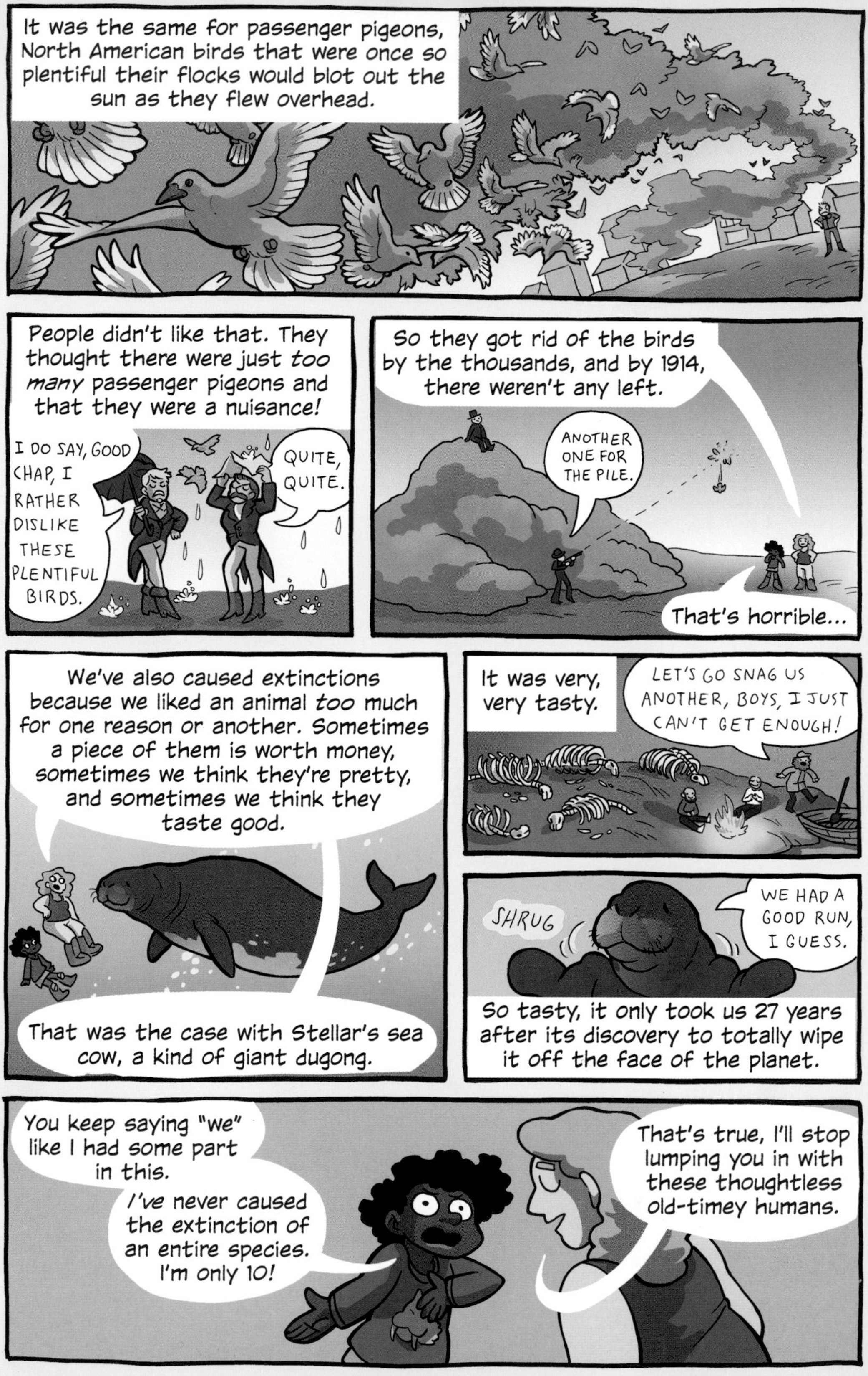
It was the same for passenger pigeons, North American birds that were once so plentiful their flocks would blot out the sun as they flew overhead.
People didn't like that. They thought there were just *too many* passenger pigeons and that they were a nuisance!
I DO SAY, GOOD CHAP, I RATHER DISLIKE THESE PLENTIFUL BIRDS.
QUITE, QUITE.
So they got rid of the birds by the thousands, and by 1914, there weren't any left.
ANOTHER ONE FOR THE PILE.
That's horrible...
We've also caused extinctions because we liked an animal *too* much for one reason or another. Sometimes a piece of them is worth money, sometimes we think they're pretty, and sometimes we think they taste good.
That was the case with Stellar's sea cow, a kind of giant dugong.
It was very, very tasty.
LET'S GO SNAG US ANOTHER, BOYS, I JUST CAN'T GET ENOUGH!
SHRUG
WE HAD A GOOD RUN, I GUESS.
So tasty, it only took us 27 years after its discovery to totally wipe it off the face of the planet.
You keep saying "we" like I had some part in this.
I've never caused the extinction of an entire species. I'm only 10!
That's true, I'll stop lumping you in with these thoughtless old-timey humans.

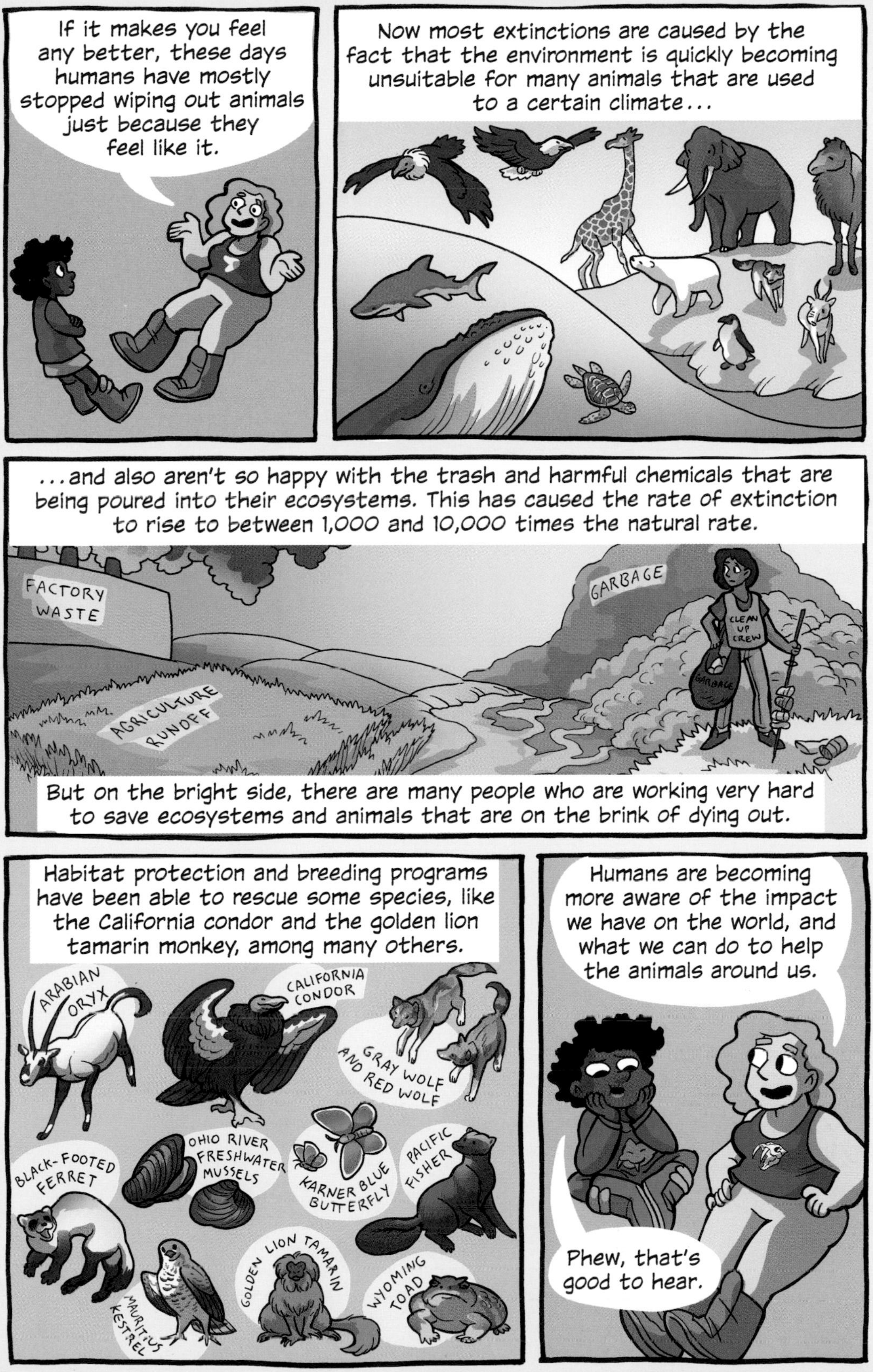
If it makes you feel any better, these days humans have mostly stopped wiping out animals just because they feel like it.
Now most extinctions are caused by the fact that the environment is quickly becoming unsuitable for many animals that are used to a certain climate...
...and also aren't so happy with the trash and harmful chemicals that are being poured into their ecosystems. This has caused the rate of extinction to rise to between 1,000 and 10,000 times the natural rate.
FACTORY WASTE
GARBAGE
CLEAN UP CREW
GARBAGE
AGRICULTURE RUNOFF
But on the bright side, there are many people who are working very hard to save ecosystems and animals that are on the brink of dying out.
Habitat protection and breeding programs have been able to rescue some species, like the California condor and the golden lion tamarin monkey, among many others.
ARABIAN ORYX
CALIFORNIA CONDOR
GRAY WOLF AND RED WOLF
BLACK-FOOTED FERRET
OHIO RIVER FRESHWATER MUSSELS
KARNER BLUE BUTTERFLY
PACIFIC FISHER
MAURITIUS KESTREL
GOLDEN LION TAMARIN
WYOMING TOAD
Humans are becoming more aware of the impact we have on the world, and what we can do to help the animals around us.
Phew, that's good to hear.

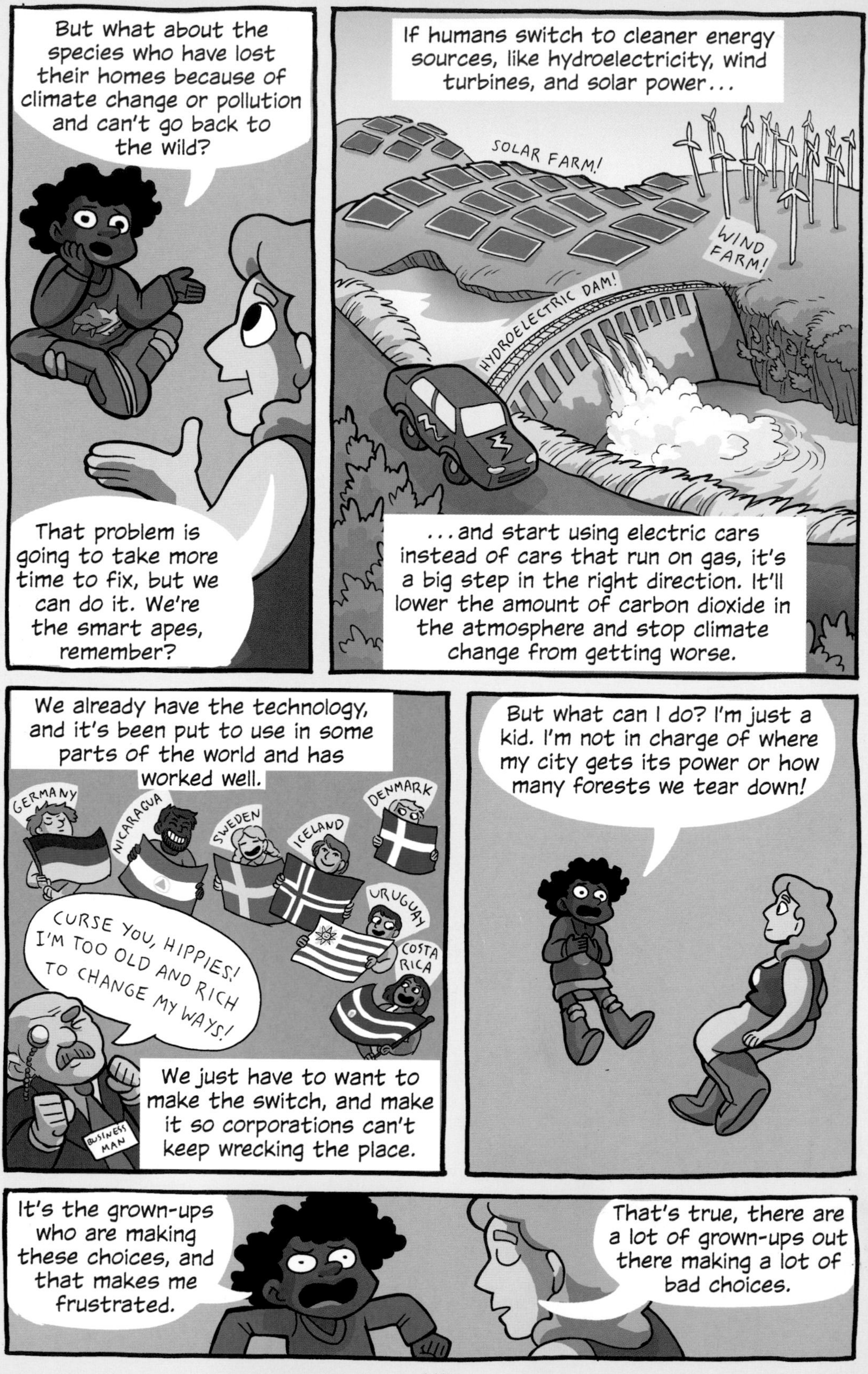
But what about the species who have lost their homes because of climate change or pollution and can't go back to the wild?
That problem is going to take more time to fix, but we can do it. We're the smart apes, remember?
If humans switch to cleaner energy sources, like hydroelectricity, wind turbines, and solar power...
SOLAR FARM!
WIND FARM!
HYDROELECTRIC DAM!
...and start using electric cars instead of cars that run on gas, it's a big step in the right direction. It'll lower the amount of carbon dioxide in the atmosphere and stop climate change from getting worse.
We already have the technology, and it's been put to use in some parts of the world and has worked well.
GERMANY
NICARAGUA
SWEDEN
ICELAND
DENMARK
URUGUAY
COSTA RICA
CURSE YOU, HIPPIES! I'M TOO OLD AND RICH TO CHANGE MY WAYS!
BUSINESS MAN
We just have to want to make the switch, and make it so corporations can't keep wrecking the place.
But what can I do? I'm just a kid. I'm not in charge of where my city gets its power or how many forests we tear down!
It's the grown-ups who are making these choices, and that makes me frustrated.
That's true, there are a lot of grown-ups out there making a lot of bad choices.

Especially big businesses and corporations, which don't seem to look beyond how much money they're making from these things that are changing the climate and making the world harder for everyone to live in.

THAT'S JUST BUSINESS, BABY!

Even for me, a grown-up, it's scary stuff, and I sometimes feel like there's not much I can do!

But there are always things you can do to help, even if it's just talking to the grown-ups around you.

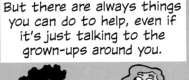

You can ask them to use compact fluorescent bulbs (the little squiggly ones) instead of incandescent bulbs, which don't last as long anyway.

HALOGEN INCANDESCENT ARE GOOD, TOO!

AND LEDS ALSO!

You can ask them to walk or use the bus instead of driving everywhere...

THIS IS CHEAPER, ANYWAY.

...and to turn off the lights and the TV when they aren't using them.

LEARN TO APPRECIATE THE DARKNESS.

DON'T BE WEIRD, MOM!

Recycling is another great thing to do, as plastic, metal, and glass can all be reused instead of becoming trash, which might pollute an ecosystem.

YO, THANKS, I APPRECIATE THAT.

ONE LESS PIECE IN A LANDFILL.

You can also ask them to help you plant a tree or a garden, which will create more air-filtering plant life.

Plus, you could get some bonus veggies out of it!

I FEEL A DEEP SENSE OF ACCOMPLISHMENT.

COW-FART-FREE MEAT ALTERNATIVES TO TRY OUT!

TOFU

TEMPEH

BEANS!

'SEITAN (TASTY!)

LAB-GROWN MEAT??

Speaking of veggies, you can also cut back on how much meat and dairy you eat, which could help limit how many cows, pigs, and chickens are out there making methane.

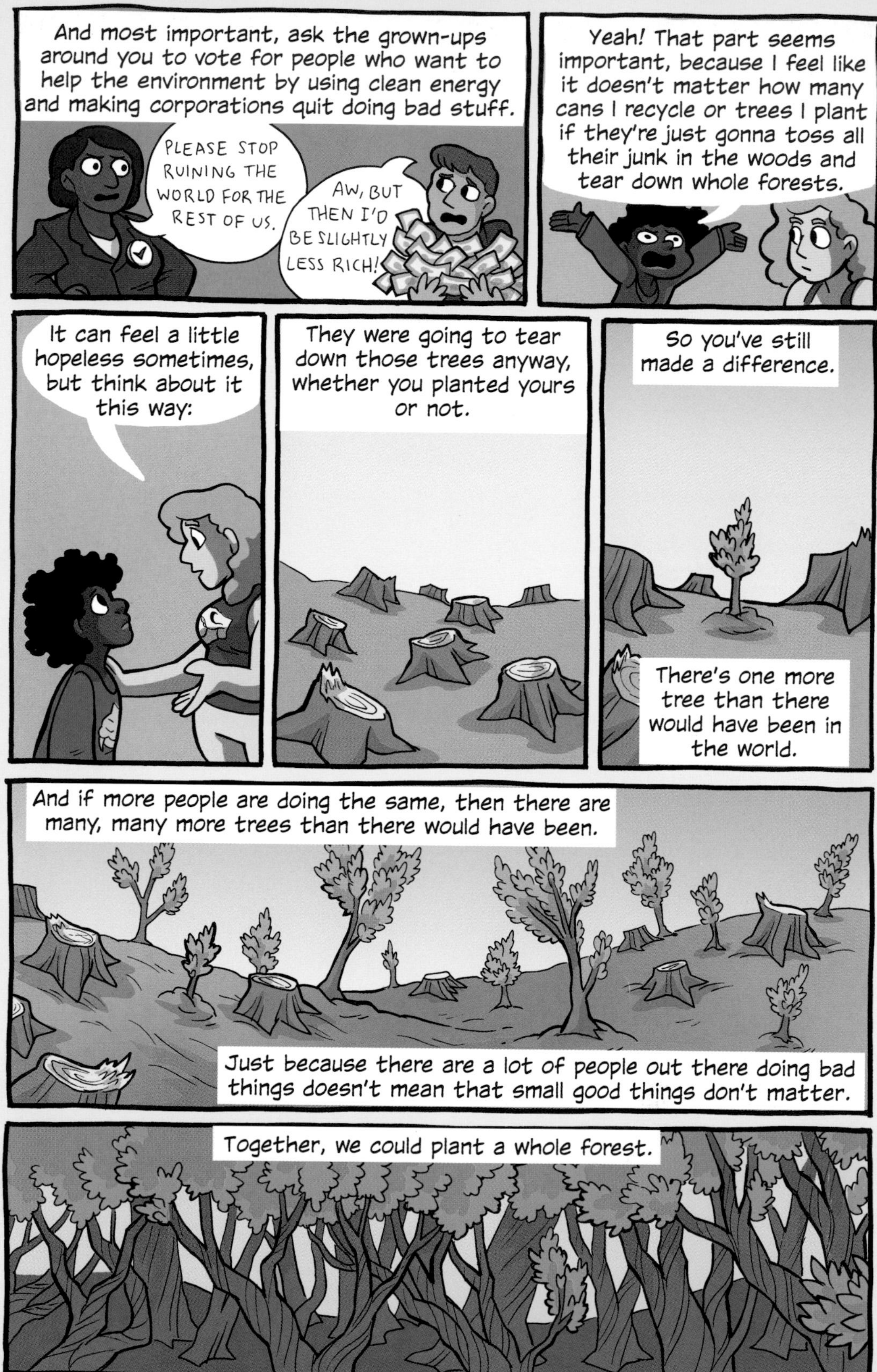

And most important, ask the grown-ups around you to vote for people who want to help the environment by using clean energy and making corporations quit doing bad stuff.
PLEASE STOP RUINING THE WORLD FOR THE REST OF US.
AW, BUT THEN I'D BE SLIGHTLY LESS RICH!
Yeah! That part seems important, because I feel like it doesn't matter how many cans I recycle or trees I plant if they're just gonna toss all their junk in the woods and tear down whole forests.
It can feel a little hopeless sometimes, but think about it this way:
They were going to tear down those trees anyway, whether you planted yours or not.
So you've still made a difference.
There's one more tree than there would have been in the world.
And if more people are doing the same, then there are many, many more trees than there would have been.
Just because there are a lot of people out there doing bad things doesn't mean that small good things don't matter.
Together, we could plant a whole forest.

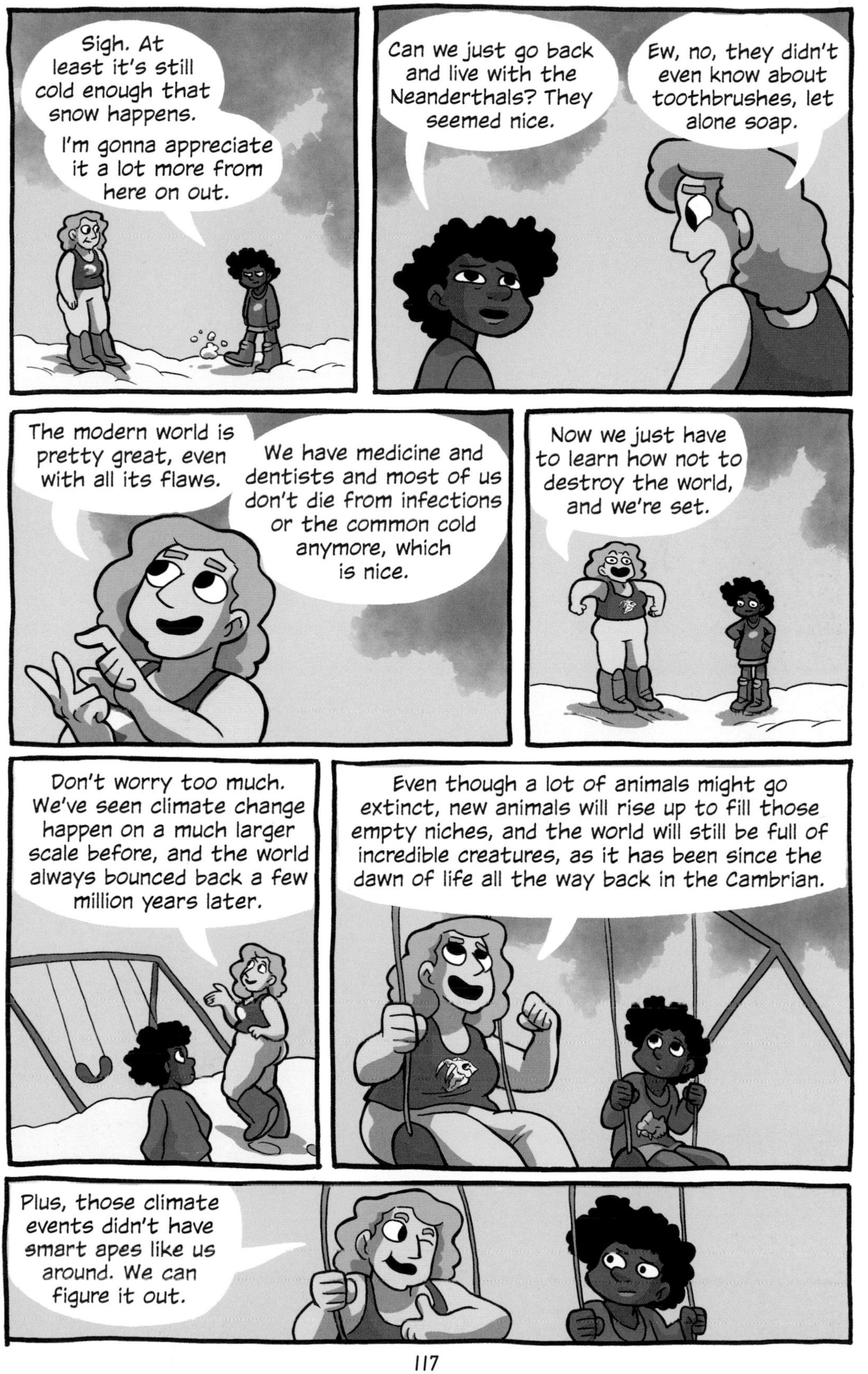
Sigh. At least it's still cold enough that snow happens.
I'm gonna appreciate it a lot more from here on out.
Can we just go back and live with the Neanderthals? They seemed nice.
Ew, no, they didn't even know about toothbrushes, let alone soap.
The modern world is pretty great, even with all its flaws.
We have medicine and dentists and most of us don't die from infections or the common cold anymore, which is nice.
Now we just have to learn how not to destroy the world, and we're set.
Don't worry too much. We've seen climate change happen on a much larger scale before, and the world always bounced back a few million years later.
Even though a lot of animals might go extinct, new animals will rise up to fill those empty niches, and the world will still be full of incredible creatures, as it has been since the dawn of life all the way back in the Cambrian.
Plus, those climate events didn't have smart apes like us around. We can figure it out.

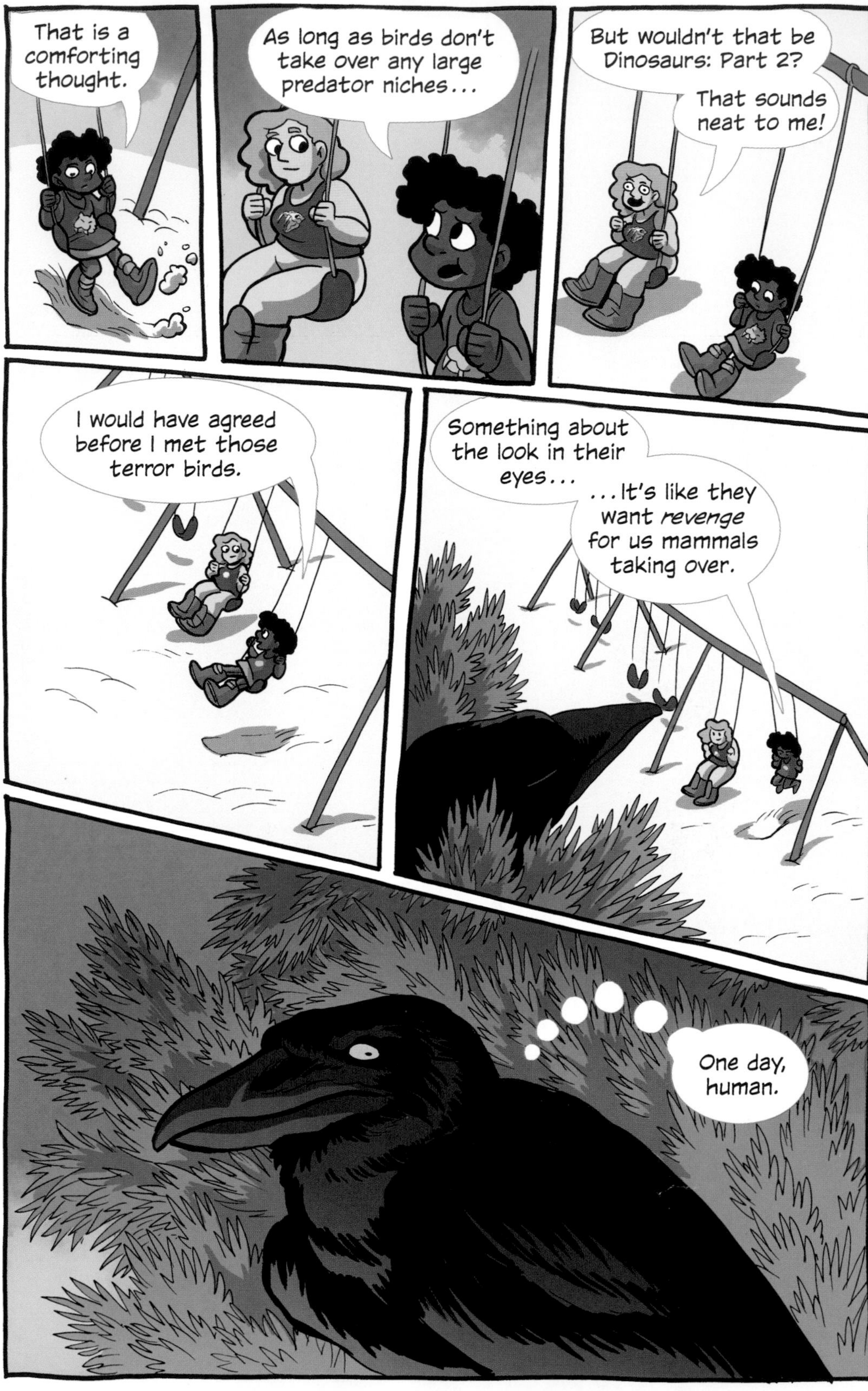
That is a comforting thought.
As long as birds don't take over any large predator niches...
But wouldn't that be Dinosaurs: Part 2?
That sounds neat to me!
I would have agreed before I met those terror birds.
Something about the look in their eyes...
...It's like they want *revenge* for us mammals taking over.
One day, human.

PHYLOGENETIC TREES!

Like a family tree, but showing how closely related different creatures are to each other! This tree shows the evolution of almost all the groups of animals discussed in the three Earth Before Us books.

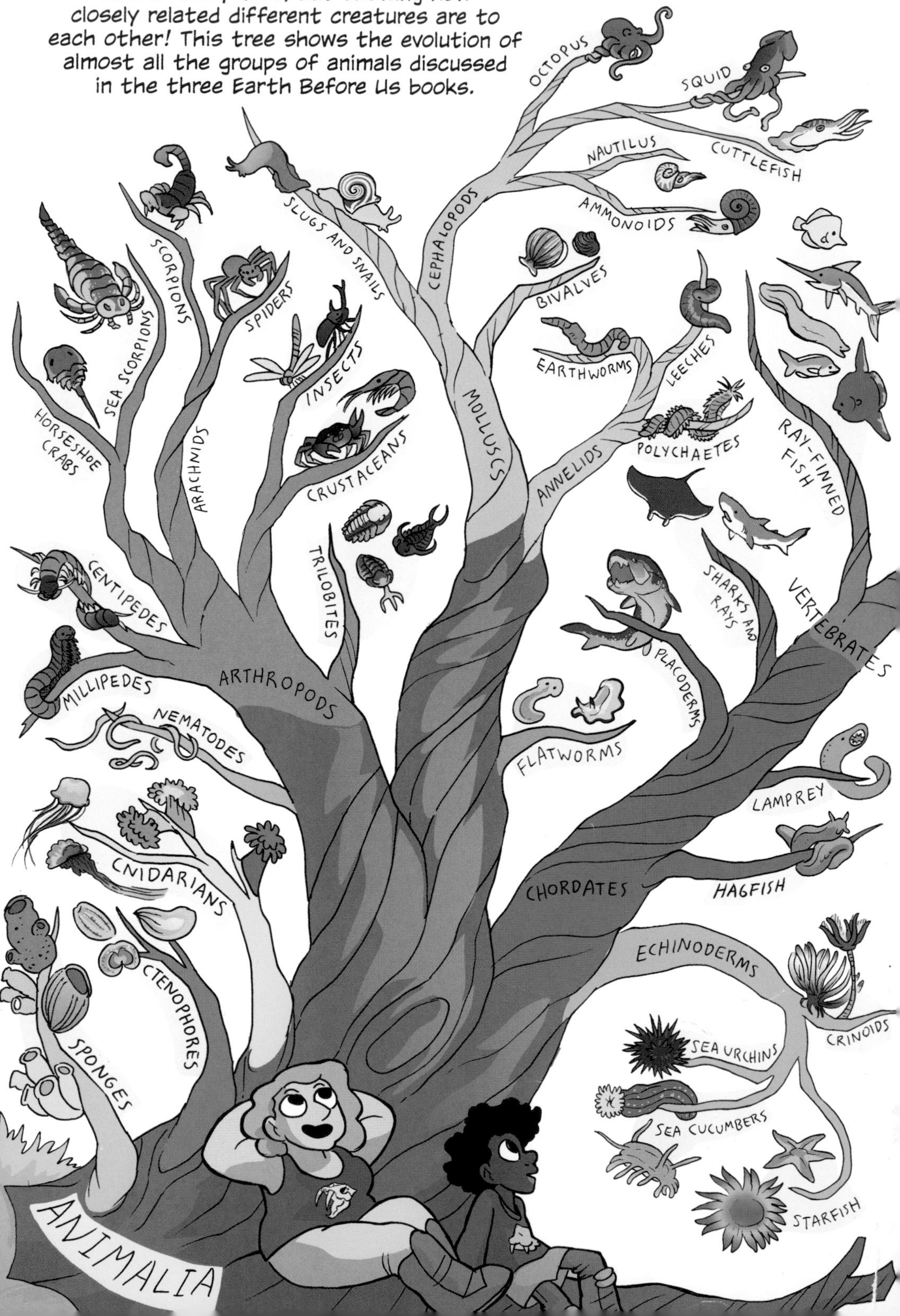

OCTOPUS
SQUID
CUTTLEFISH
NAUTILUS
AMMONOIDS
CEPHALOPODS
SLUGS AND SNAILS
SCORPIONS
SEA SCORPIONS
SPIDERS
HORSESHOE CRABS
INSECTS
BIVALVES
EARTHWORMS
LEECHES
MOLLUSCS
ARACHNIDS
CRUSTACEANS
POLYCHAETES
RAY-FINNED FISH
ANNELIDS
TRILOBITES
SHARKS AND RAYS
VERTEBRATES
CENTIPEDES
MILLIPEDES
ARTHROPODS
PLACODERMS
NEMATODES
FLATWORMS
LAMPREY
CNIDARIANS
CHORDATES
HAGFISH
ECHINODERMS
CTENOPHORES
SPONGES
SEA URCHINS
CRINOIDS
SEA CUCUMBERS
STARFISH
ANIMALIA

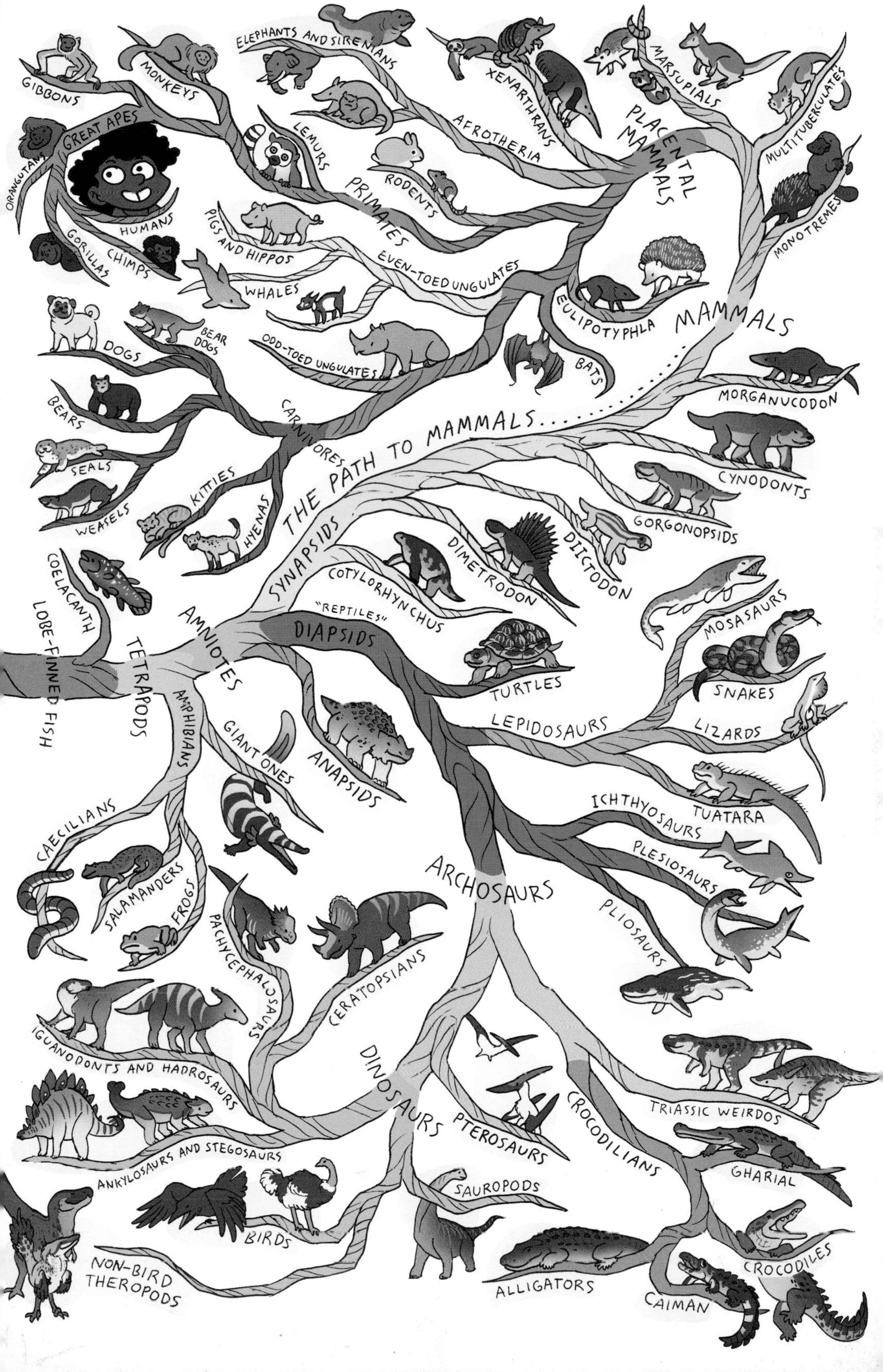

GIBBONS
MONKEYS
ELEPHANTS AND SIRENIANS
XENARTHRANS
MARSUPIALS
MULTITUBERCULATES
GREAT APES
ORANGUTANS
HUMANS
LEMURS
AFROTHERIA
PLACENTAL MAMMALS
RODENTS
PRIMATES
GORILLAS
CHIMPS
PIGS AND HIPPOS
EVEN-TOED UNGULATES
MONOTREMES
WHALES
EULIPOTYPHLA
MAMMALS
DOGS
BEAR DOGS
ODD-TOED UNGULATES
BATS
MORGANUCODON
BEARS
CARNIVORES
THE PATH TO MAMMALS
SEALS
CYNODONTS
KITTIES
WEASELS
HYENAS
GORGONOPSIDS
DIICTODON
DIMETRODON
SYNAPSIDS
COELACANTH
COTYLORHYNCHUS
"REPTILES"
MOSASAURS
LOBE-FINNED FISH
AMNIOTES
DIAPSIDS
TURTLES
TETRAPODS
SNAKES
AMPHIBIANS
GIANT ONES
LEPIDOSAURS
LIZARDS
ANAPSIDS
TUATARA
CAECILIANS
ICHTHYOSAURS
PLESIOSAURS
ARCHOSAURS
SALAMANDERS
FROGS
PLIOSAURS
PACHYCEPHALOSAURS
CERATOPSIANS
IGUANODONTS AND HADROSAURS
DINOSAURS
CROCODILIANS
TRIASSIC WEIRDOS
PTEROSAURS
ANKYLOSAURS AND STEGOSAURS
GHARIAL
SAUROPODS
BIRDS
NON-BIRD THEROPODS
CROCODILES
ALLIGATORS
CAIMAN

GLOSSARY

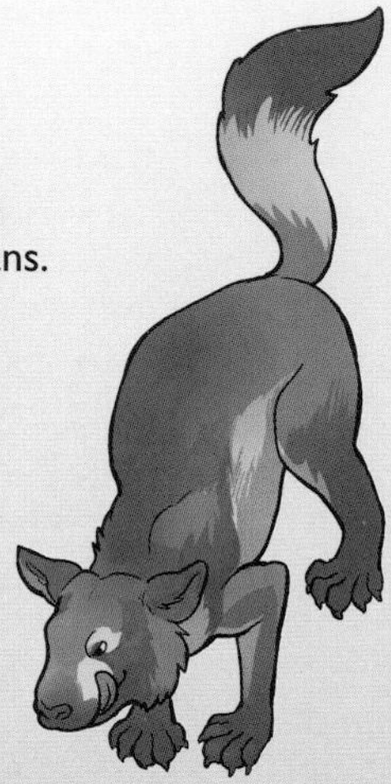

Afrotheria: The group of mammals containing elephants, dugongs, aardvarks, and hyraxes, among others. This group originated in Africa, which is why they're called "afro" therians.

Cactus: A kind of plant that has very few and often zero leaves. It has a thick, water-filled stem and is usually covered in spikes to defend itself against thirsty animals in the deserts these plants inhabit.

Cenozoic era: The era that came after the Mesozoic and continues until modern day. We are currently in the Cenozoic, which translates to "new life." It is a time dominated by mammals.

Climate change: When the average temperature of the world shifts and either becomes cooler or warmer than the creatures living on it are used to.

Convergent evolution: When unrelated organisms evolve similar traits, despite not being closely related. This usually happens when they occupy similar niches. Sharks and dolphins, for instance, are unrelated: Sharks are fish and dolphins are mammals, yet they look strikingly similar.

Entelodonts: Giant piglike omnivores that have no modern descendants. Many entelodonts were the largest predators in their region.

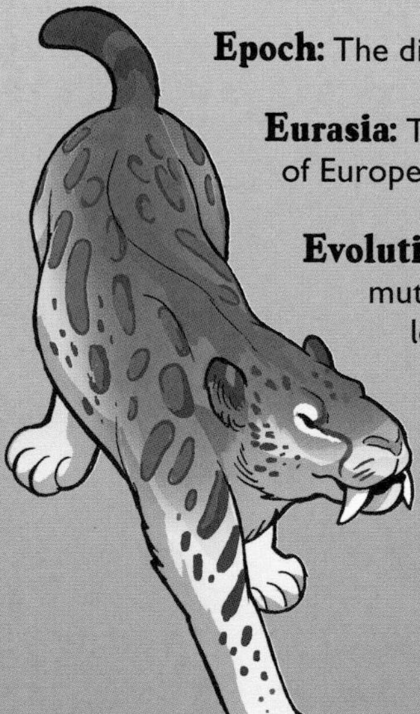

Epoch: The divisions of time within a period.

Eurasia: The supercontinent that contains the continents of Europe and Asia.

Evolution: When a group of animals changes due to mutations. Usually, the changes help them survive long enough to make more babies than they could before being mutated. This means the mutation gets passed on to more creatures and the change continues to be passed on until it becomes a trait and the group has evolved.

Fossil: Any trace of an organism preserved in rock.

Great American Interchange: An event that occurred at the start of the Ice Age, when sea levels started to subside because water froze at the poles. A land bridge formed between North and South America, and animals were free to pass between the continents.

Homo sapiens: The scientific name for our species of humans.

Ice Age: A long period of decreasing temperatures, usually accompanied by the formation of large sheets of ice in the colder parts of the world (ice caps). We are currently in an ice age.

Marsupials: The sister group to placental mammals. This group gives birth to very small, defenseless young, which continue to grow in a pouch of skin on the mother's stomach. Kangaroos and opossums are marsupials.

Mass extinction: When a significant percentage of species go extinct over a relatively short amount of time.

Mesozoic era: The era that came after the Paleozoic and before the Cenozoic. It means "middle life," as it is between the era that had the oldest known life and the era that has the newest. All non-bird dinosaurs lived and died in the Mesozoic.

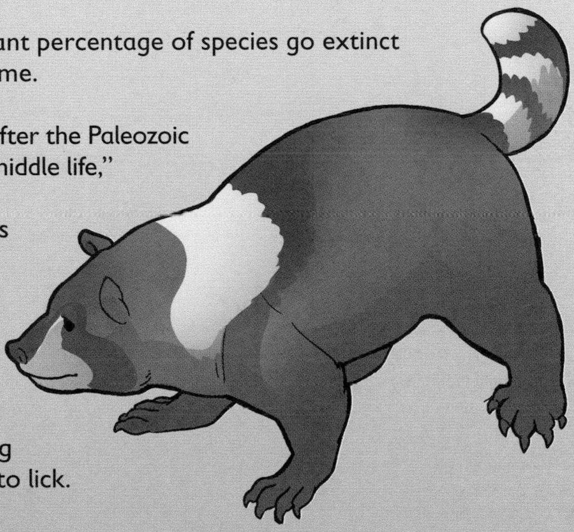

Monotremes: The sister group to placental and marsupial mammals. These mammals lay eggs and lack nipples, instead leaking milk from their skin for their babies to lick.

Niche: Where a creature lives, what it eats, and what eats it.

Paleontology: The study of fossils.

Paleozoic era: The era that came before the Mesozoic. It means "ancient life" because most of the oldest known animals evolved during this era.

Period: The divisions of time within an era.

Phorusrhacidae: Also known as the terror birds. These were giant carnivorous birds that roamed South America and, after the Great American Interchange, North America.

Placental mammals: A group of mammals that have a placenta, an organ that provides nutrients to a baby while it's inside its mother. This organ lengthens how much time a baby can stay inside its mother, so placental mammals usually give birth to more developed young than marsupials or monotremes.

Precipitation: Water that falls to the ground, such as rain, snow, or hail.

Proboscidea: A group of afrotheres that have a very long nose called a "trunk," as well as elongated teeth called "tusks." Elephants are the only living proboscids.

Rafting: When creatures are swept out to sea on "rafts" of plant matter and arrive on another island or continent.

Ungulate: A group of mammals known as the hoofed mammals, such as the even-toed ungulates (pigs, goats, whales, giraffes, etc.) and the odd-toed ungulates (horses, rhinos, and tapirs).

Xenarthra: A group of mammals that evolved on the isolated continent of South America. Their modern descendants are the anteaters, sloths, and armadillos.